Wine Country

California's Napa & Sonoma Valleys

John Doerper
Photography by Charles O'Rear

COMPASS AMERICAN GUIDES
An Imprint of Fodor's Travel Publications, Inc.

Wine Country: California's Napa & Sonoma Valleys

Copyright 1998 Fodor's Travel Publications, Inc.
Maps Copyright 1996, 1998 Fodor's Travel Publications, Inc.
Second Edition

Library of Congress Cataloging-In-Publication Data
  Doerper, John
  Wine Country: California's Napa & Sonoma Valleys/John Doerper;
  photography by Charles O'Rear.
    p. cm. — (Compass American guides)
  Includes bibliographical references and index
  ISBN 0-697-00032-1 (alk. paper)
  1. Wine and wine making—California—Napa Valley—Guidebooks.
  2. Wine and wine making—California—Sonoma County——Guidebooks.
  3. Napa Valley (Calif.)—Guidebooks
  4. Sonoma County (Calif)—Guidebooks
  I. Title. II. Series: Compass American Guides (Series)
  TP557.D64 1998
  641.2'2'0979419—dc21   97-52229 CIP

Editors: Kit Duane, Julia Dillon, Debi Dunn   Designers: David Hurst, Christopher Burt
Managing Editor: Kit Duane   Map Design: Mark Stroud, Moon Street Cartography
Photo Editor: Christopher Burt
Production house: Twin Age Ltd., Hong Kong   Printed in China

Compass American Guides, Inc., 5332 College Ave, Suite 201, Oakland, CA 94618, USA
10 9 8 7 6 5 4 3 2 1

COMPASS AMERICAN GUIDES ACKNOWLEDGES the following institutions and individuals for the use of their photographs and/or illustrations: **Kerrick James** pp. 77, 87, 109, 242; **Bancroft Library**, U.C. Berkeley p. 19; **Buena Vista Winery** pp. 24, 64, 160; courtesy **Caroline Martini** p. 37; courtesy **Joe Heitz** p. 38; courtesy **John Trefethen** p. 74 (bottom); courtesy **Willinda McCrea**, photo by Emile Romaine p. 39; **John Doerper** pp. 53, 199 and flower and grape varietal illustrations on pp. 68-69, 198-225; **Napa County Historical Society** p. 113; **Richard Gillette**, courtesy **St. Supéry** pp. 26-27; **Schramsberg Vineyards** pp. 28, 30, 110, 121, 122, 126; **Sebastiani Vineyards** p. 32, 33, 159; **Sonoma County Wine Library**, Healdsburg pp. 11, 35, 197; Trustees of the **Ansel Adams Publishing Rights Trust** 1961, courtesy of **Mumm Napa Valley**, Rutherford, California—collection of Joseph E. Seagram & Sons, Inc. pp. 42, 47, 61, 67, 85.

The Publisher also wishes to thank **Millie Howie** for acting as professional reader, **Candace Coar** for proofreading, **Jessica Fisher** for indexing, and **Kelly Stockton** for contributing wine labels.

*To my wife, Victoria,
whose deep understanding of wines and
words has ever been of inestimable support.*

C O N T E N T S

Topical Essays & Sidebars

Literary Excerpts

Maps

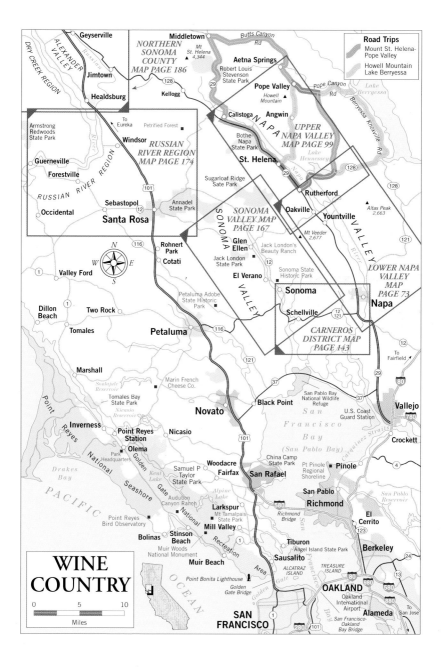

WINE
COUNTRY

ACKNOWLEDGMENTS

A BOOK IS MORE THAN JUST the product of a single mind. I would therefore like to thank the many people who have made this guide possible: Christopher Burt, Kit Duane, Julia Dillon, and Debi Dunn of Compass American Guides for asking me to write this book, and for making me feel like I could do it. In this context I would especially like to thank Kit Duane for doing such a great job editing the book and for making it seem so easy.

I would like to express my special gratitude to Zita Eastman of the Sonoma County Wine Library in Healdsburg, for easing the travails of historical research, and to Mildred Howie for answering a lot of troublesome questions that popped up at unexpected moments. I would like to thank Antonia Allegra for showing me the real Wine Country, the homespun community behind the facade of visitors' attractions, and I would like to thank Madeleine Kamman for showing me that great Wine Country food can indeed be simple. I also appreciate the way Pam Hunter and Ann Marie Conover kept me updated on wineries and Wine Country happenings during the last decade, and I am indebted to Lee Hodo and Tom Fuller for keeping me involved. Very special thanks go to the vintners and winery staff whose wines have warmed my soul and whose smiles have made feel welcome. These include, among many, Marty Bannister, Forrest Tancer, the Cakebread family, Virginia Van Asperen, Charlie Abela, Mark Swain, Revelee Hemken, John Williams, Bob Iantosca, Francis and Francoise DeWavrin-Woltner, and Nyna Cox. I owe a very special gratitude to Marie Gewirtz for introducing me not only to great Sonoma County wines but also to that gastronomic paradise's great foods. I would also like to thank Jim Caron and Darryl Nutter, as well as Michele Anna Jordan, for guiding me to Sonoma County food producers, and to Alan Hemphill for giving me glimpses of the business side of wine. Last, but not least, I must thank my wife, Victoria, for the patience and understanding with which she has supported yet one more book project.

At a celebration in San Francisco in the 1950s, a group of merry-makers from the Beringer Winery demonstrate the other traditional use of champagne. (Sonoma County Library)

INTRODUCTION

THE PATIO LIES IN THE DEEP AFTERNOON SHADE of live oaks, but the vineyard across the road is lit up by the setting sun, which is giving the ripening cabernet grapes a final boost of sugars. I have returned to my favorite Wine Country cottage to relax, to taste the young, still fermenting wines of the current vintage, and to eat good food. Only an olive grove separates me from one of the Wine Country's busiest thoroughfares, yet everything here is peaceful. I can listen to birds chirping in the blackberry thicket behind the winery and hear the splash of a heron as it lunges after fish in a pool left in the summer-dry creek. A hummingbird flits past, stalling intermittently to extract nectar; quail call from the vineyard. The heady aromas of fermenting must waft through the air, mingling with the dusty smell of the vineyard and the perfume of autumn roses. Later that night, after dinner, I sit by the open window, sipping a glass of well-aged zinfandel. A screech owl calls, interrupted now and then by the unearthly howl of wandering coyotes. This is the Wine Country at its best.

❖

I first visited Napa's and Sonoma's wine valleys in 1968, driving across the hills from Davis, where I had just started graduate school. The Wine Country has changed since then, but in many ways it has remained the same. There are more wineries now—many more—and more visitors, but the spirit of the land remains intact. This, I remind myself, is still one of the best places to visit—as the great number of "wine tourists" would seem to prove. While some locals decry the influx of so many visitors, wine tourists are a special breed. For the most part, they are eager to learn more about wine, willing to taste and evaluate, eagerly picking up advice from the staff at winery tasting rooms. They are a happy bunch, these visitors, united by a common appreciation of fine wine.

There is an instant rapport, a communion of spirits, among lovers of fine wine that is unequaled in any other profession or hobby. It is open to all who embrace its spirit, and its members readily and freely share information. No serious scholar of wine will keep secrets from fellow students. The discovery of a great wine is knowledge to be shared. Tasting rooms are places where anecdotes are told and tips are given.

A soft light illuminates a Domaine Chandon vineyard in the lower Napa Valley.

I learned about California wines during my undergraduate years in southern California, where I belonged to a circle of friends who shared bottles of wine over dinner. We eagerly searched out the bottlings of (now closed) local wineries in San Bernardino's Cucamonga and Guasti districts—always hoping for that truly special wine that would justify our efforts. We found it one day over lunch in a small Basque restaurant just off Route 66. The proprietor, after discussing the short wine list with us and listening to our wine talk, excused himself and vanished through a cellar door. He returned a short while later, carrying a pitcher of deeply colored red wine. He poured a little of the wine into each of our glasses, and we sipped, sniffed, and exclaimed. This wine, made by the restaurateur from local grapes, was some of the best red any of us had ever tasted straight from the barrel. I don't remember the name of the restaurant or the variety of grapes from which the wine was made, but I can still vividly recall its heady aroma and complex flavors.

When I first saw Northern California's Wine Country, I was underwhelmed. Where I had expected a sea of vines, there was hardly a vine in sight, except on the valley floor near Rutherford and north of St. Helena, where wineries had hung on even during Prohibition and the Great Depression. But the wines I tasted at the few wineries open to the public at the time were very good. Food, however, was a real disappointment. You could get a hamburger, of course, or greasy fried chicken, or unidentifiable meat smothered in brown sauce, but no meal to incite culinary passion.

In those days, few people had learned to appreciate cabernet sauvignon, and even fewer had heard of chardonnay, which existed in limited plantings in only a few vineyards—at rarefied places like Stony Hill, high above the Napa Valley floor. Sylvaner (labeled "riesling" by local custom), green hungarian, and carignane were varieties everyone drank. The latter might be labeled claret, "burgundy," or whatever name struck the vintner's fancy. The great red wines of California—cabernet sauvignon from Beaulieu and Inglenook, zinfandel from Ridge—were rare and hard to find.

But change was in the air. Stately old wineries like Beaulieu and Christian Brothers, as well as Robert Mondavi's new place in Oakville, attracted increasing numbers of visitors. Wine had become socially acceptable—not only to the upper ten thousand, who always drank good wine, but also to millions of American middle-class gourmets. New converts flocked to the wineries to learn more about wine and to taste the elixirs at their source. New wineries sprouted from the vineyards with every vintage. Old stone buildings, abandoned during Prohibition, were resurrected. Neglected farmhouses were saved from oblivion, restored, and turned into tasting rooms. Within a decade, the Napa Valley's focus had shifted from mundane agricultural pursuits to a search for excellence in winemaking. Sonoma County was not far behind. Soon there were outcries that too many wineries were ruining the pastoral valleys. That, of course, was not at all true. To my eyes, the wine-producing valleys—Napa, Sonoma, Russian River, Alexander, Knights', and Dry Creek, as well as the gentle hills of the Carneros—are prettier than they were before, with vineyards supplanting pastures and prune orchards, and with beautifully designed and constructed wineries replacing rusty equipment sheds. These human touches in a naturally beautiful region certainly add elements of interest which make the area more appealing to visitors.

As local wineries gained international respect for their wines, the Napa and Sonoma vineyards took their rightful place among the great wine-producing districts of the world. Today, there is more good wine than ever but, best of all, the quality of food and lodging has caught up with the wine, making the valleys and mountains of Napa and Sonoma some of the best places to visit—anywhere.

In the autumn of 1995, the quest for culinary excellence in the Wine Country received a major boost. The matching of local wines to food had started in the home kitchens of vintners and gained international recognition when French master chef Madeleine Kamman started her program for professional chefs at Beringer Vineyards in the late 1980s. Then, in 1995, New York's Culinary Institute of America, one of this nation's prime schools for chefs, opened its West Coast campus in the old Greystone Winery building north of St. Helena.

The outlooks for both local wine and local food are bright. Commenting on local wines, Napa Valley winegrower Andy Beckstoffer points out that the quality of the average wines produced in Napa and Sonoma counties is now so high that the gap between them and premium wines has narrowed to where grape growers and wine-makers feel they have to widen it—to keep distinctive wines truly distinct—by raising the quality of premium wines ever higher. I can hardly wait to taste them.

Wine is more than a beverage. To fully understand it, you should know its background. We are inviting you on a tour of the landscape where some of the world's best wines are produced. We shall give you a short history of the region and introduce you to the men and women who grow the grapes and make the wine, as well as to the chefs who create the dishes that enhance wine's place at the table. Pour yourself a glass of wine, sit back, and relax, and we'll be on our way.

THE SETTING

THE NORTHERN CALIFORNIA WINE COUNTRY is unlike any other area in the world, with its beautiful landscape and equable climate. It has tall mountains and sandy beaches, rocky, storm-tossed cliffs and quiet rivers, waterfowl marshes and redwood forests. Above all it has vineyards which produce some of the finest wines in the world. Most of the wineries, even the famous ones, welcome visitors, and the small towns which dot the countryside make everyone feel welcome.

While the Northern California Wine Country is much like southern France and northern Italy—Provence and Tuscany—in its climate and in the temperament of its people, it also has touches of Bordeaux and Champagne, of Burgundy and the Rheingau. Plus a dash of sunny Mexico. Because of its exciting cultural tapestry, the Wine Country's restaurants are among the best and most interesting in America.

All of this is expressed in a truly Mediterranean joie de vivre. Like many of the wines, the foods, too, are Mediterranean in spirit. For this is a food country as much as it is a wine country. Like Mediterranean peoples everywhere, those in the Wine Country are ever willing to discuss their food—over a glass of wine, of course—and they have every reason to be proud of it. Farmers' markets teem with fruits and vegetables. Cattle, goats, and sheep thrive in the hillside pasture and give rich milk which is made into a greater variety of cheese than you'll find anywhere else. Figs and oranges can be eaten right off the tree. If this makes the Wine Country sound like a veritable garden of Eden, it is.

But there's more to the Wine Country than wine and food. It has more exciting places to explore and things to do than anyone can manage in a lifetime. Visitors can walk quiet trails under ageless redwoods, stroll in sunny wild-

flower meadows, or silently glide over hills and vineyards in a hot air balloon or sail plane. Visitors can explore an old Spanish mission and fortress, linger in Mexican plazas, or submerge themselves in the boisterous atmosphere of an old-fashioned stern-wheeler on the Napa River. Visitors are always welcome to join residents at small-town fiestas, community barbecues, and wine festivals. Which brings us right back to food and wine, the region's prime attraction. The region's wines are well worth tasting. This book will guide you to some of Napa's and Sonoma's top wineries, but we hope you will also follow us as we explore the region's history, meet its wildlife, hike the trails, and drive the back roads. And we hope you'll join us for a picnic, as we sit on the ferny bank of a placid stream, with flowers in our hair, breaking our fast with a loaf of bread and a bottle of wine.

STEPPING INTO HISTORY

Wine comes in at the mouth
And love comes in at the eye;
That's all we shall know for truth
Before we grow old and die.

—*William Butler Yeats*

THE AFTERNOON HAS TURNED VERY HOT and you search for a shady spot. You find it on rough-hewn wooden steps running from the balcony to the dusty patio. You sit down and look around. This is truly a courtyard that time forgot. Behind you rise the thick, whitewashed walls of an adobe building. In a gloomy passageway, you can just make out the silhouette of an old cannon. To your right, a white adobe wall, topped with red tiles, cuts off the outside world; to your left rises an exotic dome structure, also whitewashed: a beehive oven for baking breads and meats. It is flanked by a *parilla* of two metal grills set into low adobe walls. A prickly pear cactus, as tall as a small tree, sprawls over the far wall of the courtyard. The edges of its paddle-shaped stems are studded with the bright red fruit Mexicans call *tuna*.

The scents of countless flowers waft through the courtyard, and a mockingbird sings in a nearby tree. As you sample the smells and sounds of a Sonoma afternoon, you remember what you have learned about local history and you imagine yourself back a century and a half, when these adobe walls were part of the great fortress of the north—the palacio of Gen. Mariano Guadalupe Vallejo. A horse whinnies in the distance. You can almost hear—mingled with the singing of the birds and the rustling of the leaves—the creaking of leather saddles, the jingling of harness rings, and the muttering of Mexican soldiers, grumbling because they have been sent to this remote northern outpost.

They had reason to grumble, for they had just returned from another fruitless chase after the Wappo of the upper Napa Valley and the Wintun of the Suisun marshes on the lower Sacramento River. With its soothing scenery and mild climate, Napa would be paradise, were it not for the tribes who refused to surrender their ancestral lands without a fight.

Gen. Mariano Vallejo poses comfortably with his daughters and granddaughters, many of whom went on to marry prominent Californians. (Bancroft Library, U.C.–Berkeley)

■ EARLY SPANISH PRESENCE

This country was settled by Europeans half a century later than was California south of San Francisco Bay. Spanish padres came first. Their San Francisco Solano mission, a stone's throw to the east, predates Vallejo's secular compound by two decades. The Spanish had constant trouble with the native tribes when they first built this mission in the land of Contra Costa del Norte Este, its hills and vales stretching from the shores of San Francisco Bay north to the impenetrable mountains of the Mayacamas range. The Mexican military commander Mariano Vallejo proved, however, that it was possible to get along with the natives. He made peace with the fiercest of his enemies, a Suisun leader known as Sem Yeto. Yeto was baptized, took the Christian name of Francisco Solano, and became one of Vallejo's most loyal friends and the leader of his native troops. Later, Solano took charge of the Sonoma palacio and its garrison.

Father José Altimira, a headstrong Catalan, was censured by his clerical superiors when he founded San Francisco de Solano mission at Sonoma in 1823, at the very end of the mission period, without permission. Altimira allied himself with

Detail of the Blue Wing Inn, across the street from the mission in Sonoma.

the secular authorities, however, and finally had the mission legitimized by his church superiors. The mission prospered despite the opposition of the native inhabitants of the land. The padres following in Altimira's footsteps established ranchos in the Petaluma, Sonoma, and lower Napa valleys, raising cattle and planting olives and grapes. Contemporary travelers reported that the wine they made was indifferent at best. But it was good enough to be served at Mass, and it made decent *aguardiente* (brandy).

Wine was first made by the padres at Mission San Juan Capistrano in 1782 from grapes planted three years earlier. But secular wine was not far behind. According to John Melville's *Guide to California Wines,* the first layman of record was Gov. Pedro Fages, who planted a vineyard alongside his orchards in 1783, not far from his residence in Monterey, Alta California. In the early 19th century Dona Marcelina Felix Dominguez, the first known woman winegrower in California, planted at Montecito near Santa Barbara a fabulous vine which would bear in good years some four tons of grapes. (Known as La Vieja de la Parra Grande, or "The Old Lady of the Grapevine," she was said to be 105 years old when she died in 1865.) Production increased, but the quality of California wine did not improve much after the missions were secularized in the early 1830s, primarily because wine continued to be made only from the mission grape.

Gov. Mariano Vallejo was the first secular grape grower in Sonoma. When he was put in charge of secularization in the North Bay country, he parcelled out much of the former mission ranchos of today's Sonoma and Napa counties—as far as the Dry Creek Valley and lower Lake County—to his relatives and friends, keeping prime properties like the Petaluma Valley and the rich lands bordering the lower Napa River for himself. He bestowed the lands bordering the warlike tribes of the upper Napa Valley on Anglo adventurers, known to be at least as fierce as the indigenous people they were to live with.

■ ANGLO ADVENTURERS ARRIVE

George C. Yount, a mountain man who had come to Sonoma Mission in the 1820s and stayed to perform odd jobs, was granted Rancho Caymus, in the heart of the Napa Valley, in 1834. He built himself a block house—equipped with rifle ports—right smack in the middle of an Indian ranchería, and managed to keep his foothold. Edward T. Bale, an irascible British physician who had married one of

Vallejo's nieces, was pushed off to the upper Napa Valley after he tried to shoot down Salvador Vallejo, the General's brother. Bale gave his rancho an oddly derived name when he changed the native name *Callajomanas* (a Wappo word of unknown meaning) to *Carne Humana* (Human Flesh). The grist mill Bale built on his ranch still stands. It has been restored, and on most weekends you can watch state park rangers grind by waterpower. Both Yount and Bale planted some grapes but were not instrumental in getting the Napa wine industry started. That was left to Bale's son-in-law, Charles Krug.

But back to Sonoma. It was here, in the plaza out front, on June 15, 1846, that a rag-tag band of American mountain men and adventurers surrounded the adobe fortress. After arresting Vallejo, his brother Salvador, and his secretary Victor Prudon, the mountain men raised a makeshift flag decorated with a star, a badly painted bear, and a strip of red flannel. While their compatriots rushed Vallejo to John C. Frémont, who was camped on the American River near present-day Sacramento, the rebels, under the command of William B. Ide, declared California an independent republic. Neither side knew that the United States and Mexico had been at war for more than a month and that U.S. troops were about to land and take possession of all of California, including Sonoma.

Ide had made his declaration from the "Fortress of Sonoma," but Vallejo was kept prisoner in another fortress—that of John Sutter at Sacramento. This must have seemed like betrayal to many of the region's Hispanic citizens, especially since we have more than a modicum of suspicion that Vallejo had rigged the rebellion because he favored annexation of California by the Americans. En route to Frémont's camp, he refused to be rescued near Vacaville by a superior Mexican force under Juan Padilla, and he was certainly not shy about his continuing pro-American sympathies after his release. Holding no grudges, he did not object when his eldest daughter, Epifania, married Capt. J. B. Frisbie, U.S. Army, commander of the barracks of Sonoma—which is what Vallejo's former *palacio* became under the new regime. Since Vallejo had to move out of his fortress, he built himself an American-style mansion down the road, where he and his wife lavishly entertained visitors. This villa, named *Lachryma Montis* for the natural springs gushing from the ground, has been well preserved and is now part of Sonoma State Park. Later, he platted the city of Vallejo and offered it to the state as the site for the new capital (Monterey, the old capital, was too far from the scene of action, the Mother Lode). After two short sojourns, the legislature ultimately preferred

The Bale Grist Mill just north of St. Helena. Grist mill owners were important and influential citizens in the Napa Valley's early days.

Sacramento, but it did grant Vallejo's wish and named the county in honor of Vallejo's Indian ally, Solano. Yet Vallejo did not rest idly on his laurels. He continued making wines. Soon they were winning honors, and among proud relics of the old grandee are numerous premiums and medals; also a solid silver pitcher, a state fair trophy for his finest claret.

■ HARASZTHY FOUNDS BUENA VISTA

While Vallejo was the first secular grape grower in the Sonoma Valley, the big push towards commercial production came from Agoston Haraszthy, a Hungarian immigrant encouraged by Vallejo (two of the general's daughters married Haraszthy's sons).

Haraszthy, the founder of Sonoma's Buena Vista Winery, is often given credit as the first to plant European grape varietals in Northern California. That has since been disproved. Napa Valley vintners, among them George Beldon Crane and Sam Brannan, may have had more to do with introducing high-quality European vinifera grapes to the region than did Agoston Haraszthy.

Agoston Haraszthy, one of the first vintners to plant European grape varietals in California. (Courtesy Buena Vista Carneros Estate)

The zinfandel grape, of mysterious European origin, has adapted well to the vicissitudes of California's climate.

Nevertheless, Haraszthy does deserve credit for two very important break-throughs. During the mission and rancho periods, grapes were grown in the low-lands, close to sources of irrigation water. At Buena Vista, Haraszthy planted grapes on dry hillsides, proving that the local climate was sufficiently moist to sus-tain grapes without irrigation. He was also the first to experiment with using red-wood barrels for aging wine—an innovation which would become the most popular storage method of the California wine industry for almost a hundred years. The adoption of inexpensive redwood over expensive oak went hand in hand with the boom in grape plantings in the Napa and Sonoma valleys. Despite the continuing efforts of several vintners, European vinifera grapes, the varietals which were eventually to make the region's reputation for first-rate wines, were slow to replace mission grapes. In the 1860s, much of the Napa Valley's wines still came from some 2,000 acres of mission grapes, and as late as 1876, Charles Krug ranted about the use of these inferior grapes for making wine. But a new red wine grape was becoming increasingly popular, both because it made excellent claret (as good red wine was then called) and because it had adapted to the vicissitudes of the Wine Country's errant climes: the zinfandel.

■ DIGRESSING TO THE PRESENT

Your historical reverie is finally broken by present-day revelry. A band in the Plaza strikes up "La Maruca," a popular Mexican mariachi tune, and the savory aroma of barbecued beef wafts under your nose. This is the day of the annual Ox Roast in the Plaza (to benefit the Sonoma Community Center—Wine Country folk have a commendable habit of combining civic duties with pleasure). You stroll over to the booth selling the meat (barbecued beef, corn on the cob, a roll with butter, and a salad, all for $8), stop at another booth to buy a glass of Sonoma zin-

The Napa Valley's topography creates a multitude of micro-climates. Fog from the northern reaches of San Francisco Bay cools the low-lying Carneros region but evaporates before reaching the lower Napa Valley. The higher elevations at the north end of the valley capture increasing amounts of Pacific moisture during the rainy season (November—March). Rainfall totals increase from around 20" per annum in the southern end of the valley to over 45" at the northern end. (Painting by Richard Gillette, courtesy St. Supéry Vineyards)

fandel, find a quiet place beneath a shady tree, and dig in. It occurs to you that here, in your hand, are combined several elements of the Wine Country's pioneer agricultural quest: grain in the form of wheat and maize, beef, and wine. During the latter decades of the 19th century, the new farmers learned the valuable lesson that wet years alternated with dry in the crazy-quilt pattern of Wine Country climes. And in drought years, wheat and corn failed and cattle faltered, but grapes survived and sometimes even produced a splendid vintage. Aside from grapes, fruit trees—especially prunes—thrived in this climate, and whenever it became economically (or politically) unfeasible to grow grapes, farmers tended to their fruit trees.

■ 19TH-CENTURY IMPROVEMENTS

The second half of the century may be called the Napa Valley's German age, since so many of the Valley's winemakers came from that country. German winemakers like Charles Krug and Jacob Schram set the tone for the style of wines made in the Napa Valley for years to come. Many 19th-century vintners were immigrants from Europe, but Americans more than held their own. Author Charles Nordhoff wrote in 1872, "I was told that the Americans, where they attend to the business, become the most skillful and successful of all. . . ." Time has proved him right. The Italians, who also were very successful, came later.

Winemaking methods had improved dramatically from the 1840s, when rancho Indians trod out the grapes in cowhide bags. Another pioneer was J. J. Sigrist, whose vineyard was a few miles from Napa. Sigrist distinguished himself by making "his wine from each variety of grape singly—Quite definitely a trend with a future." These pioneers experimented with more than grapes and winemaking; they also pioneered a new style of architecture. Most of the imposing stone wineries which still dominate hillsides in the Wine Country were built during this period.

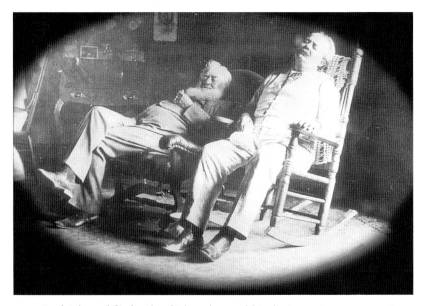

Jacob Schram (left), founder of Schramsberg, and friend enjoy a quiet nap at the vintner's mansion. (Courtesy Schramsberg Vineyards)

When Gustave Niebaum built a new winery at Inglenook in Rutherford in the 1880s, he gave the quality of Napa wines a further boost, not only by planting prime vinifera grapes and by practicing meticulously clean methods of vinification, but also by bottling wines at the winery in large quantities for shipping, instead of having them bottled at the shipper's office in San Francisco. This ran counter to the prevailing practice of shipping the wine in barrels (or even railroad tank cars) to a shipper in San Francisco, the Midwest, or the East Coast, where the wine would be aged and bottled. Un-

Charles Krug was one of the valley's pioneer vintners.

fortunately not all of those shippers were honest, and some wine reached the market in adulterated form.

Charles Krug and other California vintners traveling to the East Coast soon learned that what happened to the wine back East did not necessarily enhance the Napa and Sonoma valleys' reputation, especially since some of the better vintages were bottled under fake European labels while indifferent wine was bottled as "California." The practice of shipping wine by the barrel allowed the shippers who stored the wine to set the purchase and sales prices of their wines and thus directly influence the money paid to the vintners. By speeding up or delaying the release of a vintage, the shippers could glut or starve the market. This ultimately led to complete control of the market by the San Francisco wine houses, who in 1894 consolidated their power by forming the powerful—and monopolistic—California Wine Association. This monopoly would dominate the California wine industry until the onset of Prohibition.

In the American West, the Chinese were considered invaluable laborers in the construction of railroads and engineering of mines during the latter half of the 19th century. Their mining skills were also put to work in the creation of wine cellars in Napa County. The man pictured above worked for Jacob Schram. (Courtesy Schramsberg Vineyards)

■ VINEYARDS EXPAND AND SUFFER

During this formative time, vineyard plantings expanded into new territories. Jacob Schram planted grapes in Sonoma's Knights Valley, starting the link of that outlying Sonoma wine valley with Napa Valley producers (that Knights Valley vineyard is today maintained by Beringer). In Sonoma County, the Korbel Brothers established a successful sparkling wine operation in the Russian River Valley; the Kunde family became major winegrowers; and the Dry Creek Valley grew into a stronghold of Italian family wineries. Napa vintners planted grapes in nearby Conn, Pope, and Chiles valleys; on Howell Mountain; on the rolling green hills of the Carneros; and in Solano County's Green Valley (which should not be confused with Sonoma County's Green Valley).

Then, around the turn of the century, the vineyards were struck by phylloxera, a vine-destroying root louse *(see* "GLOSSARY," *page 290).* The only way to fight this bug was to replant the vines on resistant root stocks—a process that was often rocky and uncertain. (In fact, it has not yet been satisfactorily resolved, and in the 1990s, as in the 1890s, Sonoma and Napa vineyards were struck again.)

Once this was accomplished, the vineyards flourished. Many of the workers who dug the caves, constructed the splendid stone wineries still dotting the Wine Country, and built the stone fences still snaking across the hillsides were Chinese. The Chinese had come to the American West to help build the transcontinental railroad, and when that job was done, they turned to agricultural pursuits. In the Napa and Sonoma valleys, they not only helped build the wineries, but also cleared the land, tilled the soil, harvested the grapes and, in some cases, made the wine.

Most Chinese were driven out of California in the early 1890s because of anti-Asian agitation in San Francisco, and Napa Valley vintners hated to see them go. Immigrant workers from Italy and other regions of southern Europe took over the jobs vacated by the Chinese. Unlike their Chinese predecessors, the Italians had a keen interest in winemaking. It was during this period that the first Italian family wineries were established in Northern California, wineries that would make a major share of Northern California's wine for the next century.

The dreaded phylloxera louse, so small it rests easily on the tip of a needle, has ruined many a vine in the Wine Country.

■ ITALIAN SWISS COLONY

The most successful of the Italian enterprises was the Italian Swiss Colony, based in Asti, on the northern frontier of the Sonoma Wine Country. The "colony" began as an investment scheme conceived by San Francisco financier Andrea Sbarboro. Sbarboro had made a success in creating several self-help investment schemes, structured much like today's credit unions, and he thought it was time to tie into the talent pool of local Italian immigrants. In 1881, he rounded up Dr. Paolo de Vecchi and other investors to found a mutual aid society whose purpose would be to buy empty land, plant it to grapes, and turn a tidy profit. The workers involved in the scheme would receive wages at first; later they could invest part of their earnings and become stockholders.

The first part of the scheme worked. The society, incorporated as the Italian Swiss Colony (the "Swiss" was added to welcome Italian-speaking settlers from Switzerland's Ticino canton) bought land along the Russian River just south of Cloverdale in 1882, where the climate was like that of northern Italy. While it was not "empty," since part had been planted to grain, it seemed highly suitable for viticulture. The

When they were introduced in the 19th century, redwood aging vats—less costly than their oak counterparts—helped create a boom in grape plantings. (Courtesy Sebastiani Vineyards)

Italian immigrants often worked as laborers before garnering enough savings to break into the wine business. The men in this photograph are mining cobblestones to pave the streets of San Francisco, as did Sonoma vintner Samuele Sebastiani. (Courtesy Sebastiani Vineyards)

project made money right from the start. Much of the land had to be cleared of madrona, manzanita, and oak, but the workers turned the wood into charcoal, which was sold at a profit. Once the land was cleared, grape acreage increased rapidly. It became clear that the "colony" would be a financial success. The only problem lay with the workers, most of whom were not interested in acquiring shares but preferred to draw salaries. The "colonists" were, in fact, the San Francisco capitalists who had started the scheme. But the directors were not to be daunted. When they realized, in 1885, that most of the investors lived in San Francisco and had no interest in occupying their share of the communal acreage, they changed the company's bylaws to adapt to the changed operating conditions. While the corporation continued to aid Italian immigrants in need of employment and economic security, emphasis was now placed on winemaking. The directors hired Pietro Carlo Rossi, an Italian immigrant, as winemaker and general manager, and proceeded to give him free rein. In 1888, the Italian Swiss Colony made 130,000 gallons of wine from such classic Italian varietals as barbera, grignolino, nebbiolo, and sangiovese; by 1895 the capacity had reached a million gallons; in 1902, after the Colony had expanded into other winegrowing districts, it reached 10 million gallons.

But quality mattered more to the Italian Swiss Colony than quantity. Following Rossi's maxim that "Pure wines are the gospel at Asti," the colony not only strived to make ever better wines, it also searched for improved ways to send them to market. Between 1904 and 1905, the Colony began bottling wines in its San Francisco facilities and shipped the wine, in the bottle, up and down the Coast—something almost unheard of at the time, despite Gustave Niebaum's earlier pioneering efforts. This new way of shipping wine was helped along by the Pure Food and Drug Act of 1906, which looked askance at wines altered by the shipper. Even then, almost no wine was shipped to the East Coast in the bottle; it still went by tank car and barrel as before.

All of these wine tank cars came in handy during Prohibition, when no wine could be legally shipped, but it was perfectly legal to ship juice (and grapes) across the country for wine manufacture by home winemakers. But by then the Colony had fallen on hard times. It was absorbed by the California Wine Association, bought by several employees when the CWA divested itself of its assets at the onset of Prohibition, and served as a grape broker for Sonoma County growers during the 1920s. But even after Repeal the winery never quite regained its former glory. In 1942—when the government outlawed the making of whisky, because grain was needed for the war effort—the Italian Swiss Colony was sold to National Distillers. After the war, it changed hands frequently until it became merely a label, like so many other old wineries. Today Asti is closed off from the world by a large gate with a sign that states:

WINE WORLD INC.
Bonded Winery # 1589. ASTI, CA.
Sorry NOT OPEN for tours or tastings.
No solicitations please.

It's a sad epitaph marking the site of a once-great empire. But changes loomed in November of 1995, when Nestlé sold its Wine World Estates Division to American investors. We can but hope that the new owners will resurrect the once honorable winery and restore the label to its former glory.

■ PROHIBITION AND REPEAL

The National Prohibition Act, which passed in 1919 under the popular name of the Volstead Act, had a very strange effect on Napa and Sonoma wineries. Several, like Beaulieu, Beringer, and the Christian Brothers, stayed in business by making sacramental wines; others survived by shipping grape juice or grapes to home winemakers, a practice which was not outlawed by the Volstead Act. Because of this anomaly, coupled with rising demand, more grapes were grown in California at the end of Prohibition than at its start. But quality had declined. Growers had grafted over their vineyards to high-yielding red varietals like the red-juiced alicante bouschet, which allowed home winemakers to make more gallons of wine per ton of grapes—especially if the juice was enhanced with a generous helping of cane sugar.

Many wineries shut down and growers planted their land with fruit and nut trees, but several wineries kept their inventories in bond. The wine magically flowed out the back door into barrels and carboys brought by customers, and just as magically it seemed to replenish itself. Now and then a revenuer would crack down, but enforcement seems to have been lax at best. Who wanted to bother with wineries when you could bust up a moonshine still?

After Repeal was passed in 1933,

Brother Timothy Diener of Christian Brothers samples grapes. Some wineries were able to stay in business throughout Prohibition by supplying sacramental wine for churches across the country. (Sonoma County Library)

restarting legitimate winemaking proved difficult: during Prohibition, wineries had lost many of their traditional customers to bathtub gin and cheap cocktails. Those still drinking wine now preferred sweet to dry. For the wine industry this meant a long struggle that did not really end until the 1960s.

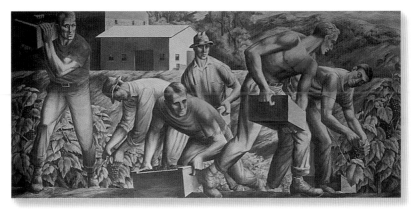

This mural, done by a WPA artist sometime in the mid-1930s, adorns the St. Helena Post Office. The painting could be interpreted as a celebration of the repeal of Prohibition in 1933.

For the 40 years after Repeal, much of the wine produced in Sonoma County was shipped in bulk, to be blended or bottled into generic brands.

During this time, several Napa Valley wineries, some of whom might be considered upstarts, brought about a wine renaissance—almost in spite of themselves. To understand what happened, we must go back to the ancient winegrowing districts of Europe, where grapes and fruit trees also alternate in the mosaic of landscapes. In Europe these planting patterns were established centuries ago, with the richer soils always being reserved for fruit trees and the poor soils assigned to grapes.

Sonoma County has greater patches of rich soil than does Napa, making it possible for farmers to make a living from fruit trees without having to bother about grapes. With prices of grapes and wines at a Great Depression low, it did not pay to replant idle patches of grape lands, but it paid to harvest those vineyards that had supplied the home winemakers' market during Prohibition. The Napa Valley, on the other hand, is laced with rocky and gravelly slopes, bench lands, and alluvial fans where fruit trees grow poorly, but where grapes thrive. A Napa Valley farmer found it more difficult to make a living on tree fruit alone, but had to find ways to make vineyards pay as well.

Fortunately, several major wineries had survived Prohibition and laid the foundation for new prosperity. Besides Beringer, these were Beaulieu, Inglenook, the Christian Brothers, Louis M. Martini, and, after the Cesare Mondavi family bought the winery in the 1940s, Charles Krug. Considering the all-time low demand for their product—and the state of the American palate—these wineries made some amazingly good wines during this period. Yet the seeds sown by these wineries were to bear fruit only much later. It was a tasting of well-aged Inglenook reds from this period that decided Christian Moueix, of Chateau Pétrus fame, to become involved in Dominus, one of the more prestigious French/Napa wines of the 1980s.

Despite the stagnation during the gray decades after Repeal, signs of hope flashed on the horizon. From 1947 until the early 1960s, the Napa Valley wine industry seemed to be running in place. In 1949, Idwal Jones published *Vines in the Sun,* a bubbly little book on California wine devoted primarily to the past, with historical anecdotes that may have owed more to fiction than fact. But his descriptions of the contemporary wine scene are lively and prove that wine was alive and well in the Golden Valleys:

> The road from Yountville to the Stevenson aerie on Mount St. Helena is the Grand Route for those curious about vineyards, which here seem to

The "baggypants vintners brigade," shakers and movers in the revival of Napa's wine industry, included (left to right): Brother Timothy Diener of Christian Brothers; Charles B. Forni of Sunny St. Helena Co-op; Walter Sullivan and Aldo Fabrini of BV; Michael Ahern of Freemark Abbey, Peter and Robert Mondavi of Krug; John Daniel Jr. of Inglenook; Louis M. Martini, Charlie Beringer, and Martin Stelling of Sunny St. Helena Co-op; and Fred Abruzzini of Beringer. (Courtesy Caroline Martini)

be numberless, and each has its "tasting room"—the parlor sometimes; and at the larger farms, the office where the dossier on every barrel is kept in a metal cabinet. But the valley is not exploited on that account; the taverns or small eating places are ordinary, and the farms are not organized for tourists.

In an oral history, vintner Joe Heitz, one of the wine revolutionaries of the 1960s, blames himself for helping to start the tourist rush to the Napa Valley in the 1950s. It was he who convinced Beaulieu, his employer at the time, to open a tasting room. He nonetheless justifies his action by adding: "If there are no customers, there's no need for wineries."

Yet we cannot deny that California winemaking, in the period from the end of Prohibition to the wine renaissance of the 1960s, was marked by confusion. While most wineries made drinkable wine, much of it was marketed under generic names such as "sauternes" or "white burgundy" for whites. White wine came in three styles: dry, medium, and sweet. What passed as "white burgundy" in California was more often than not a blend of any white wine grapes at hand, just like the latter-day California whites known as "chablis" or "Rhine wine."

Red "burgundy" was blended in a similar fashion, but from red wine grapes, which included anything but pinot noir, the noble grape of France's Bourgogne (Burgundy) wine-growing district. "Claret" and "chianti" could also be made from any convenient red wine grape. The known style of an individual winery was more important than the generic name of the wine. To overcome this anarchy of meaningless proprietary and generic names, the better wineries began labeling their finer wines with the name of the grape: what was once called "sauternes" became "sauvignon blanc," and "claret" became "cabernet sauvignon."

Joe Heitz, a great vintner in his own right, was one of the early promoters of wine tourism in Napa Valley.

Eleanor and Fred McCrea created Stony Hill Vineyard, and a legendary chardonnay that set the standard for quality California white wines. (Photo by Emile Romaine, courtesy Stony Hill)

■ RENAISSANCE

The first proof of real change appeared in 1952, when Eleanor and Fred McCrea released the first of their now legendary chardonnays from Stony Hill Vineyard, a gravelly patch of land high up on Spring Mountain, near a summer home they purchased in 1943. This wine set a new standard for California whites (and still does) and may have inspired millionaire James Zellerbach to build Hanzell, a tiny Sonoma Valley winery dedicated to the production of true Burgundian-style wines. Before Zellerbach died in 1963, his winery had pioneered two methods that have now become standard practice in California winemaking: fermentation in stainless steel tanks rather than redwood or oak tanks, and the aging of chardonnay in small French Limousin oak barrels (the same oak from which Burgundian wine barrels are traditionally made).

Wine was about to become respectable: American soldiers returning from France after World War II and the droves of college students who'd traveled on the

Continent in the 1950s and '60s brought back the belief that the enjoyment of wine was part of a sophisticated lifestyle. James Zellerbach had shown that it was all right for respectable folk to dabble in wine. In 1965, Jack and Jamie Davies refurbished Jacob Schram's old cellars and began making first-rate sparkling wines from Napa Valley chardonnay grapes rather than from the colombard or riesling used by other local producers. In 1966, after a quarrel with his brother Peter, Robert Mondavi left Charles Krug, the family winery, and built a place of his own in Oakville—the first new winery built in the Napa Valley since Repeal. It was the right move at the right time, just as market demand for high-quality varietals was beginning to rise. He was emulated by Donn and Molly Chappellet on Pritchard Hill in 1969, by Charlie Wagner at Caymus in Rutherford and by David S. Stare at Sonoma County's Dry Creek Vineyard in 1972, by John and Janet Trefethen in Napa and by Fred Fisher on the Sonoma side of the Mayacamas range in 1973, and by many other vintners since. Napa Valley wines got a psychological boost in 1973, when the renowned French champagne house of Moet & Chandon bought vineyards and platted a winery site in 1973 to make French-style sparklers with Napa Valley grapes.

Stainless steel vats (above, at Domaine Chandon) used for fermentation are gradually replacing those made of wood (left, at Round Hill).

■ PARIS WINE TASTING OF 1976

The watershed event that changed the Wine Country forever happened in Paris in 1976. To celebrate the American Bicentennial, wine merchant Steven Spurrier put on a comparative tasting of California red and white wines against French cabernets and chardonnays. The tasters were French and included both journalists and producers. The 1973 Stag's Leap Wine Cellars came in first among the reds; the 1973 Chateau Montelena edged out the French whites. When the shouting died down, the rush was on. Both tourists and winemakers streamed into the Napa Valley. Wine prices rose so much that they even helped revitalize the Sonoma County wine industry; in Sonoma as in Napa, prune orchards were supplanted by vines.

The rustic lifestyle of the vineyards of yore was captured beautifully by this Ansel Adams photo, Man Plowing Vineyard, 1961. *(Courtesy Mumm Napa Valley)*

■ Precious Land

In the 1980s, the Napa Valley's rustic lifestyle seemed doomed by weekend home buyers who didn't mind plunking down a million dollars or more for a place among the vines. But as the Valley's popularity increased, so did opposition to untrammeled development which might threaten the very vineyards and wineries that made the Napa Valley such a special place to visit. By 1988, the battle lines were drawn between pro-growth and farm-preservation factions. The growth faction won a hotly contested county supervisor election in the fall of 1988, but when the newly elected supervisors moved too rashly in changing the face of the land, the pro-farm faction rallied and put together a proposition (Proposition J) that would allow no modification of the Valley's agricultural preserve and watershed for the next 30 years without the voters' approval. The measure passed by a wide margin in the 1990 election.

Sonoma County, too, saw increased urban sprawl, but Sonoma has more land: when Landmark Vineyards was pushed out of the Windsor area by suburban development, the winery moved into the upper Sonoma Valley. Other Sonoma wine regions are far enough from the madding crowd that they may not have to worry about urbanization for decades, if ever.

■ Real California Wines

Victory on the agrarian front has not brought complacency to the valleys. As you travel through the Sonoma and Napa wine valleys today, tasting the wines, talking to the winemakers, you sense a change in the air. No longer are wineries going all out to make the best French-style wine they can: they are striving to make the best possible California wine. This involves harvesting grapes at the optimum time, not only for grape sugars (which will be fermented into alcohol) but also for freshness and complexity. Where there used to be an almost desperate struggle to keep the alcohol level down to 12 percent by volume (the French norm—and a difficult task in California, where grapes ripen better than they do in France), by harvesting grapes too young, before their complex flavors had fully developed, there is now an acceptance that California is different. Today's wines often have an alcohol content of 13.5 percent—unacceptably high for France, where winemakers may have to augment their fermenting must with sugar to reach even 12 percent. Our

Barrels of aging wine are labeled in an old stone cellar.

winemakers no longer apologize for the extra alcohol. It does not detract from the wines' flavors and, as one vintner maintains, "it helps them age better."

Fermentation, too, is undergoing a revolution. Instead of importing the European yeasts used to make Champagne, Montrachet (the finest white Burgundy), or Bordeaux reds, the winemakers try to capture the wild yeasts of their own vineyards to imbue their wines with the particular quality of the place.

But our vintners are no longer sure that undiluted cabernet sauvignon and chardonnay, the war-horses of the '70s and '80s, are the best grapes for the region. As a result, blends are back, most of them under the catch-all label "Meritage," or under a proprietary name. While white Meritage is mostly a blend of sauvignon blanc and semillon, red Meritage may be made from cabernet sauvignon with a liberal admixture of merlot, cabernet franc, malbec, petit verdot, or any number of other Bordeaux varietals. Other blends might not contain any cabernet at all, such

Homemade wine is lovingly nurtured in Napa Valley along with its commercial counterpart.

as a series of new reds based on red Rhone varietals like mourvèdre, syrah, or grenache. Traditional Italian varietals, barbera, grignolino, nebbiolo, and sangiovese, cousins of the grapes first planted by the Italian Swiss Colony at Asti a hundred years ago, are also making a strong comeback. Even the Robert Mondavi winery, a leader in the promotion of inky cabernet sauvignons, is planting several varietals from the Rhone and from Italy.

But don't worry if you've just learned to tell Howell Mountain from Carneros chardonnay or Dry Creek from Chiles Valley zinfandel. Change comes slowly in the Wine Country, and you'll still have all your old favorites to taste as you explore the new varietals. The really good news is that no matter where you travel in the Wine Country, whether you stop at a small winery or a large one, you're bound to discover a superb bottle of wine.

WINE COUNTRY GEOLOGY:
SAUVIGNON SOIL, SILVER ORE, SERPENTINE

The diverse patterns of soils below Napa Valley's crags befuddle even the most experienced geologist or grape grower. Some of the soils are composed of dense, heavy sedimentary clays washed from the mountains; others are very rocky clays, loams, or silts of alluvial fans. You'll find similar soils in the winegrowing valleys of Sonoma County. These soils are best for growing grapes when they are composed largely of rocks and pebbles and are thus very porous. Grapes do not like their feet wet. But even here you will find that different grape varietals thrive under different conditions: cabernet sauvignon does best on well-drained, gravelly soils. If the soils are too wet or contain too much heavy clay or organic matter, the wines will have an obnoxious vegetative quality which even the best winemaking techniques cannot remove. Merlot grapes, on the other hand, can take more clay and still be made into wine that tastes rich and complex. Sauvignon blanc grapes do quite well in heavy clay soils, but the winegrower has to open up the canopy and cut back on irrigation to rid the grapes of such vegetative flavors as green pepper and asparagus—once thought to be varietal characteristics of this white grape, but now considered unacceptable.

A streak of light-colored, almost white soil runs across the Napa Valley from the Palisades to St. Helena and in Sonoma County from the western flanks of the Mayacamas Mountains to Windsor. These have been described as limestone—which would be a desirable rock in any wine country, since vines prefer basic soils to acidic ones. But these are actually volcanic ashes, tufas or tephras, of plutonic (volcanic) rather than neptunic (oceanic) origin. The "limestone" into which Napa Valley wine caves were dug in the 19th century and the pale building stone of Beringer's Rhine House and other Wine Country mansions and wineries was born of volcanic activity, and is thus not limestone at all.

Volcanic ash can be seen in several road cuts along the Napa Valley's Silverado Trail. A particularly good cut is near its northern end, below Glass Mountain, where broad bands of light-colored ash are speckled with flecks of black obsidian. Curiously, volcanic ash, obsidian, and rhyolite rock all have the same chemical composition—even though their outward appearance differs dramatically. They also have the same composition as the light-colored granite—also of plutonic origin—of the Sierra Nevada. These various rocks differ in appearance because the igneous granite slowly cooled under the earth, allowing its minerals to settle out, while the volcanic rocks of the Wine Country cooled rapidly above the earth, keeping the minerals in suspension. Like the Sierra Nevada, the mountains of the Wine Country have produced quantities of silver and gold. The Silverado Mine on Mount St. Helena was made famous by writer Robert Louis Stevenson, but the less romantic Palisades Mine east of Calistoga produced the greater amount of silver and gold and was, for a short time, one of the richest mines in the country. It closed in 1941, but there's still enough of the precious metals in the soil to reopen the mine if the price of silver rises.

As you drive through the mountains of the Wine Country, you may notice almost barren patches of landscape where scrub oak and gray pine predominate, even though nearby slopes are blanketed by lush meadows or woods. These sere patches are underlain by a gray-green to blue-green rock with a smooth, almost soapy surface. This is serpentine, a rock rarely seen elsewhere on the surface of our planet. If you look closely, you may notice that this odd-colored rock—with a color like petrified essence of ocean waves—does not merge into neighboring rock, but is cut off from it along a fairly sharp edge. That is because serpentine is a rock originating deep within the earth's crust that has been squeezed, unchanged, from its native matrix like paint from a tube. Why? How? No one knows. Unweathered serpentine contains chemicals noxious to most plants and will thus support only a limited number of trees and shrubs. But its nature changes as it weathers. When serpentine is exposed to the air for long periods of time, it turns red and eventually decomposes into soil which, thankfully, supports the growth of trees and—best of all—vines.

Old Wine Press on Patio at Mountain Winery, 1961 *by Ansel Adams. (Courtesy Mumm Napa Valley)*

VISITING WINERIES
TASTING & TOURING

Wine is a peephole on a man.
—Alcaeus, ca. 625–575 B.C.

Wine is the most healthful and most hygienic of beverages.
—Louis Pasteur, 1822–1895

LET US ASSUME THAT YOU HAVE PARKED YOUR CAR under a ramada of blooming wisteria vines. The winery, a rambling building sheathed in naturally weathered redwood, rises to your left from thickets of roses in full bloom. Several climbing roses cover the entrance trellis. You pause before you enter, because the view down the valley across vineyards and oak copses is breathtaking. Mountains covered with a dark evergreen forest rise straight from the valley floor on the far side of the vineyards. Behind the winery, the vineyard abuts a rocky slope studded with blue oaks and gray pines. A pair of ravens circles overhead and a covey of quail chatters and clucks among the willows and cottonwoods lining a creek bed. A quail's distinctive call rises from a scrub oak thicket on the hillside and is answered by another from a willow tangle. A cow lows in the distance. You tear yourself away from this pastoral scene and enter the winery's tasting room.

■ INTO THE TASTING ROOM: APPRECIATING WINE

Tasting rooms are very common among wineries in California's Wine Country; they're generally well marked and easy to find. Visiting them is essential to any trip through Napa and Sonoma counties. Don't worry if you know nothing about wine or the whys and wherefores of "tasting." Tasting rooms are very relaxed places. And they're designed to introduce novices to the pleasures of wines as well as to give the more accomplished a chance to expand their knowledge. If you're a novice, everyone will be glad to help—wine is a very social beverage. Besides, there's no magic to tasting wine. All you need is a palate and a little common sense. Wine is evaluated by appearance, aroma, and flavor, as follows.

■ THE WINE'S APPEARANCE

The first thing to judge when tasting wine is its appearance. No matter whether it's white, rosé, or red, a wine should be clear, without cloudiness or sediments. Hold the wine up to a window to let more natural light flow through the glass and show up any cloudiness. Next, check the color. Is it right for the wine? A white should be clear golden: straw, medium, or deep, depending on the type. The latter is acceptable only in rich, sweet, dessert wine but out of place in a chardonnay or sauvignon blanc. A rosé should be a clear pink—not too red, and without touches of orange or brown. A brown tinge in white and rosé wines usually means that the wine is too old, over the hill, or has been stored badly. Reds may have a violet tinge when young, a hint of amber when well aged (at that stage it is permissible for reds to have deposits, but the wine should be decanted before being poured: a glass is not the proper place for settling out deposits). A definite brown color is a flaw in reds, as is paleness—unless you're looking at a pinot noir. Good wine made from this grape can be quite pale yet still have character.

Natural light is best in checking wine for clarity and color.

■ THE WINE'S AROMA

After you have looked the wine over, swirl it gently in your glass and stick your nose into the glass. Aroma may well be the most important part of wine: your nose actually plays a larger role in tasting wine than your palate does, because the human palate can only perceive four basic tastes. One reason wine tasters swirl wine in the glass is to release the aromas. The more aromas and the more complex their interaction, the more interesting the wine.

Most of the aromas in wine are appealing. You might smell apricots, peaches, ripe melon, honey, and wildflowers in a white wine; black pepper, cherry, violets, and cedar in a red. Rosés are made from red wine grapes and thus have scents similar to those of a red wine, but on a more gentle scale and with hints of raspberry, geranium, and, sometimes, a touch of pomegranate. Each grape varietal has its own distinct aroma. With experience you'll learn to recognize it. Wine with good varietal character is better than wine with indistinct aromas.

Of course, there are times when you are in the mood for a wine with a light aroma rather than a heavy, complex one. There's nothing wrong with this. A wine does not have to be "great" and complex to be thoroughly enjoyable. But the aroma of such a wine should be clean and pleasing. It should never be "off" or smell of such things as sauerkraut, wet cardboard, garlic, wet dog, or skunk— strange, unpleasant odors all listed on the official Wine Aroma Wheel of the American Society for Enology and Viticulture, along with such scents as moldy, horsey, mousey, and sweaty. If you're tasting a heavier wine, you'll want to sniff at this time for such chemical faults as sulfur, or excess wood vanillin from the oak.

After you've judged the aroma, it's time to evaluate the acidity. All wine has acid. It's necessary to balance the fruit of the wine and give it backbone. But it should be an acidity you taste later, and not smell. If the wine smells acetic, it means it has started turning into vinegar. Don't drink it. Use it to make salad dressing.

■ FLAVORS FOUND IN WINE

You're now ready to take your first sip of the wine. How does it feel in your mouth? Does it feel pleasant? Do you like it? If not, don't drink it. You should never drink a wine you don't like. Although you may learn to appreciate a wine you don't understand, a wine will never really appeal to you unless you like it.

The human palate can process only four tastes: salt, bitter, sour, and sweet. Salt is not a natural component of wine, of course. If you taste some light bitterness in young reds, taste again, and you'll soon discover that the wine's tannic tartness can fool the palate. True bitterness is a fault, and it's thankfully rare in wine. Incidentally, there is no such thing as a "sour" wine—at least not in the opinion of the experts. What you perceive as sour is called astringent, acidic, or tart by enophiles. Taste for sugar. Sweetness—perceived or real—is found in many wines, even in some wines claiming to be dry. Many wines have become sweeter in recent years, perhaps because the American consumer does have a sweet tooth. But it's a very light sweetness, barely at the threshold of perception. A dinner wine should have no perceptible sweetness; a dessert wine commonly has quite a bit.

As you taste wine you'll notice more than just the four basic flavors, because your nose continues to "taste" the aromas. A wine taster swirls the wine in his or her mouth, or chews it, to release more aromas, which the nose picks up and analyzes.

When you swirl the wine around in your mouth, how does it feel? Does it seem to fill your mouth, or is it thin and weak? It should be well balanced and feel good. Do you like the flavor? Does it relate to the aroma? If not, something is out of balance. Swallow. Does your throat feel like it's puckering up?

Most importantly, you should ask yourself if you liked the wine. Your appreciation of its general quality is just as important as the individual parts. A wine can be technically perfect but seem very boring nevertheless. Remember: you're the one to decide. It's your taste that matters.

Keep several other things in mind as you taste wine in a tasting room. First, don't overdo it, especially if you drive. Those little sips add up. And don't feel like you have to buy a bottle of wine just because the winery has given you a taste or two. You're not expected to. Tasting rooms are set up to make customers familiar with a winery's name and product, and it's the winery's hope that you will like the wine enough to buy it at your favorite wine shop or supermarket. Which, by the way, is where you should buy wine, because wine sold at wineries often carries a higher price. This does not mean, of course, that you shouldn't stock up on hard-to-find vintages or varietals. Sometimes these can be bought only at the winery. If you're an out-of-region visitor, ask about the wineries direct-shipment program. Most wineries now ship wine directly to consumers in the 14 states with reciprocal agreements.

How Fine Wine Is Made

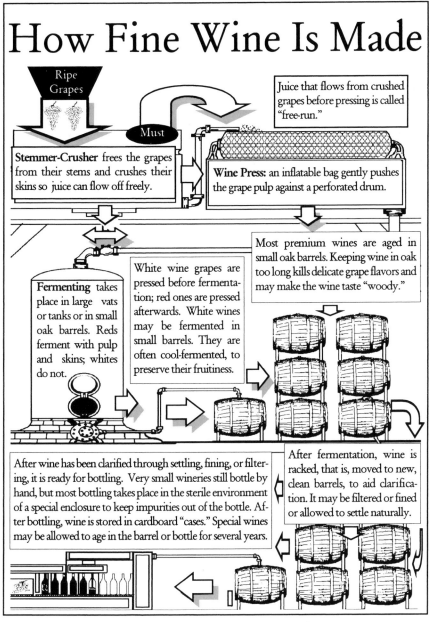

Ripe Grapes

Must

Stemmer-Crusher frees the grapes from their stems and crushes their skins so juice can flow off freely.

Juice that flows from crushed grapes before pressing is called "free-run."

Wine Press: an inflatable bag gently pushes the grape pulp against a perforated drum.

Fermenting takes place in large vats or tanks or in small oak barrels. Reds ferment with pulp and skins; whites do not.

White wine grapes are pressed before fermentation; red ones are pressed afterwards. White wines may be fermented in small barrels. They are often cool-fermented, to preserve their fruitiness.

Most premium wines are aged in small oak barrels. Keeping wine in oak too long kills delicate grape flavors and may make the wine taste "woody."

After fermentation, wine is racked, that is, moved to new, clean barrels, to aid clarification. It may be filtered or fined or allowed to settle naturally.

After wine has been clarified through settling, fining, or filtering, it is ready for bottling. Very small wineries still bottle by hand, but most bottling takes place in the sterile environment of a special enclosure to keep impurities out of the bottle. After bottling, wine is stored in cardboard "cases." Special wines may be allowed to age in the barrel or bottle for several years.

■ Taking a Winery Tour: How Wine is Made

If you have enjoyed your taste of wine, you might want to tour a winery and see how their wine is made. Such a tour will be most rewarding between August and October, when most of the grapes ripen and are crushed and fermented into wine. At other times of the year, winery work consists in monitoring the wine, "racking" it—that is, transferring it from one tank or barrel to another to leave deposits behind—or bottling and boxing the finished wine.

Winery tours can be exciting, but they are all pretty much alike. You can make tours more interesting by visiting different types of wineries. A large winery will make wine in a somewhat different fashion from a small family winery, and sparkling wine is made by a different process. Some wineries age their wines in warehouses, others have *caves* (say "kovz," as in French) which are long tunnels bored into the hillsides where the wine is kept naturally at an even temperature. Even if you've taken tours before, you might take another now and then, to refresh your memory.

Crushing grapes the old-fashioned way . . .

■ THE WINE CRUSH

Most winery tours start out at the **crush pad.** This is where the grapes are brought in from the vineyards. Grapes are brought to the winery in large containers called **gondolas,** which gently drop the grape bunches onto a conveyor belt. Grapes must be handled with care, so none of the juice is lost. Some wineries pick their grapes by machine, while others still pick by hand. It depends on the terrain and on the **varietal,** or type of grape. Some delicate white varietals like chardonnay are picked at night with the help of powerful floodlights. Why? Grapes contain natural fruit acids, which not only bring out the fruit but also give the wine its "backbone"— the element that holds it together during fermentation and aging. Grape acids are reduced during the heat of the day, when the sun warms the grapes, but they in-crease during the cool hours of the night. When a vineyard picks its white wine grapes at night, it gets the grapes at their highest fruit-acid content. Nighttime picking is not a consideration with red wine grapes, as red wines depend upon acids from the grape skins.

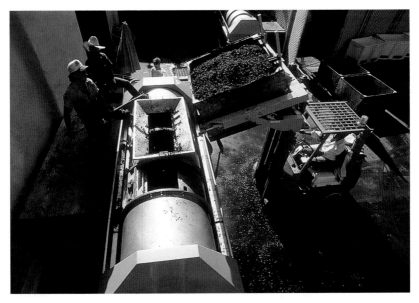

. . . and the newfangled way.

The conveyor belt drops the grape clusters into a **stemmer-crusher,** which has a drum equipped with steel fingers that knock the grapes off the stems, and pierce their skins, so the juice can flow of freely. The grapes and juice fall through a grate and are carried via stainless steel pipes to a press or vat. The stems and leaves drop out and are recycled to the vineyards as natural fertilizer.

■ FERMENTING AND AGING WHITE WINES

What happens to the crushed grapes at the next stage depends on what variety of grape has been crushed and what type of wine is being made—white, rosé, or red. The juice of white wine grapes is first sent to settling tanks, where the skins and grape solids settle to the bottom, separating from the clear free-run juice on top. From here the free run is pumped directly to a fermenter—either a stainless steel tank (which may be insulated to keep the fermenting juice cool) or to an oak barrel. The grape skins and other solids which have sunk to the bottom of the tank still contain a lot of juice. They are dropped into a press in which the juice is gently extracted by air pressure. Modern presses have a perforated drum with a Teflon-coated bag inside. As this bag is inflated slowly, like a balloon, it pushes the grapes against the outside wall—slowly and gently—and the liquids are squeezed from the solids and flow off. Press juice and free-run juice are fermented separately, but a little of the press juice may be added to the free-run juice to give it added complexity. But not too much, since press juice tends to be too strongly flavored and may contain undesirable flavor components. Press juice is always fermented in stainless steel tanks; free-run juice may be handled differently. In the case of chardonnay and some sauvignon blanc, free-run juice is fermented in small oak barrels, in individual batches, with each vineyard and lot kept separate. That's the way the very best wine is made, and that's why good white wines are so expensive. It's a very labor-intensive process: the oak barrels, imported from France, are very expensive and can be used for a few years only. California wineries like to use French oak because that's the wood traditionally used for aging wine, but some are experimenting with American oak as well.

Barrel aging rooms are kept dark, because electric lights generate heat, and wine does not like to be too warm. Nor does wine like bright light—if exposed to too much light, wine can change in unexpected ways. Supermarket displays of wine on open, brightly lit shelves may allow shoppers to read labels and prices more easily, but it's rough on the wine. Fluorescent overhead lights can be just as damaging to wine as bright sunlight can, and supermarket air conditioning systems tend to dry out the corks. It's even worse if the bottles are stored upright, with no wine touching the corks to keep them moist. If the cork dries out, it shrinks, allowing oxygen to enter the bottle and spoil the wine.

Large stainless steel tanks are used for fermenting wine and for storing white wine. They may be equipped with wraparound cooling sleeves. Sauvignon blanc and riesling are commonly fermented cool to develop more fruit aromas and delicacy. Chardonnay, as well as some reds, may be fermented in small oak barrels, which makes for a richer wine. Fermentation in small barrels creates more depth and complexity, as the wine picks up vanilla and other harmonious flavors from the wood. When the wine is finished, several batches are blended together. Careful blending gives the winemaker an extra chance to create a perfect wine.

When the wine has finished fermenting—whether in a tank or barrel—it is **racked:** it is moved into a clean tank or barrel to separate it from the lees, the spent yeast, and any grape solids that have dropped out of suspension. At this stage the wine may or may not be filtered, depending on how the winemaker feels about it. Sometimes chardonnay and special batches of sauvignon blanc are left on the lees for extended periods of time—at the winemaker's discretion—to pick up extra complexity. If wine is aged for any length of time, it will be racked again and may be **fined**—or clarified by the introduction of fining agents such as a fine clay called bentonite, or albumen, from egg white. These substances help clarify the wine. Some wineries filter their wines, especially white wines, while others just fine. Some reds are left unfined for extra depth. Wine may be filtered after fermentation, before bottling, or whenever the winemaker thinks it necessary. After the wine is bottled, most of it is not kept in storage for long. It goes to a cooperative warehouse from which it is shipped on demand. Many wineries age only their reserve wines in their own cellars.

■ FERMENTING AND AGING RED WINES

Red wine production is slightly different. Red wine grapes are crushed just like white wine grapes, but they are not separated from the grape skins and pulp during fermentation. It is this step which gives red wine its color. After crushing, the red wine must and the grape pulp and skins are pumped into vats where they are

(continues on page 60)

Creating the oak barrels that age the wine is a craft in its own right. At Demptos Napa Cooperage, a French-owned company that employs French barrel-making techniques, the process involves several elaborate production phases. Below, the staves of oak are formed to the barrel shape using metal bands. At right, semi-finishing takes place to smooth the rough edges off the bound staves. Finally, the barrels are literally toasted (left) to give the oak "flavor," which will in turn be imparted to the wine.

Three types of barrels are made: those of 100 percent American oak; those of 100 percent French oak; and those that are a blend of both.

fermented together. The must is "left on the skins" for varying periods of time, depending on how much color the winemaker wants to extract. Reds are more robust than whites because the fermentation extracts not only color but also flavors and tannins (special acids that help the wine age) from the skins. Red wine fermentation occurs at a higher temperature than that for whites—reds ferment at about 70 degrees F to 90 degrees F (21 degrees C to 32 degrees C). As grape sugars are converted into alcohol, great amounts of carbon dioxide (CO_2) are generated. CO_2 is lighter than wine but heavier than air, and it forms an "aerobic cover" which protects the wine from oxidation. As the wine ferments, grape skins rise to the top and are periodically mixed back in so the wine can extract the maximum amount of color and flavor. This is done either in the traditional fashion by punching them down, or by pumping over the wine and the skins. The former is preferable since it keeps the CO_2 cover intact and minimizes exposure of the wine to oxygen.

At the end of fermentation, the free-run wine is drained off. The grape skins and pulp are sent to a press where the remaining wine is extracted. As with the whites, the winemaker may choose to add a little of the press wine to the free-run wine—if he feels it will add complexity to the finished wine. Otherwise the press juice goes into bulk wine. After the wine has been racked, it ages in oak barrels for a year or longer. Unlike the barrels used for aging chardonnay, the barrels used for aging red wine are not always new. They may already have been used to age chardonnay, which has extracted most of their flavors. Oak, like grapes, contains natural tannins, and the wine extracts these tannins from the barrels. Oak also has countless tiny pores through which water in the wine slowly evaporates, making the wine more concentrated. To make sure the aging wine does not oxidize, the barrels have to be regularly topped off with wine from the same vintage—which is another reason why aged wine is more expensive.

The only way even the best winemaker can tell if a wine is finished is by tasting it. A winemaker constantly tastes wines while they are fermenting, while they are aging in barrels, and regularly, though less often, while they age in bottles. The wine is released—or "sent to market"—when the winemaker's palate and nose say it's ready.

■ MAKING ROSÉ WINES

Rosé or blush wines are also made from red wine grapes—but they are left on the skins for a matter of hours, not of days. The winemaker decides how long. When the juice has reached the desired color, it is drained off and filtered. The yeast is added and the juice ferments like any other wine. Because it stays on the skins for a shorter time, it also attracts fewer tannins and is thus not as heavy as red wine. You might say that rosé is a lighter, fruitier version of red wine, not a pink version of white. If it is made right, it will have some of the flavors of the grape. Rosés can be great food wines—if they are not too sweet. They're also great for sipping on the back porch on a hot afternoon or warm summer evening.

Expect to find slight variations of these methods at some wineries. Most wineries are open for tours and tastings, though some are only open on weekends or by appointment. Call ahead to be sure. (See "WINERY MASTER LIST," *page 294, for phone numbers.)*

Man Riddling Bottles of Champagne, *a 1961 silver print by Ansel Adams from "The Story of Wine," an exhibition at Mumm Napa Valley. (Courtesy Mumm Napa Valley)*

GROWERS AND WINEMAKERS, VINEYARDS AND WINERIES

Is wine made in the vineyard or in the winery? French winemakers, who believe in the importance of the *terroir* (the soil, the micro-climate, the growing conditions), would argue the former. California winemakers—not all of whom grow grapes of their own—generally claim the latter. Ideally, of course, all winemakers would grow the grapes they need to make their own wine. But that's not always possible—especially in the Northern California Wine Country, where prices for prime vineyard land have soared in recent years. While the vineyard was once considered the first—and necessary—investment of every winery, few wineries opened since Prohibition began their operations with a vineyard. Instead, many winemakers purchase their grapes from independent growers. Not surprisingly, growers have become key players in the wine industry in Napa and Sonoma counties, and an understanding of their complex, ever-changing relationship with winemakers is helpful information for any lover of the region's wine.

Andy Beckstoffer, lord of his realm.

THE GROWERS

Andy Beckstoffer, a prominent Napa Valley grower, estimates that only about 50 percent of the grapes harvested in Northern California's Wine Country are grown by wineries; the other half come from independent growers. Where grape quality is concerned, the growers may have the edge over many wineries, because they must be in the forefront of viticultural innovation in order to sell grapes to finicky winemakers.

And right now, everything is being questioned—even the soils in which the vines are planted. According to vineyard specialist Beckstoffer, from 30 to 50 percent of Napa Valley vineyards are planted in bottomland soils that are too rich: vines are among the few plants that give their best fruit when they grow in poor soils. Ideal vineyard soils, says Beckstoffer, drain well. "You need lots of things," he says, "but permeability is on top. The permeability of the soil is more important than its mineral content. You can always change the mineral content."

There's another challenge for growers to contend with: the phylloxera root louse is slowly killing local vines, and most of the region's vineyards will have to be replanted—and done so efficiently—within the next decade. As a grower replants, he has to carefully select vine clones and match the most desirable clones to the best root stocks. Because growing is all they do, independent growers can usually respond more quickly and expertly than can winemaker/growers. But even when replanting, growers must continue to anticipate the needs of their winemaker

An enologist draws wine into a pipette to measure its acidity.

clients. For instance, **Robert Young Vineyard**, the Alexander Valley vineyard famous for its chardonnay grapes, had to be uprooted because of phylloxera. The vineyard is being replanted not just with chardonnay, but with cabernet sauvignon, merlot, cabernet franc, and even sangiovese, because the Youngs discern a market trend toward red wines.

Saralee's Vineyard. The 150 acres of this vineyard in the Russian River appellation were carefully selected by Rich and Saralee Kunde for their soil and cool climate. More than just a grape supplier for wineries, the vineyard serves also as a research facility for another family business, **Sonoma Grapevines,** a major supplier of rootstocks and vines both to other grape growers and sometimes to wineries who have vineyards of their own. Many parts of Saralee's Vineyards meet international standards for worldwide shipment of propagation wood—meaning the vines are free from communicable diseases. The Kundes must employ the most up-to-date vineyard techniques to stay competitive.

(continues)

Sangiacomo Vineyards. Another one of Sonoma County's best-known vineyards lies to the south of the city of Sonoma, along Sonoma Creek. Like Rich and Saralee Kunde, the Sangiacomo family owns no winery but is a grower exclusively. Farming over a thousand acres of grapes in the cool Carneros region, the Sangiacomos are best known for the chardonnay grapes their vineyards produce. But they also grow pinot noir and a few merlot vines. It may be the latter which will ultimately produce the best wine. One indicator is the intense 1993 Ravenswood merlot, made from Sangiacomo grapes. Besides Ravenswood, the Sangiacomos sell their grapes to such top wineries as Chateau Souverain, Clos du Bois, Domaine Chandon, Gundlach-Bundschu, Matanzas Creek, Saintsbury, and Simi. Even Buena Vista, the Carneros district's biggest winery and grapegrower, buys some grapes from the Sangiacomos. Without producing a single bottle of wine, large growers like Kunde or Sangiacomo are pivotal to the success of the region's wine industry.

SMALL WINERIES

Small wineries with only a few acres of grapes are limited in their scope, because different grape varieties like different types of soils and micro-climates. Which is, of course, the

Bottling wine in the 1870s at Buena Vista . . .

reason why so many small wineries buy grapes, even if they have vineyards of their own. Chardonnay likes well-drained vineyards but will take heavy soil, and merlot likes clay with gravel. Sauvignon blanc will grow in much richer soil but needs special handling, such as leaf-pulling and other viticultural techniques, to make up for the richness of the soil (which can give the grapes and wine a "weedy" flavor).

If, on the other hand, a small winery has the right location, and grows only those grapes best suited to its special soil and micro-climate, it can produce spectacular wines from small vineyards. That's what Chateau Woltner does with chardonnay, Storybook Mountain with zinfandel, and Livingston with cabernet sauvignon. If such a small winery wants to expand production, it needs to buy another vineyard or buy grapes from other growers.

Some winemakers and growers feel that this complexity can be achieved only by growing grapes in the proper soils. Others are convinced they can achieve complexity through careful rootstock and clone selection.

WINEMAKERS
Buying grapes from a grower does not necessarily reduce a winemaker's labors, but it may

(continues)

. . . and performing the same chore at Freemark Abbey in the 1990s.

change the type of work he or she does. A good winemaker will carefully monitor the grapes from different growers' vineyards throughout the season, from spring pruning (which determines the vigor of the vines) through fruit thinning (to make the remaining grapes more intense in flavor), to leaf-pulling (to give the grapes even exposure to the sun), and to determining the proper day for picking. If the vineyards from which a winemaker buys grapes are spread out over several appellations—as often happens—a winemaker will spend a considerable amount of time on the road, traveling back and forth between the different plots of vines. The winemaker's presence is especially critical at harvest, when he or she will regularly check the grapes' ripeness by tasting as well as checking the sugar levels by testing.

Winemakers try to sign long-term contracts with reliable growers to control the consistency and quality of the fruit—as though they had their own vineyard run by a vineyard manager. But that's not always possible, especially when a grower sells to more than one winery.

Ironically, the winemaker also faces the problem of making wine that is too good and too popular. For as the demand for the wine—and its price—rises, so will the price of the grapes. In some cases, other wineries will bid up the price of the grapes from the grower who grew the grapes that made the acclaimed wine, so that a winemaker can no longer afford the grapes that made his or her winery famous. This competitiveness among winemakers for a specific batch of grapes brings us right back to the French notion that, ultimately, great wine is made in the vineyard. Which might lead us to believe that the grower is at least as important as the winemaker. Yet when you taste wines made by different winemakers from grapes produced in one vineyard, you'll notice right away that there's more to making wine than growing grapes. The quality of these wines may range from merely good to truly great. Winemaking is, after all, more than an agricultural pursuit. It is an art.

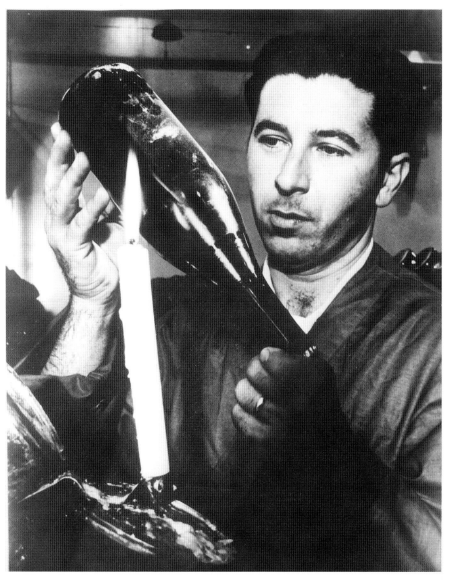

The uninspiring title of this Ansel Adams silver print is Man Looking at Bottle (with Candle), 1961. *It appears in an exhibition at Mumm Napa Valley. (Courtesy Mumm Napa Valley)*

GRAPE VARIETIES

Chardonnay
This noble grape variety of Burgundy can give great wine in California, when grown in austere soils of cool vineyards.

Riesling (also called **Johannisberg Riesling** or **White Riesling**)
This cool-climate grape has been up-staged by chardonnay and viognier, but it can make great wine in California—when conditions are right.

Pinot Blanc
When grown in well-drained soils of cool vineyards this white grape can give a wine that rivals chardonnay.

Sylvaner
A white wine grape makes good, easily enjoyable wine and thrives almost everywhere in California.

Sauvignon Blanc
This white grape does very well almost anywhere in the California Wine Country—even in fertile bottom lands—and often makes more interesting wine than chardonnay.

Pinot Noir
This finicky grape is giving great wine in the cool growing regions of the Carneros district and the Russian River Valley.

Cabernet Sauvignon

This noble red wine grape of Bordeaux also gives great wine in California, when grown in austere, well-drained soils.

Zinfandel

When grown in the austere red soils of northern Sonoma or Napa, this "native" California grape gives complex, well-balanced wine that ages as well as the best French clarets.

Cabernet Franc

Cabernet franc gives aromatic red wines, soft and more subtle than those of the closely related cabernet sauvignon.

Sangiovese

This versatile Tuscan wine grape grows well in Sonoma County and can give light-bodied as well as long-lived, very complex reds.

Merlot

This dark, blue-black grape is quickly becoming California's most popular red wine grape, because its wine is soft yet complex, even when young.

Illustrations by John Doerper

LOWER NAPA VALLEY

One barrel of wine can work more miracles than a church full of saints.
—Italian proverb

THE NAPA VALLEY IS A LONG, NARROW TROUGH between mountain chains with more wineries per mile than than any other place in America. Because there's so much to see and taste, we have broken our trip recommendations into two sections, each of which is perfect for a day of self-guided touring. Since the lower valley is close to tidewater and thus stays cool on a hot summer day, you might plan your visits accordingly. The upper valley can get very hot in summer but is pleasantly mild in spring and autumn.

Our first drive follows a loop route, heading north from the city of Napa, visiting Yountville and Oakville, and turning east at Rutherford Cross Road to return south by way of the Silverado Trail and the Stags Leap District. Our second drive, described in "UPPER NAPA VALLEY," following, starts with a visit to Rutherford, and includes wineries found along the route to St. Helena and Calistoga.

Before you set out to tour the Napa Valley wineries, please keep in mind that you cannot visit them all. So be selective. Three or four per day is plenty, not only in terms of your energy levels, but in terms of alcohol consumption. Plan ahead but also leave time to pay a spontaneous visit to a winery not on your list. Before beginning, consult "VISITING WINERIES," page 49.

■ OVERVIEW OF THE NAPA VALLEY

Highway 29, the Napa Valley Highway, heads north from Vallejo first as a busy four-lane highway with traffic lights (which always turn red just as you approach them), then as a freeway, and finally as a two-lane highway. At the juncture where CA Highway 29 becomes a freeway heading north into the Napa Valley, a freeway sign points the driver north to "Napa" along CA 121. This sign refers to the town of Napa, but it's best to continue north on CA 29 to reach the main part of the Napa Valley.

The state had made plans to extend the freeway all the way to Calistoga, but local winegrowers stopped that plan by turning the Napa Valley into an agricultural

Looking south along the length of Napa Valley from an altitude of 30,000 feet. The north end of San Francisco Bay is just visible at the top of frame.

preserve, and now the freeway only extends to Yountville. Beyond that CA 29 remains a narrow, two-lane road. But, narrow and congested as this thoroughfare is, it has not stopped an ever-growing number of visitors eager to see the Napa Valley and taste its fabled wines. It has, however, halted most development away from the highway so that today, except for a new winery or two, the valley looks much as it did a quarter of a century ago.

In the 35-mile drive from tidewater to the foothills of Mount St. Helena, you will pass through several different climate zones; driving into the mountains to the east and west will add a few more. Looking at the vineyards, you may notice that the soils change often. This variety explains why the valley makes so many different wines and makes them so well. Several parts of the Napa Valley have been recognized as being sufficiently unique to warrant their own sub-appellations. Two of these, Oakville and Rutherford, stretch clear across the valley floor. Stags Leap encompasses a small district on the east side of the valley, while Mount Veeder, Spring Mountain, and Howell Mountain encompass parts of—but not all of—the mountains from which they take their name. The rest is simply known as Napa Valley. Plan to visit one of these appellations at a time or pick a winery in each, or ignore them altogether, as you explore the valley. The Napa Valley gets warmer as you drive north (unless you visit in winter, when the pattern is reversed). The Carneros is coolest; Calistoga gets hottest. St. Helena, where the valley narrows, is the dividing point. You may not, however, notice this climatic change in the wines you will taste, for most of the wineries grow grapes in several of the regions or buy them from growers in other sub-appellations. Thus Mumm Napa Valley gets the grapes for its sparkling wines from the cool Carneros region, while the grapes in the vineyards surrounding the winery go to Sterling, another of its parent company's wineries. As you taste the wines, feel free to ask where the grapes for a particular wine came from. It's a part of understanding wine.

The main route, CA 29, goes north toward Yountville. A second, less traveled route diverges at Dry Creek Road (take Redwood Road from the town of Napa) and leads to the **Mount Veeder** appellation, which parallels the highway to the west *(see page 94).*

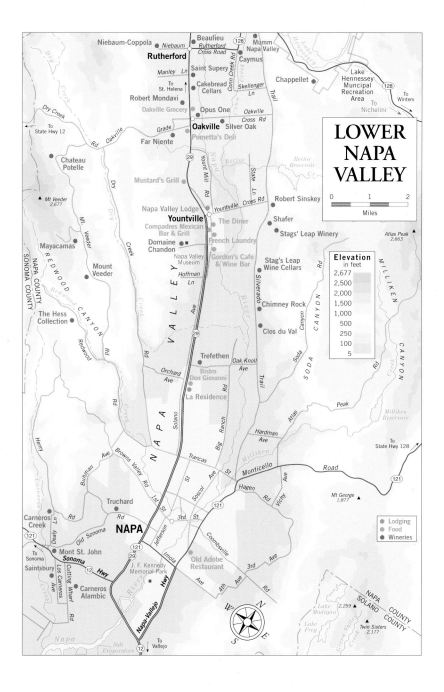

LOWER NAPA VALLEY

Niebaum-Coppola • Niebaum
Beaulieu • Rutherford Cross Road
128
Mumm Napa Valley •
Rutherford
Caymus •
Manley Ln
Saint Supery •
Chappellet •
Lake Hennessey Muncipal Recreation Area
128
To Winters
To St. Helena
Cakebread Cellars •
Skellenger Ln
Robert Mondavi •
Oakville Grocery •
Opus One •
Oakville Cross Rd
To Nichelini
To State Hwy 12
Oakville Grade
Oakville • Silver Oak
Pometta's Deli
Far Niente •
29
Rector Reservoir
Chateau Potelle •
Mustard's Grill •
Robert Sinskey •
▲ Mt Veeder 2,677
Napa Valley Lodge •
Yountville Cross Rd
Yountville
Atlas Peak 2,663 ▲
Compadres Mexican Bar & Grill
The Diner •
Shafer •
Mayacamas •
Domaine Chandon • ■
French Laundry
Stags' Leap Winery •
Napa Valley Museum
Gordon's Cafe & Wine Bar
Stag's Leap Wine Cellars •
Mount Veeder
Hoffman Ln
The Hess Collection •
Chimney Rock •
Clos du Val •
Trefethen •
Oak Knoll Ave
Bistro Don Giovanni •
La Residence •
Peak
To State Hwy 128
Orchard Ave
Hardman Ave
Truchard •
Monticello
Road
121
Mt George 1,877 ▲
Carneros Creek •
121
NAPA
To Sonoma
Mont St. John •
Sonoma Hwy
J. F. Kennedy Memorial Park
121
Coombsville
Saintsbury •
Old Adobe Restaurant
Carneros Alambic •
Lake Madigan
2,259 ▲
NAPA COUNTY
SOLANO COUNTY
Lake Frey
Twin Sisters 2,177
To Vallejo

Elevation
in feet
2,677
2,500
2,000
1,500
1,000
500
250
100
5

0   1   2
Miles

● Lodging
● Food
● Wineries

■ From Oak Knoll to Rutherford Bench

Because the highway passes through unpleasant urban sprawl as it leaves Napa, visitors rush north to Yountville, where they feel the real valley starts. Which is why they may miss one of the Napa Valley's most important wineries, Trefethen Vineyards.

Trefethen Vineyards. The big, Tuscan-red building is the old Eshcol Winery, built in 1886. This huge, three-story gravity-flow winery is, unlike other old Napa Valley wineries, built from wood rather than stone—making it somewhat of a rarity. It has weathered the last century well, although the upper floors were strained when a budding Domaine Chandon used it for storing sparkling wine.

Eshcol closed during Prohibition and was reopened for a short time after Repeal; then the vineyards were leased to Beringer. Gene Trefethen, executive vice president of Kaiser Industries, and his wife, Catherine, bought the property in 1968 as a retirement home. Some retirement *that* turned out to be. Like so many folks retiring to the Napa Valley, they began replanting the vineyards and restoring the winery. Then an event occurred that no one could have foreseen: Moët-Hennessy, the French champagne house, decided to open a

Janet and John Trefethen.

winery in the Napa Valley and settled on Yountville as the facility's location. While plans were made for building the winery, Moët-Hennessy's master of champagne was eager to make wine from local grapes to learn which would be best for sparkling wine production. But to make commercial wine, you need a bonded winery. As historian Jamie Laughridge tells it, Robert-Jean de Vogüé, the Chairman of M-H, and John Wright, the project manager, met Catherine Trefethen at a party. She invited them to lunch the next day. They discovered that Trefethen had a perfectly usable but empty winery building, and a deal was worked out.

M-H kept some of its operations at Trefethen until 1977, when both wineries went their separate ways. The Trefethen winery, now run by John Trefethen and his wife, Janet, soon gained recognition for the excellence of its wines: a 1976 Trefethen chardonnay placed first in a 1979 tasting held in Paris by Gault Millau. Today the Trefethens make excellent chardonnay, cabernet sauvignon, and merlot, as well as riesling. Their two proprietary wines are Eshcol Chardonnay and Eshcol Cabernet Sauvignon. *1160 Oak Knoll Avenue, Napa; (707) 255-7700.*

Domaine Chandon. A few miles up the road, to the west of Yountville's only freeway underpass, sprawls the expansive, sparkling-wine complex of Domaine Chandon. The winery is constructed as a series of huge half barrels, open to the south—so you can hardly see it from the highway, even though it's just off the road. No other winery quite blends into the landscape the way Domaine Chandon does in the rear, where it goes underground, and shows as dramatic a front to the world where it opens up in serried arches. When the winery was built, the ancient oaks on the property were spared. Today, 20 years later, the oaks are more beautiful than ever. Unfortunately, Domaine Chandon recently violated its standards by erecting an unappealing, slab-sided warehouse north of the old winery.

Sparklers here are made only by the labor-intensive—and costly—*méthode champenoise,* meaning the wine is fermented individually in the bottle and individually disgorged *(see page 125 for more on disgorging).* All of the wines are *cuvées* (blends); the top of the line Etoile is a cuvée of older vintages. It is a splendid accompaniment for the exquisite dishes served at Domaine Chandon's restaurant—a Wine Country first that caused quite a stir when it opened in June of 1977 *(see* "RESTAURANTS," *page 252).* The winery is especially nice to visit. *One California Drive, Yountville; (707) 944-8844.*

❖

Not open to the public is **Dominus Estate,** the Napa Valley venture of Christian Moueix, owner of Bordeaux's prestigious Chateau Petrus. In *Guide to the Best Wineries of North America,* André Gayot comments on the creation of Domaine Chandon, Opus One, and Dominus that "collectively these three joint ventures signaled the Napa Valley's unassailable eminence in the wine world." Some folks in Sonoma might disagree.

You will not notice a change in the scenery or the vineyards as you cross from the Oakville sub-appellation into the Rutherford one, yet Robert Mondavi lies in the former, and Cakebread, just a stone's throw up the road, lies in the latter.

Winemaker Chris Phelps tastes a new batch at Dominus Estate.

Japanese plum trees bloom along the road leading to the Niebaum-Coppola Estate. (Kerrick James)

■ YOUNTVILLE

Yountville, at the southern edge of the St. Helena district, became a wine-growing center back in 1870, when wealthy San Francisco immigrant Gottlieb Groezinger built a large winery here. The brick winery building still stands, but has since been turned into a shopping complex called Vintage 1870. The town was founded by George Calvert Yount, a mountain man from North Carolina. Yount changed his name to Jorge Concepcion Yount when he converted to Catholicism in order to obtain the grant of Rancho Caymus from Mariano Vallejo in 1836.

Today, Yountville has several of the Valley's best restaurants, including The French Laundry, The Diner, and, north of town, Mustard's Grill (see "Restaurants" beginning on page 250). The town's lodging facilities match the quality of the food (see "Lodging" beginning on page 262). Yountville Market on Washington Street dates back to 1916. It's a good place for local bread, produce, wines, and picnic lunches. You can picnic at either the **Yountville Park** (picnic tables, barbecue grills, public restrooms) at the north end of town or at the **Napa River Ecological Reserve** off the Yountville Cross Road (no picnic tables here—you'll have to sit on a grassy bank or gravelly beach, but you can dangle your feet in the river, when it has water). While strolling through Yountville, you might want to visit the **Pioneer Cemetery and Indian Burial Ground** off Jackson Street, which were established in 1848. George Yount is buried here, and the cemetery is still used by the remaining members of the local Wappo tribe. The Veterans' Home southwest of Domaine Chandon was established in 1881 for disabled veterans of the Mexican War and the Grand Army of the Republic. The marvelous new **Napa Valley Museum** has been built on Veterans' Home property. Its permanent exhibit, *California Wine: The Science of an Art,* offers a user-friendly introduction to exactly that: how the sciences of geology, agriculture, and wine-making technology join forces with the inspiration, creativity, and experience of the winemaker to create a memorable bottle of wine. The museum is accessible directly through the Veterans Home or by gate from the Domaine Chandon winery. *55 Presidents Circle; (707) 944-0500.*

Yountville is close to the Stags Leap District, whose vineyards lie beneath the towering volcanic palisades and crags and produce superb cabernet sauvignon grapes. To get there directly, take Yountville Cross Road to the Silverado Trail and turn south. Or follow our more leisurely route north to Rutherford, then cut across to the Silverado Trail and follow it down.

■ OAKVILLE WINERIES

Just north of Yountville lies the hamlet of Oakville. Stop here and check out the local deli fare. **Pometta's Deli** on the west side of the road, where the Oakville Grade meets the highway, has great barbecued chicken and sandwiches. Its specialty is the Napa Valley muffaletta sandwich: ham, salami, two cheeses, and the house olive spread. A couple of hundred feet farther up CA 29, on your right, just after the Oakville Cross Road turns off to the east, is the **Oakville Grocery**—a gourmet shop small in size but prodigious in depth. This is the perfect place for picking up picnic fixings as well as hard-to-find local wines (house wines are made by Joseph Phelps, the grocery's owner). The grocery has a full-fledged restaurant next door, the former Stars.

Take the Oakville Cross Road east and look for **Silver Oak Wine Cellars** on the right. This small winery, started by Ray Duncan and former Christian Brother Justin Meyer, makes nothing but cabernet sauvignon—but what wine! The grapes come from Sonoma County's Alexander Valley, from the small Bonny's Vineyard in Oakville, and from other Napa Valley vineyards. The wines age well but are not inexpensive. *915 Oakville Cross Road; (707) 944-8808.*

The golden fields and green hills of a Napa Valley vineyard.

Robert Mondavi Winery. A short distance north of the Oakville Cross Road, on the west side of the highway, rise the tower and large entrance gate of the Napa Valley's best-known winery. Earlier in this century, the huge To-Kalon Winery dominated this part of the Napa Valley, both with the quantity and the quality of its wines. Today, its place—and some of its vineyards—have been taken over by Robert Mondavi Vineyards. No other winery has done more to promote the excellence of Napa Valley wines throughout the world—though, curiously, Mondavi wines were missing from the 1976 Paris tasting that brought the Napa Valley such fame.

Robert Mondavi forever changed the nature of the wine known as California sauternes by taking sauvignon blanc grapes, leaving them on the skins after the crush, fermenting the juice in stainless steel, and aging it in French oak barrels. He called his creation fumé blanc (a play on blanc fumé, the steely-crisp wine made from sauvignon blanc in France's Loire Valley). Both the style and the name caught on: dozens of wineries in both Napa and Sonoma counties now make fumé blanc. When you take a tour at Robert Mondavi, you will see an oak barrel with the wood of one end replaced by a panel of plexiglass to let you see the wine age on the lees (the deposits thrown off as the wine ages). But while the fumé blanc has been Mondavi's most copied wine, it has been the reserve reds that have made

Robert Mondavi (foreground) entertains guests at a dinner in his vineyards.

the winery's reputation.

Recently, the Mondavi winery, now run by Robert's sons Michael and Tim, has crossed another frontier, by experimenting with wine made from Italian and Rhone varietals. *7801 St. Helena Highway, Oakville; (707) 963-9611.*

Far Niente, another prominent Oakville winery, occupies a stone building erected in 1885 and restored from 1978 to 1982 by Gil Nickel. Its 15,000 square feet of caves were dug in 1990. The winery produces a much-coveted chardonnay and cabernet sauvignon, but it is not open to the public.

Opus One is a joint venture of the Napa Valley's Robert Mondavi and France's Baron Philippe Rothschild. Operations are not progressing as quickly as had been hoped, because phylloxera has devastated the winery's vines. The winery is a modern building that looks a bit like a flying saucer that got stuck in the mud. It was planned as a semi-subterranean facility, to take advantage of the cool earth keeping the aging cellars at constant temperature. Instead, the builders found a hot spring. It was too late to look for another building site, and the winery is now cooled by mechanical rather than natural air conditioning. Open for tastings by appointment. *7900 St. Helena Highway, Oakville; (707) 944-9442.*

The Robert Mondavi Winery has grown to be one of the Napa Valley's most eminent producers of premium wines.

Jack Cakebread is an accomplished photographer as well as winemaker.

Cakebread Winery. This great winery is run by one of the nicest and most creative families in the business. Jack Cakebread, who founded the winery in 1973 with his wife, Dolores, is also a renowned photographer; Dolores is a superb cook who has played a major role in making the Napa Valley a food as well as a wine region. Her kitchen garden—where she grows vegetables and herbs for entertaining important guests—occupies a prominent (and perhaps symbolic) spot between the winery and the vineyards. Their son Bruce makes the wines, a sauvignon blanc of great character and depth, a beautifully complex cabernet sauvignon, and a luscious chardonnay.

The winery, which was designed by William Turnbull, is truly beautiful, with an attention to detail in the wood and brick work that's unmatched anywhere else. But see for yourself. The tasting room is open to the public. Tours are by appointment. *8300 St. Helena Highway (CA 29); (707) 963-5221.*

Saint Supéry Vineyards & Winery. Set well back from the road, Saint Supéry is a study in contrast. The first building you see after you park your car in the rather large parking lot (you could plant a lot of vines in this "Rutherford dust") is the beautifully restored Atkinson farmhouse. The next building is a vast concrete edifice that looks like a cross between a college hall and a factory. Ignore the ugly exterior. Inside, you'll find one of the most thoughtfully appointed visitors centers in the Wine Country. Besides a relief map of the Napa Valley and other displays, you'll appreciate the sniffing station, an ingenious contraption that lets you smell some of the flavor elements that determine the character of red and white wines—the cherry, black pepper, bell pepper, and cedar aromas of reds, and the wildflower, new-mown hay, green olive, and grapefruit of white wine aromas. It's a good way of checking up on your nose—it's one of the peculiarities of human physiology that not everyone smells the same things. You can do a self-guided tour or take the formal tour, which includes the 1881 farmhouse.

By now you will have realized that a lot of money goes into creating an operation like this. Saint Supéry is owned by Skalli, a large French food corporation and negociant. In 1982, Skalli purchased the Dollarhide Ranch in Pope Valley; they planted grapes in 1983 and built the winery in 1989. The winery takes its name from Edward St. Supéry, a French winemaker who lived in the farmhouse from the early 1900s until Prohibition. Primarily a "red wine house," Saint Supéry makes very good cabernet sauvignon and merlot from its Pope Valley grapes, wines which will get even better as the vines mature. A 35-acre vineyard next to the winery is planted exclusively with cabernet sauvignon. There's also a well-structured sauvignon blanc and chardonnay. *8440 St. Helena Highway (CA 29); (707) 963-4507.*

■ RUTHERFORD CROSS ROAD

Caymus Vineyards. Head east on the Rutherford Cross Road to visit Caymus. There's a special quality about a winery that owns its own vineyards. The soil, vines, and climate, all well-understood by the winemaker, combine to make a wine quite unlike one made at a hobby winery which buys grapes on the spot market. The Wagner family began farming in the Napa Valley in 1906, when it grew prunes as well as grapes. In 1972, Charlie Wagner converted an old barn into a winery and

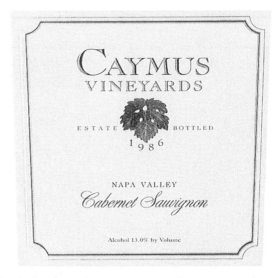

started making wine. After he hired Randy Dunn as winemaker, Caymus cabernet sauvignon gained national stature. Dunn left in 1986 to run his own winery on Howell Mountain *(see* "COUNTRY ROADS," *page 215),* and Charlie's son took over the winemaking—with no discernible drop in quality. The Caymus reds are as good as ever. The winery also produces an interesting white called Conundrum a blend of sauvignon blanc, semillon, viognier, chardonnay, and muscat. Tasting by appointment only; no tours. *8700 Conn Creek Road; (707) 963-4204.*

■ DOWN THE SILVERADO TRAIL

Return to the Silverado Trail, turn right across the Conn Creek Bridge, and drive south until you see a low barnlike structure on your right, below road level. That's Mumm Napa Valley.

Mumm Napa Valley. You don't realize how large this unobtrusive, beautifully de-signed winery is until you walk right up to it and find yourself going and going. Built in 1986, long after other French winemakers had become entrenched in the Napa Valley, Mumm—a joint endeavor of Seagram and the French champagne house—had some catching up to do. It did so with the winery's layout and with the quality of its sparkling wines. The winery contains an art gallery, which has a permanent exhibit of photographs Ansel Adams took when Seagram commis-sioned him to photograph the making of wine. There are hourly tours of the win-ery. And you do want to taste the sparklers, even though there is a fee. They're worth it. *8445 Silverado Trail, Rutherford; (707) 942-3300.*

Mumm Napa Valley houses an exhibition of Ansel Adams silver prints from the collection of Joseph E. Seagram & Sons. This print was created in 1961 and is titled Old Vine. *(Courtesy Mumm Napa Valley)*

The rocky cliffs east of Yountville are known as Stags Leap. (Kerrick James)

■ STAGS LEAP DISTRICT

From Mumm, turn right onto the Silverado Trail and drive south. You'll know when you enter the Stags Leap District because there's a sign by the road that tells you, but you might notice anyway, because the landscape changes. It becomes somehow more austere, as though Mother Nature were trying to tell you that here is a special ecosystem, with unique soils and a unique micro-climate. There are several versions of how the rocks we know as Stags Leap got their name: one claims that a stag, pursued by hunters, leaped off the rocks to safety; the other claims he leapt to his death. A third version has several stags leaping. Take your pick.

Robert Sinskey Vineyards. The first winery you'll come upon, off to your left, is as austere as the landscape. It looks like an oversized horse barn, and the vineyards grow on old pasture land. We shall have to admit that the quality of the wines came as a surprise to us—almost a shock. They are amazingly good for a winery that's barely a decade old. Even though the winery is in the Stags Leap District, the grapes were grown in the Carneros. Thereby hangs a tale. As Rob Sinskey tells it,

Ballooning in the valley is a popular sport. This event took place at the Mumm winery.

his father, Robert Sinskey, M.D., got together with two friends, Mike Richmond and Jerry Goldstein. They put up some money and became limited partners in Acacia Winery. Robert Sr. got himself seriously bitten by the wine bug, and in 1982, he bought 32 acres along Las Amigas Road in the Carneros. In 1985, by the time the vineyard was ready to bear fruit, the partners decided to sell Acacia to Chalone. Sinskey had his vineyard—all he needed was a winery to put his grapes to use. He bought land in Stags Leap and construction began. The first two vintages were crushed at Flora Springs, while his winery was under construction. The first crush in the new winery occurred in 1988. Sinskey's son Rob took some time off to help in the winery. "I think a week had passed," he says, "when I discovered that that my father's avocation had become my obsession." Rob is now the winery's president.

We met him at a recent Napa Valley Wine Auction, when he sat down at our table during the Big Dinner and started pulling corks. After the first sniff and sip, we knew we were on to something good. That was ᴉ ne pinot noir. The merlot was even better. From Carneros grapes? we asked. Sinskey enlightened us by telling us that the Carneros was cool by California standards, but still warmer than some of the world's other growing regions like, for example, St. Emilion and Pomerol, where some of the world's greatest merlots are produced. Sinskey has planted grapes in Stags Leap that should also produce great wine, once they grow up. *6320 Silverado Trail, Napa; (707) 944-9090.*

Stags' Leap Winery. One winery you can't see as you pass by on the Silverado Trail is Stags' Leap Winery. This is where one very special petite sirah comes from. It's grown in a vineyard atop the alluvial fan that slopes downhill from the famed Stags Leap palisades, a cluster of volcanic crags. The vineyard lies in a small side valley, between the Stags' Leap Winery and mansion built here

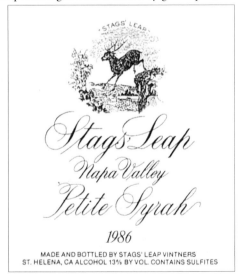

Stags Leap

Napa Valley

Petite Syrah

1986

MADE AND BOTTLED BY STAGS' LEAP VINTNERS
ST. HELENA, CA ALCOHOL 13% BY VOL. CONTAINS SULFITES

in 1888 by Chicago financier Horace Chase. Chase didn't hang on to his fortune for long, and his winery soon lay in ruins. The mansion had a somewhat checkered career as the Stag's Leap Hotel (and establishments of less repute) until Carl Doumani rescued it in the early 1970s and reopened the winery as well. During the rebuilding, the workmen found a deep wine cave that had been dug into the hill behind the winery. No one had suspected its existence under the mound of rubble that hid its entrance. It now serves as an aging cellar.

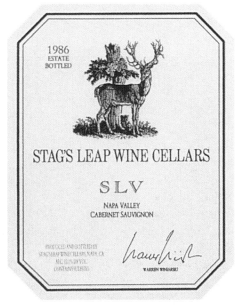

Because of a trademark battle, the apostrophe moved one space to the right, so that you now have the Stags' Leap Winery on the old Stag's Leap Winery property, while the winery down-valley is called Stag's Leap Wine Cellars and the appellation is known as the Stags Leap District. If this seems very confusing, please remember that these distinctions were decided on by winemakers—who spend their lives judging nuances.

Stags' Leap Winery is justly famous for its estate-grown petite sirah, which has been compared, in its intensity, to the best syrah wine from France's Rhône Valley. The winery also produces a cabernet sauvignon which is lean, complex, yet restrained—like a first-rate red Bordeaux, in fact. The Stags' Leap grounds are beautifully landscaped. This is a very romantic place. It is unfortunate that it is not open to the public. *6150 Silverado Trail, Napa; (707) 944-1303.*

Stag's Leap Wine Cellars. After you return to the Silverado Trail you'll see, on your left, the low, earth-colored buildings of Stag's Leap Wine Cellars They seem rather plain and look more like a modern country school than a winery of such eminence. But the place is livened up with flowers. There's a small picnic area in a garden.

Warren Winiarski is proprietor of the world-renowned Stag's Leap Wine Cellars.

Warren and Barbara Winiarski's winery is the home of the 1973 cabernet that won the red wine section of the famous 1976 Paris tasting (as well as the home of the famed "Cask 23" cabernet sauvignon), and the place tends to be overrun with serious enophiles. Relax. Let the snobs show off how much winespeak they can talk. Taste the wines: not just the cab, but also the sauvignon blanc and chardonnay. This is good wine. Even the wine sold under Stag's Leap's second label, Hawk Crest, is well worth sniffing and sipping. *5766 Silverado Trail, Napa; (707) 944-2020.*

Chimney Rock Winery. As you head south on the Silverado Trail, you can't help noticing a low white building to the east (unless the poplar trees surrounding it are in full leaf and hide it from view). It's built in the somewhat ornate Cape (as in Cape of Good Hope) Dutch style of the 17th century and seems a bit out of place in the austere Stags Leap landscape. That's Chimney Rock Winery. But you've just got to love a winery that is built and planted on part of a bulldozed golf course, putting the land to a much nobler use. That's exactly what Hack Wilson, a former soft drink executive, did in 1984, when he bought the Chimney Rock Golf

Course, decided part of the land had just the right soils for a fine vineyard, and sent in the bulldozers. There's still a Chimney Rock Golf Course, but it only has nine holes. All Chimney Rock wines are estate-grown. The cabernet is more elegant than wines of its caliber tend to be hereabouts, and there's also a very fine fumé blanc. But decide for yourself. Chimney Rock has a very pleasant tasting room. It's quite elegant, in fact. *5350 Silverado Trail, Napa; (707) 257-2641.*

Clos du Val. With the exception of Chimney Rock, architectural understatement seems to be the rule in the Stags Leap District. The next winery down the road, Clos du Val, has the plain, severe lines of a Bordelais chais (wine-aging cellar) and does not at all look like a chateau. The winery, built in 1972, is owned by French-American businessman John Goelet. It was started by Bernard Portet, a French winemaker whose father was technical director at Château Lafite-Rothschild.

Portet, who is also the winery's president, began with the intention of making only cabernet sauvignon and zinfandel, but has since branched out into merlot, pinot noir, and chardonnay. Clos du Val's wines are very French in character and structure, not revealing their complexity until after they have been aged in the bottle for a considerable amount of time. Be sure to taste the reserve, if you get the chance— it is produced only in exceptional years. *5330 Silverado Trail; (707) 259-2200.*

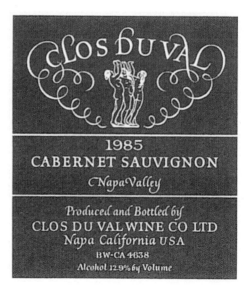

From Clos du Val, you can continue south on the Silverado Trail to Trancas Avenue, then turn right to return to CA 29 in Napa. Or backtrack to the Yountville Cross Road and drive west to Yountville (you might want to stop at the parking area at the bridge and dangle your feet in the Napa River—if it has water), or take a walk in the shade of the riverside trees.

■ TOWN OF NAPA

Not many years ago, Yountville could rightly be considered the southernmost wine commune of the Napa Valley, because the city of Napa had turned its back on the Wine Country. That is no longer true—and it was certainly not the case before Prohibition. Today, with the revitalization and expansion of the Carneros vineyards, Napa suddenly finds itself right in the heart of the Wine Country—which makes it a perfect stopping-over place, especially since hotel rates are considerably lower than those in Yountville, St. Helena, or Calistoga (*see* "LODGING," *page 262).*

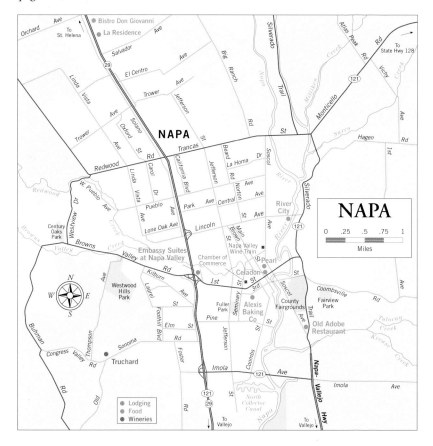

In the 19th century, Napa River was used extensively for commercial purposes, including the transport of wine from Napa to warehouses in San Francisco.

Napa is the oldest town in the Napa Valley, founded in 1848 in a strategic location on the Napa River, where the Sonoma-Benicia road crossed at a ford and at the head of navigation. The first steamship arrived in 1850, and according to one historian, "the Dolphin was very small—about the size of a whaleboat"—so small, he comments: "It is said that when coming up the river, the Captain (who is very tall) came in sight before the smoke stack." The first house, a saloon, was built in 1848. Before then, a few Mexican adobes were the only houses in the region (one of these, built in the 1840s, survives at the corner of Soscol Avenue and the Silverado Trail as the **Old Adobe Bar & Grille)**. Not surprisingly, you can order either Mexican dishes or steaks.

In subsequent years, Napa became a favorite wintering place for gold miners from the Mother Lode. Saloons remained the major local industry in Napa for quite some time to come. The first commercial Napa Valley wine was made by a British brewmaster named Patchett in the 1850s from grapes planted in a vineyard in what is now downtown Napa. Patchett also built the first stone cellar in the Napa Valley and shipped wine regularly from 1857 on. Although Napa's first cash crops were cattle and wheat, by the late 1800s, large wineries like Charles Carpy's Uncle Sam Wine Cellars lined the river. Large Napa bulk wineries dominated the trade until Prohibition, but unlike the small family-owned wineries up-valley, they never recovered.

While Napa is not exactly a small town anymore, and gone are the days when sailboats tacked up the river on weekend excursions from San Francisco, Napa's downtown still preserves the old river-town atmosphere. The early residential areas, in which many Victorian houses survive, evoke a simpler, less hectic time. The business district has preserved a few historic buildings, like the Opera House from 1879, the turn-of-the-19th-century courthouse, and several warehouses on the Napa River waterfront. Napa County Landmarks will set you on the right trail for a self-guided tour of older buildings. *1026 First Street; (707) 255-1836.*

Napa has several good restaurants, most notably the **Alexis Baking Company, Bistro Don Giovanni, Celadon, and Pearl** *(see* "RESTAURANTS," *page 250 for details.)* Napa also has several excellent parks (some with river access), which alone make the town worth a stopover.

Because of its central location between the Carneros and Mount Veeder districts to the west, the valley to the north, and the back-road wineries of the Vaca Hills to the east, Napa is a good base from which to explore this part of the wine country.

■ MOUNT VEEDER APPELLATION

The wineries in this southwestern Napa Valley appellation can be reached from the town of Napa and CA 29 via Redwood Road, then Pickle Canyon to Mount Veeder Road; or from the north via the top of the Oakville Grade, then Dry Creek to Mount Veeder roads. South of the Oakville grade, the Mayacamas Range is deeply cut by several creeks which flow from northwest to southeast; farther south, the mountains break up into a series of hillocks, ridges, and mountain glades. Even though this region gets more rain than the Napa Valley (as witnessed by surviving stands of redwoods), soils are poor and rocky and the water runs off quickly, forcing any grapes planted here to grow deep roots. Vines thus stressed produce grapes of exceptional character, as proved by the sparkling wines made from Domaine Chandon's Pickle Canyon vineyard as well as by the cabernet sauvignons and chardonnays produced by the handful of wineries which eke out a living in this austere terroir.

The Hess Collection. Not all of the wines made by the Hess Collection are austere, since grapes from other growing regions are used as well, but when Swiss brewer and soda merchant Donald Hess took over the Christian Brothers Mont

LaSalle winery in 1986, he also planted vineyards on ridges and mountaintops. Some of these sites are so steep that the grapes have to be picked by hand and brought down to the winery by four-wheel-drive pickup truck. This extra caretaking in growing the grapes definitely shows in the quality of the estate wines.

Curiously, the Hess Collection offers free, guided tours of the Hess's splendid, world-class collection of modern art, yet it charges for tasting the wines. But the wines are worth it—although chances are that, after you leave, you will remember the art more than the cabernets or chardonnay: it's hard to forget Leopold Maler's striking *Hommage 1974*—a literally flaming typewriter, created as a protest piece against the repression of artistic freedom by totalitarian regimes.

There are also some spectacular views from the terrace into the heart of the Mayacamas range, with hills as tortured as those in a Chinese landscape painting. And yes, those green patches on the mountaintops are vineyards. This is an especially nice winery to visit. *4411 Redwood Road, Napa; (707) 255-1144.*

Mayacamas Vineyards. If you thought the drive to the Hess Collection was convoluted, you will really enjoy the drive up Mount Veeder Road to Mayacamas

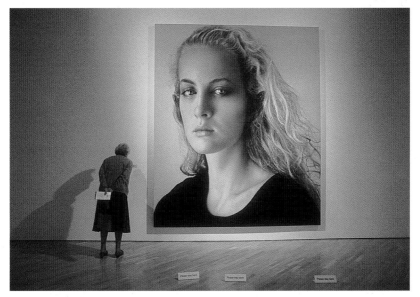

Johanna II *by artist Franz Gertsh is part of the Hess Collection.*

Trees draped with Spanish moss near the summit of the Oakville Grade.

Vineyards, which has been known to try the faint of heart. The old Fischer stone winery, built in 1889, was resurrected in 1941 by Jack and Mary Taylor, early pioneers of the Napa Valley wine renaissance who demonstrated what great wines can be made from cabernet sauvignon and chardonnay grapes grown high in the mountains. The winery, owned by Bob and Elinor Travers since 1968, now makes sauvignon blanc as well, plus a little pinot noir. The wines are big, flavorful, and concentrated. Production is limited to some 5,000 cases a year. Be sure to call ahead and make an appointment before you visit. *1155 Lokoya Road, Napa; (707) 224-4030.*

Chateau Potelle. The road to this small (25,000-case) winery is steep, but the wines are worth every inch of the 1,800-foot elevation. The winery uses only natural fermentation for its estate and Napa Valley grapes. The splendid estate zinfandel proves that even the French (owners Jean-Noel and Marketta Fourmeaux de Sartel are from France) can make a great wine from California's native grape. *3875 Mount Veeder Road, Napa; (707) 255-9440.*

". . . Fifty rows of vines were promised too, each one to bear in turn. Bunches of every hue would hang there ripening, weighed down by the god of summer days." — Homer, Odyssey

UPPER NAPA VALLEY

And Noah often said to his wife
when he sat down to dine,
"I don't care where the water goes, if it
doesn't get into the wine."
—G. K. Chesterton, 1874–1936

THE ST. HELENA WINE DISTRICT—which stretches from Yountville to the vineyards north of St. Helena—became an enological hotspot in the 1880s when the vineyards of France were destroyed by phylloxera, and the demand for California wine rose to an all-time high. Napa Valley wines gained international renown when enologist George Husmann took an assortment to the 1889 World's Fair in Paris. Napa Valley wines collected 20 medals and awards, causing the *San Francisco Chronicle* to hail Napa as the "California Medoc."

Business boomed. Vineyard plantings increased dramatically. Not until recent decades would as many Napa Valley acres be planted to grapes.

From the Repeal of Prohibition in 1933 until the 1960s, St. Helena and the associated crossroad villages of Rutherford and Oakville a few miles to the south kept the spirit of wine alive. The new age in California wine began in 1966 when Robert Mondavi left his family's Charles Krug Winery to start a winery of his own in Oakville. Today the main north–south Napa Valley Highway, CA 29, is lined with wineries and vineyards.

■ RUTHERFORD

The tiny community of Rutherford is made up of a few houses near the intersection of two Wine Country roads, but this may well be the most important wine country intersection in the country. For here, on either side of the highway, stand two ivy-clad wineries that kept the reputation of California wines alive during Prohibition. Both of these wineries, Inglenook and Beaulieu, still make world-class wine, although the former has changed its name. But hereby hangs a tale.

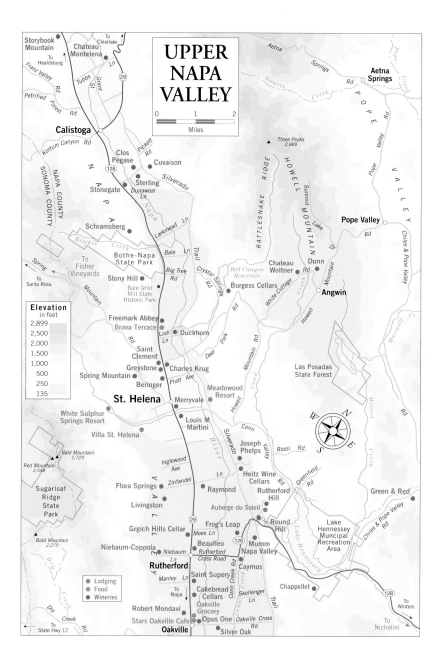

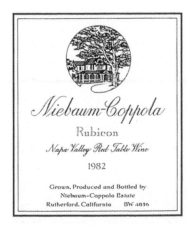

Niebaum-Coppola

Rubicon

Napa Valley Red Table Wine

1982

Grown, Produced and Bottled by
Niebaum-Coppola Estate
Rutherford. California   BW 4836

■ THE INGLENOOK SAGA

Niebaum-Coppola Estate. When you look across the valley at the great Inglenook chateau, you might be tempted to utter the Biblical lament on "how are the mighty fallen," for the Inglenook label, which once graced the Napa Valley's most distinguished wines, has been reduced to a Central Valley bulk wine label. But there may be reason for hope. Filmmaker Francis Ford Coppola and his wife, Eleanor, purchased the old Niebaum Estate, west of the winery, from Inglenook in 1975. Coppola converted Niebaum's old stables to a winery and started making wine as Niebaum-Coppola Estate. It was obvious from the beginning that this was going to be a high-quality operation, not a money mill. The first wine, from the 1978 vintage, was not released until 1985. The wine, named Rubicon, showed that it was in the same class as the old Inglenook reds—of which the 1887, 1888, and 1889 vintage are still alive and well. (Though you can hardly expect to find a bottle.)

Things were not going as well at Inglenook. The winery had been founded in 1879 by Gustave Niebaum, a Finnish sea captain, who made his money in the Alaska fur trade after his Russian employers sold that state to the United States. John Daniel, a grand-nephew, took over the winery at Repeal and restored it to its former eminence. The red wines he made were of such high quality that they

Gustave Niebaum in 1880, the year the Finnish sea captain completed his purchase of Inglenook.

attracted the attention of the French, who began to invest in the Napa Valley in the 1970s. In 1964, he sold the winery to United Vintners, who promptly transferred winemaking to a larger facility the company owned nearby. In 1969, United Vintners, including Inglenook, was sold to Heublein, a producer of spirits. Later that year, Heublein bought Beaulieu, Rutherford's other venerable winery. While Heublein made some halfhearted attempts to keep up the quality at Inglenook, the winery's reputation continued to deteriorate. In 1989, Heublein bought out the Christian Brothers, more for the Brothers' Central Valley brandy operations than for their Napa Valley wineries, and gained another 1,200 acres of Napa Valley vineyards in the transaction. Heublein, which had been sold to the British conglomerate Grand Metropolitan in 1987, now owned almost 4,600 acres of vines in the Napa Valley—about one in every seven acres planted to vines. By the early 1990s, there were definite signs of overload—there was even talk that Grand Metropolitan might get out of the wine business altogether. The Inglenook label was sold to Canandaigua Wine Company of New York in 1994. The winery, its once vast vineyard holdings reduced to a few acres by piecemeal sales to various landowners, was put up for sale in the fall. It was bought by Francis Coppola early in 1995, reuniting Niebaum's two historic Napa Valley properties.

Coppola felt that local residents, who wanted to see Inglenook restored to its former glory, helped him persuade Heublein to sell the winery to him. To thank them, he threw the biggest block party the Napa Valley has ever seen. The invitations were illustrated with a drawing of the Inglenook winery, its cupola blown off by dancing music notes. The Niebaum-Coppola tasting room is at *1991 St. Helena Highway; (707) 963-9099.*

■ THE BEAULIEU STORY

Beaulieu Vineyard. You can't miss the ivy-covered edifice of Beaulieu Vineyard in the center of Rutherford. Beaulieu was founded by French vintner Georges de Latour in 1900. His wife, Fernande, a Californian of French parentage, may have had as much to do with the winery's success as Latour, for it was she who introduced Latour to the San Francisco social circles where his wine became fashionable. According to novelist Gertrude Atherton, it was Fernande de Latour and not Georges who named the winery "Beaulieu" (Beautiful Site). The winery stayed open during Prohibition making—according to Atherton— "wines for sacramental and governmental purposes." Governmental purposes? Is this something we should know about? Did the government drink during Prohibition? After her husband's death in 1940, Fernande de Latour kept the winery going. Her heirs sold it to Heublein in 1969.

The late André Tchelistcheff, Beaulieu's winemaker from 1936–1973, firmly placed Beaulieu among the world's great wineries. He may well have been the most influential American winemaker ever, for he not only set an example by making great wine, but advised winemakers from California to the Pacific Northwest. Look at the historical records of the West Coast's most successful wineries, and Tchelistcheff's name is sure to pop up. The style of the wine you drink with your dinner is more likely than not influenced by his ideas and ideals, from varietal selection to fermentation techniques to barrel construction.

Heublein has maintained the integrity of Beaulieu's top wine, the Georges Latour Private Reserve cabernet sauvignon, first created by Tchelistcheff in the 1930s. The winery also makes good cabernet sauvignon, chardonnay, and pinot noir. The "Beautour" reds are good wines at reasonable prices. But no one knows what the future will hold. By all means, take the tour. It is very good. Enjoy Beaulieu wines one vintage at a time and hope for the best. *1960 St. Helena Highway, Rutherford; (707) 963-2411.*

The late and much respected André Tchelistcheff, the doyen of the California wine industry.

■ NORTH OF RUTHERFORD

Grgich Hills Cellar. Just north of Rutherford and Inglenook, look for Grgich Hills, a small, ivy-covered winery on the west side of the highway. In 1977, shortly after his Chateau Montelena chardonnay bested several top French white Burgundies at the famous 1976 Paris tasting, Miljenko (Mike) Grgich opened a winery of his own in partnership with Austin Hills, heir of the Hills Brothers coffee fortune. It's almost too bad that Grgich won early fame with chardonnay, a grape which has almost been turned into a Napa Valley cliché, because the cabernet sauvignon, fumé blanc, and zinfandel Grgich makes are every bit as good, if not better. Taste them at the winery, then surprise your friends by planning a meal around a Grgich Hills fumé and zin. You might also want to lay away a few bottles. Wines made by Grgich in the early 1970s are still very much alive and a few could even go a bit longer. *1829 St. Helena Highway; (707) 963-2784.*

Raymond Vineyards & Cellars. Roy Raymond Sr. went to work for Beringer as winemaker in 1933; in 1936 he married Martha Jane Beringer, granddaughter of one of the founders. After spending some 30 years at Beringer he retired, and in 1971, established his own 80-acre vineyard on Zinfandel Lane, east of CA 29. His sons Roy Jr. and Walt joined him in the winery, which made its first wine during the 1974 vintage. Today, Roy Jr. manages the vineyards at Raymond Vineyards & Cellars, and Walt makes the wine. The wines are still good, but not as exciting as the cabernets made by Raymond in the early 1980s. Perhaps it was the special touch of Roy Sr., now retired, that made those wines so distinct. Or the winery may have suffered when the Raymonds sold it to Kirin Breweries of Japan in 1989 (the Raymonds are now managing partners with a minority interest). But who knows? Upcoming vintages might surprise us all. Keep tasting. *849 Zinfandel Lane, St. Helena; (707) 963-3141.*

A NAPA VALLEY
RED TABLE WINE

TRILOGY
1986
A classic blend
of three traditional
claret varietals
specially selected
for this bottling.

Flora Springs

Estate Grown, Produced and Bottled by
Flora Springs Wine Co. St. Helena, CA

Flora Springs Wine Company. Clear at the other end of Zinfandel Lane, at the edge of the western foothills of the Mayacamas range, this old stone winery, built in the 1880s by the Scots Rennie Brothers, served as home for Louis M. Martini from 1930 to 1976, and was purchased in 1977 by Jerry and Flora Komes as a retirement getaway. This turned into a typical Napa Valley "retirement." By 1979, the Komes's adult children had joined them in making the first wine from grapes growing on the property, a chardonnay. In recent years, Flora Springs has made more of a splash with its reds, however, especially a sangiovese, and a red Meritage called Trilogy because it is blended from three traditional Bordeaux grape varietals: cabernet sauvignon, cabernet franc, and merlot. There's a good reason for the quality of the wines: the grapes grow in some of the best vineyard soils of the famed Rutherford appellation. The winery itself is not open to the public, but the tasting room is: *677 S. St. Helena Highway, St. Helena; (707) 967-8032.*

❖

Just south of Flora Springs, sitting on an alluvial fan of "Rutherford Bench" deposits, is a very special small winery that makes truly great cabernet sauvignon. Unfortunately, **Livingston Wines** is not open to the public. But you might want to call *(707) 963-2120* and arrange to buy a few cases of the wine, to lay away for a special occasion. Some grapes for the wines come from the Moffett Vineyard on the property; others, from gravelly patches of vineyards up and down the valley—all of which make outstanding cabernets. (These are labeled as "Stanley's Selection.") Just south

The other "Rutherford Bench."

Louis P. Martini inspects grapes in one of his vineyards.

of the family home and the old barn that serves as the winery's office stand the stone wall ruins of the old H. W. Helms Winery of 1883, which the Livingstons plan to restore. Wine caves the Livingstons have dug in the hill are laid out in such a way that they will connect with the winery when the restoration is complete. Helms's winery was famous in its day for the quality of its wines; you'll understand why when you taste the Livingston wine.

❖

Louis M. Martini. Back on CA 29, you head north to St. Helena. But just before you reach town, look for the Louis M. Martini winery on the right side. This winery, founded in 1922 by the late Louis M. Martini as a grape-growing farm, started making wines under his name after Repeal. His son Louis P. brought the winery to prominence. It is now run by Louis P.'s daughter Caroline; his son Michael makes the wine. This winery, known primarily for "sound wines and honest prices," as one guidebook states it, has always kept a low profile, both in its physical plant and in its public image. Which is really too bad, since a lot of credit owed Louis M. Martini has gone to others. This is truly one of the Wine Country's pioneering wineries. Louis M. Martini was among the first to identify and propagate vinifera clones and to release vintage dated varietal wines, and it was the first large winery to invest in Carneros as well as in Mayacamas mountain vineyards. Martini's best wines are its reds, especially the barbera and zinfandel. Both profit from bottle aging. *254 South St. Helena Highway; (707) 963-2736.*

■ ST. HELENA

You'd think that with a town that started near a grist mill, the emphasis would be on grain farming. (At the recently restored **Old Bale Mill** north of town you can watch grain being ground by water power on weekends, and buy some freshly milled flour to take home.) Not so. While that was true for other parts of the Napa Valley until far into the latter part of the 19th century, St. Helena took to vines almost instantly. The town got its start in 1854 when Henry Still built a store. Still wanted company and donated lots on his town site to anyone who wanted to erect a business house. Soon his store was joined by a wagon shop, a shoe shop, hotels, and churches. In 1857, the town was large enough to be officially recognized. Dr. George Crane planted a vineyard in 1858 and was the first to produce wine in commercially viable quantities. A German winemaker named Charles Krug followed suit a couple of years later.

Downtown St. Helena in 1906, soon after the introduction of an electric rail line.

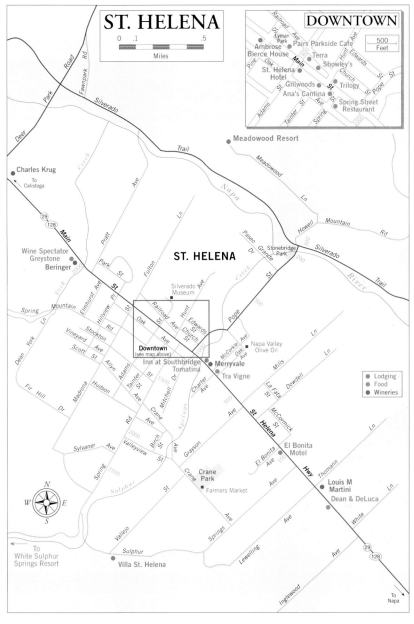

ST. HELENA

0   .1   .5

Miles

DOWNTOWN

500 Feet

Lyman Park

Railroad Ave

Pairs Parkside Cafe

Ambrose Bierce House

Terra

Pine St

Oak St

Main

Showley's

St. Helena Hotel

Gillwoods

Trilogy

Ana's Cantina

Adams

Tainter St

Spring

Spring Street Restaurant

Hunt

Edwards

Church St

Pope St

Meadowood Resort

Trail

Meadowood

Napa

Ln

Charles Krug

To Calistoga

Creek

Ave

Pratt

Ln

Howell

Mountain Rd

Silverado

River

Trail

Passeo Grande Dr

Stonebridge Park

Wine Spectator Greystone

Beringer

29 128

Main

York Ln

Park St

Fulton

Pope

Creek

St

ST. HELENA

Silverado Museum

Railroad Ave

Hunt St

Edwards St

Church St

Spring

Mountain

Elmhurst Ave

Hillview Pl

Rd

Oak Ave

McCorkle

Oak Ave

Napa Valley Olive Oil

Vineyard

Stockton

Ave

Ln

Ln

Scott St

Allyn Ave

Adams St

Tainter St

Downtown (see map above)

Inn at Southbridge

Tomatina

Merryvale

Mills St

Dowdell

Dean

Madrona

Hudson

Charter Ave

Tra Vigne

La Fata St

McCormick St

Fir Hill Dr

Rd Ave

Crane Ave

Birch St

Springs Ave

500

● Lodging
● Food
● Wineries

Sylvaner Ave

Valleyview St

Grayson Ave

El Bonita Ave

St Helena Hwy

El Bonita Motel

Thomann Ln

Spring

Sulphur St

Crane St

Crane Park

Farmers Market

Louis M Martini

Dean & DeLuca

White Ln

N
W   E
S

Vallejo

Sulphur

Springs Ave

Ave

29 128

To White Sulphur Springs Resort

Villa St. Helena

Lewelling Ave

Inglewood Ave

To Napa

PROUD OF ITS WINE

*S*t. Helena . . . is proud of the great quantity of rich wine-grapes grown in the district it serves and of its many old wine cellars. Many of the inhabitants of St. Helena and environs are Swiss, Germans, and Italians from vineyard sections of Europe. Here as abroad they hold their new-wine festivals each fall—with certain American additions in the form of floats with figures of Bacchus and his followers. Beside State 29 on the northern outskirts is the **Beringer Brothers Winery** (*open*), in whose underground storage cellars . . . hundreds of thousands of gallons of wine are aging in great casks.

—WPA guide to California, 1939

Other wineries soon followed in his wake. Success came from an unexpected quarter. Just as phylloxera, a devastatingly deadly bug (to vines) introduced from America's heartland, began its destruction of France's vineyards, Napa Valley wines caught the world's attention. At the 1889 World's Fair in Paris, Napa Valley wines walked away with an impressive array of awards, and demand for them increased exponentially. In St. Helena, rapid business growth spawned a building frenzy. Many of the stately mansions still gracing the town's residential neighborhoods were built during this decade. Many homes also served as wineries, and many basements were designed as wine cellars. Today, by an odd twist, several old stone wineries have been converted into private homes: the 1886 Dowdell Winery, 1870 Edge Hill Vineyard winery, and the 1880 Castner and 1876 Weinberger wineries.

❖

Shortly after you enter St. Helena, you'll see the pastel-colored stone buildings of the **Tra Vigne restaurant** complex on your right. Just beyond, is **Merryvale Vineyards**, founded in 1983 by Robin Lail (a daughter of Jack Daniel, the founder of Inglenook) and other investors at what was originally the Sunny St. Helena Winery (which gave the Mondavis their Napa Valley start). Among the wines a red Meritage blend called Profile is worth tasting, as is a white Meritage. The tasting room is an easy stroll from Tra Vigne and offers a pleasant diversion while you wait for a table. *1000 Main Street; (707) 963-2225.*

What gives St. Helena its special ambience is the warmth of the sun-mellowed stone of old downtown buildings on Main Street, mostly between Adams and Spring streets, and along Railroad. Of these, Steve's Hardware dates back to 1878, the I.O.O.F. Building to 1885, and the very elaborately decorated Masonic Lodge to 1892. Other notable structures include the Noble Building at Main and Spring and the *St. Helena Star* offices. Several of these buildings sport modern facades, but you can study the old structures by strolling the back alleys. Other old downtown buildings include the **St. Helena Hotel,** built in 1881, which has a room dedicated to the British actress Lillie Langtry, who is said to have stayed here on her way to visit her ranch at Guenoc, in Lake County. (Other accounts claim she stayed at the Miramonte near the railroad tracks.) Several of the nearby wineries are also built from local stone, most notably Beringer and Freemark Abbey, just north of town, and V. Sattui just to the south.

In the late 1800s, there were even attempts at turning St. Helena into an industrial center to supply the needs of local viticulturists for specialized machinery. Several stone warehouses were built near the railroad tracks downtown, and in 1884 the firm of Taylor, Duckworth, and Company put up an impressive stone building to serve as a foundry for building wine presses, and as a planing mill and box factory for grape boxes. The enterprise had failed by 1890 and the structure

The old-fashioned Italian grocery at St. Helena's Napa Valley Olive Oil Mfg. Co. (Kerrick James)

was subsequently used as an electric plant, glove factory, storage shed, and hatchery. For a while, it housed the Robert Louis Stevenson Museum, which moved adjacent to the public library in 1979. The old foundry building is now occupied by offices and by Terra restaurant.

The **Ambrose Bierce House,** built on Main Street in 1872, has been lovingly restored. It now serves as an inn and has a collection of memorabilia of the cantankerous writer who lived here for 13 years before vanishing in Mexico in 1913.

The Silverado Museum, just east of downtown at the public library on Library Lane, has one of the best collections of Robert Louis Stevenson memorabilia in the world. The collection is so good that Scottish television crews have come several times to shoot documentaries there.

Many visitors never get away from Main Street and its wineries, restaurants, and shops, but leave it behind, and you're instantly in quiet residential neighborhoods where time seems to have stood still for decades. A few blocks to the west, and you're surrounded by vineyards which merge into the ragged wilderness edge of the Mayacamas Mountains. A few blocks to the east on Pope Street and you're at the Napa River, which separates St. Helena from the Silverado Trail and Howell Mountain. Here too, you enter the countryside within a mile or less. Don't be surprised if a deer comes down to the edge of the road, or if a heron rises from a riparian pool.

Off Main Street, St. Helena is a very private city, but this is the part of town that's the most fun to explore. Stroll along the tree-shaded streets before dining at one of the town's renowned restaurants. Of these, **Trilogy, Terra,** and **Spring**

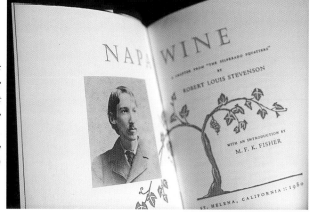

Robert Louis Stevenson spent time in Napa Valley at Jacob Schram's estate north of town. (Courtesy Schramsberg)

Tra Vigne restaurant is one of several that have transformed St. Helena into a gourmet's paradise.

Street are in easy walking distance from the public parking area along Railroad, downtown, one block east of Main Street. **Tra Vigne** is a longer walk to the south and **Brava Terrace** a short drive north. For casual fare, drop in at **Ana's Cantina** on Main Street near Spring, or pick up the makings for a picnic at the **Napa Valley Olive Oil Mfg. Co.** at the east end of Charter Oak Avenue. You can settle down at one of the picnic tables just outside the white, barnlike structure, amid grape vines and orange trees, or head for **Lyman Park** downtown (public restrooms), or to **Stonebridge Park** where the stone-arch Pope Street Bridge (1890) crosses the Napa River.

■ NORTH OF ST. HELENA

Two of St. Helena's most famous wineries, Beringer Vineyards and Charles Krug, stand on either side of CA 29 just north of town.

Beringer Vineyards. The entrance gate to Beringer Vineyards is at the north end of town, on the west (left) side of the road, just before the tunnel of elm trees that spans the highway. This winery, founded in 1876 by Rhine Valley emigrants Jacob and Frederick Beringer, had fallen on hard times when it was rescued by the Swiss Nestlé corporation in 1971. Beringer is proof that corporate purchase of a winery does not necessarily mean a decline in quality. Nestlé sold its wine interests in late 1995 to American investors. The new owners plan to keep the old staff, making us hope that no major changes are to be expected—at first. The Napa Valley cabernet and chardonnay—especially the reserve wines—have returned Beringer to the ranks of California's top wineries; the Knights Valley cabernet and sauvignon blanc are in a class by themselves.

This is one tour you should not miss, if only to see the stone tunnels dug by Chinese laborers in the 19th century. They now serve as storage cellars for the reserve cabernets. A guide may tell you that the tunnels were cut into limestone, but it's not limestone at all—it's compacted volcanic ash. So much for that. The old winery, built from squared stones, is much too small for current operations and a new state-of-the-art winery has been built across the street (that part of the operation is not open to the public). Beringer is the Napa Valley's oldest winery in continuous operation since its first vintage (during Prohibition, the winery made sacramental wines, as well as a little brandy for "health purposes").

The Beringer estate and winery is probably the biggest tourist attraction in Napa Valley.

Frederic Beringer (fifth from right) poses in this 19th-century portrait in front of his winery.
(Napa County Historical Society)

The winery grounds have been beautifully landscaped, and there's also an old mission fig tree growing on the north side of the Hudson House, near the overflow parking lot. No one seems to harvest the figs. You can tell when they're ripe by the black splotches they leave on lawn and pavement each autumn. Try them—they're delicious.

The two mansions on the grounds have been beautifully restored. The Rhine House, built in the 1880s to resemble the Beringers' ancestral home, was Frederick's residence and now contains the tasting rooms. Jacob and his family lived in the Hudson House, north of the redwood grove. It was built by the property's first settler and now houses Beringer's School for American Chefs, a program that brings carefully selected professional chefs to the winery for a very intensive two-week course taught by renowned cooking teacher and writer Madeleine Kamman. Through her courses, Kamman has done more than anyone else to put the Napa Valley on the national food map (*see* "FOOD AND WINE," *page 235, for details*).

The winery is an especially charming place to visit. *2000 Main Street; (707) 963-7115.*

The **Charles Krug Winery**, just up the road on the right, is the Napa Valley's oldest winery. It was founded by immigrant winemaker Charles Krug in 1861 and quickly rose to prominence as the valley's largest and most important winery. Krug went bankrupt before his death. If you wonder why, just look at the size of his rather ostentatious carriage house (which is now used to store wine). The winery was closed during Prohibition and did not reopen until it was rescued by Cesare Mondavi and his sons Robert and Peter in 1943. The Mondavis reestablished the winery's prominence through the quality of the wines they made. Robert left the family winery in 1966 to open a place of his own in Oakville. It sometimes seems as though he took all of the family's good credit as well. After Robert Mondavi left, Charles Krug seemed to slip into oblivion. Yet under Peter Mondavi's stewardship, the Charles Krug Winery has continued to make good wine, especially reds. *2800 Main Street, St. Helena; (707) 963-2761.*

❖

The huge stone building across the street, known as **Greystone**, was built in 1889 by William Bourn, an investor who had made his money in gold mines. It was bought by the Christian Brothers in 1950, and is now no longer a winery. In 1995 it became the advanced studies campus of the **Culinary Institute of America** or the CIA. The stone edifice was completely renovated with teaching kitchens, a two-acre organic garden was planted, and a 125-seat classroom restaurant opened in mid-October. It is expected to develop into one of the Napa Valley's premier dining places. The emphasis of the restaurant, under the guidance of executive chef Paul Sartory, will be on foods from countries on the Mediterranean Sea. A scholarship program set up by Napa Valley wine pioneers Jack and Jamie Davies (of Schramsberg fame) will give grants to chefs to spend extra time in the valley after their regular course ends to study wine, winemaking, and the matching of wine and food.

❖

Just north of Greystone, on the same side of the road, is **Saint Clement Vineyards**, a Victorian mansion built in 1876 as a family home by Fritz Rosenbaum atop a small stone winery. He called his property "Johannaberg." The mansion was bonded in 1968 by Southern California real estate speculator Mike Robbins as Spring Mountain Vineyards. Robbins sold the Rosenbaum mansion in 1975 to Dr. William Casey, a San Francisco eye surgeon, who renamed it St. Clement and who later sold it to Sapporo, USA, the U.S. subsidiary of the Japanese brewery.

(previous pages) Mustard blooms in the late winter, providing a colorful carpet below the barren vines.

Greystone being built in 1889. The massive structure became Christian Brothers Winery in 1950 and now accommodates the Culinary Institute of America's West Coast school.

The winery is worth visiting for a tour of the stone cellar, a taste of the sauvignon blanc and merlot, and for its splendid views. *2867 St. Helena Highway; (707) 963-7221.*

In the meantime, in 1974 Robbins bought Tiburcio Parrot's old Miravalle estate on Spring Mountain. In 1976, he built a new winery beside the mansion and named *it* **Spring Mountain Vineyards.** This may well be the best-known winery in the Napa Valley, not because its chardonnay came in fourth in the famous Paris tasting, ahead of three renowned white burgundies, but because it served as a setting for the television soap opera "Falcon Crest." Robbins even released a Falcon Crest wine in 1982. Robbins sold the winery in 1992 and retired to a life of playing golf. The new owner, tired of all the gapers, has closed the winery to the public. *2805 Spring Mountain Road.*

North of Lodi Lane, on the east side of CA 29, is a large complex that includes **Brava Terrace** restaurant.

(Top) Vineyard hot pots protect vines from spring frosts. (Above) Winery pomace is composted for garden fertilizer. (Opposite) A vineyard worker prunes back some vines.

Freemark Abbey. Established by old-time Napa Valley vintners and friends in 1967 in the old Lombarda stone winery building erected in 1886, Freemark Abbey takes its name from a winery occupying the site from 1940 to 1959. This

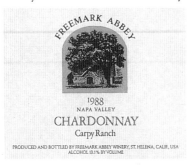

1988
NAPA VALLEY
CHARDONNAY
Carpy Ranch
PRODUCED AND BOTTLED BY FREEMARK ABBEY WINERY, ST. HELENA, CALIF, USA
ALCOHOL 13.1% BY VOLUME

had nothing to do with religious orders but got its name from three investors whose names were Charles FREEman, MARK Foster, and Albert Ahern, whose boyhood nickname had been ABBEY. The Lombarda winery, incidentally, started out as the Tychson winery, the first Napa Valley winery built by a woman. John Tychson and his wife Josephine had planted grapes and were planning their winery when Tychson committed suicide in 1885. Mrs. Tychson went ahead and supervised the building of the winery in 1886. In 1900, the winery was acquired by Antonio Forni, who renamed it Lombarda (and eventually sold it to Ahern).

The winery's latest reincarnation appears to be its luckiest one. It started making great wines from the first vintage on and has been notable for cabernets ever since. All the grapes are estate-grown, with the exception of a cabernet, whose grapes comes from the Bosché vineyard from the Rutherford Bench and which is bottled separately. The winery has also gained a reputation for its late-harvest riesling. *3022 St. Helena Highway North; (707) 963-9694.*

STONY HILL
NAPA VALLEY
CHARDONNAY
1985
Grown, produced and bottled 600 feet above the floor of the Napa Valley by Stony Hill Vineyard, St. Helena, Calif.
ALCOHOL 13% BY VOLUME   CONTAINS SULFITES

Stony Hill Vineyard. A narrow, unmarked road leads up Spring Mountain to Stony Hill Vineyard. This is another Napa Valley winery that started out as a weekend retreat and became a winemaking legend—except that it precedes the other "legends" by some 30 years. Eleanor and Fred McCrea fell in love with a goat farm and bought it as a summer home on Spring Mountain in 1943, planted chardonnay vines in 1948 (when that grape was virtually unknown in the Northern California Wine Country—University of California viticulturists tried to persuade them to plant more popular varieties), and sold their first wines in 1954. Fred McCrea died in 1977; Eleanor in 1991. The winery is now run by their descendants, but production is still minuscule, and the quality has not suffered one bit. The winery also makes a little riesling, which, sip by sip, is as good as the chardonnay. If you have not yet tasted a Stony Hill wine, find a way to do so—even if you must cajole, bribe, or beg. Or simply go to one of the six restaurants in Napa Valley where Stony Hill wines are served: Auberge de Soleil, Brava Terrace, The French Laundry, Meadowood Restaurant, Showley's at Miramonte, and Terra Restaurant.

This is one of the loveliest spots in the valley to visit—perhaps it's the perfect integration of farm and nature that makes it so beautiful. It's necessary to call ahead for a tour or tasting appointment and for directions. *(707) 963-2636.*

Schramsberg Vineyards. Five miles north of St. Helena, turn left onto Peterson Road, then right onto Schramsberg Road. But be sure to call ahead and make an appointment first. The road is very narrow and winding. Watch for wildlife and other cars.

Jacob Schram built this mansion for his wife after she complained about the small cabin they had been living in since the vineyard's founding in 1862. (Courtesy Schramsberg Vineyards)

Tucked into an idyllic dell on the slope of the mountain is the legendary Schramsberg Vineyards. Founded by Jack and Jamie Davies, the winery occupies the 19th-century cellars, stone winery, and home of Napa Valley pioneer winemaker Jacob Schram. Schram founded his winery in 1862, a year after Charles Krug started his. He gained literary fame when Robert Louis Stevenson visited in 1880 to taste the wines and wrote about his experience in *Silverado Squatters.*

What made the Davies' excursion into sparkling wine production so unique is not only that they made their wine by the traditional *méthode champenoise*—others, like Hanns Kornell, on Larkmead Lane, had done that before—but that the Davies also insisted on using the traditional grapes of Champagne: chardonnay and pinot noir, very few of which had been planted in the Napa Valley at that time. Schramsberg has not looked back since President Richard Nixon served Schramsberg sparkling wine at a reciprocal state dinner he gave for Chinese premier Chou En-lai in Beijing. Production has increased, but the quality is still as good as ever.

(chapter continues on page 127)

Annie Schram (seated above) poses with vineyard workers and family members in front of a new wine cellar. The champagne cellars of Schramsberg today (right) extend into the hillside in a network of tunnels totaling almost one kilometer in length.

CHAMPAGNE AND SPARKLING WINES

If you don't like dry Champagne say so. A moderately sweet (or moderately dry) Champagne is a human kind. A Brut is not. It is an acquired taste.

—Hilaire Belloc

Sparkling wines are, despite the mystique surrounding them, nothing more or less than wines in which carbon dioxide is suspended, making them bubbly. Sparkling wines were invented in Champagne, France's northernmost wine district, where wines tend to be a bit acid because grapes do not always fully ripen. That's why sparkling wines have traditionally been naturally tart, even austere.

Because of their progenitor's birthplace, many sparkling wines are often called "champagne." But since the term designates a region of origin, it really shouldn't be used for American sparkling wines. But that's not to say that Napa and Sonoma County sparkling wines are in any way inferior to French ones—many are even better. Perhaps they should conquer the world under regional names of their own! The French Champagne houses are fully aware of the excellence of the California product, and have already been quick to cash in on the laurels gathered by such pioneers as Hanns Kornell, Schramsberg, and Iron Horse by establishing sparkling wine cellars in Sonoma and Napa with American partners *(see page 148).*

Keep in mind that although we no longer need drink pricy imported champagne, quality American sparklers don't come cheap. Good sparkling wine will always be expensive because a great amount of work goes into making it.

Harvest. It starts with the harvest. White sparkling wines are made from both white and black grapes, which allows them to achieve very complex flavors. Growers pick the black grapes very carefully, to avoid crushing the berries and minimizing contact between the inner fruit and the skins, where the purply-red color pigments reside. The grapes are rushed to the winery, crushed very gently, and strained off the skins right away, again, to prevent the juice from coming in contact with pigments and turning red. (The juice of the black grape's inner fruit is usually white.) Even so, some sparklers have more of a pink tinge to them than the winemaker intends.

Sparkling wines are traditionally made from pinot noir (and, in France, from pinot meunier as well) and from chardonnay grapes. In California, pinot blanc, riesling, and other white wine grapes may also be used.

Fermentation. The freshly pressed must is fermented with special yeasts that preserve the wine's fruit. Before bottling, the finished "still" wines (wines without bubbles) are mixed with a *liqueur de tirage,* a blend of wine, sugar, and yeast. This mixture causes the wine to ferment again—in the bottle—for six to twelve weeks. It produces carbon dioxide as a by-product, which is trapped in the bottle and dissolves in the wine (instead of escaping into the air, as happens during fermentation in barrel, vat, or tank). It is this captive carbon dioxide which transforms the still wine into a sparkling wine. The second fermentation also raises the wine's alcohol level by about one percent—which is one reason why grapes for sparkling wines are picked at low sugar levels that ferment out initially to 11 percent alcohol, instead of the 12 percent (or more) regular wines ferment to.

Aging. The bottles of new sparkling wines are stored on their sides in deep cellars. The wine now ages *sur lie,* or on the lees (lees are the dead yeast cells and other deposits trapped in the bottle). This aging process enriches the wine's texture and embellishes the complexity of its bouquet. The amount of time the sparkling wine ages *sur lie* bears a direct relation to its quality: the longer the aging, the more complex the wine.

The lees must be removed from the bottle before the sparkling wine can be enjoyed. This is achieved in a process whose first step is called "riddling." In the past, each bottle, head tilted slightly downward, was placed in a riddling rack, an A-frame with many holes of bottleneck size. Riddlers gave each bottle a slight shake, every day if possible, and a downward turn. This continued for six weeks, until each bottle rested upside down in the hole and the sediment had collected in the neck, next to the cork. Simple as this sounds, it is actually very difficult to do. Hand-riddling is a fine art perfected after much training. But today, most sparkling wines are riddled in ingeniously designed machines called gyro palettes which riddle up to 500 or more bottles at one time. The machines also do the work in as little as a week to ten days. Yet some bottles resist the caressing touch of the machines and must still be riddled by hand.

Disgorging. After riddling, the bottles are "disgorged." The upside-down bottles are placed in a deeply chilled brine solution which freezes the sediments in a block that attaches itself to the crown cap sealing the bottle. The cap and frozen plug are removed, the bottle is topped off with a wine and sugar mixture called "dosage," and recorked with the traditional champagne cork. It is this dosage which determines the final sweetness of a sparkling wine.

Brut to Doux. Sparkling wines with 1.5 percent sugar or less are labeled "brut"; those with 1.2 to 2.0 percent sugar are called "extra dry"; those with 1.7 to 3.5 percent are called "sec"; and those with 3.5 to 5.0 percent, "demi-sec." "Doux" (sweet) sparkling wine has more than 5.0 percent sugar. If all of this odd labeling seems a bit deceiving, it is. Most sparkling wine drinkers refuse to admit that they like their bubbly on the sweet side, and this labeling convention allows them to drink sweet while pretending to drink dry. It's a marketing ploy invented in Champagne at least a century ago. A sparkling wine

(continues)

to which no dosage has been added will be bone dry (and taste "sour" to some) and may be called "extra-brut" or "natural."

Vintage Dating. Most sparkling wines are not vintage dated but are "assembled" (that's the term sparkling winemakers use instead of "blended") from different wines and sometimes different vintages to create a cuvée consistent with the house style. However, sparkling wines may be vintage dated in very great years.

Bulk or Charmat Process. Sparkling wine—though not Champagne—may also be made by time- and cost-saving bulk methods. In the bulk or Charmat process, invented by Eugene Charmat early in this century, the secondary fermentation takes place in large tanks rather than individual bottles. Each tank is basically treated as one huge bottle. After the bubbles have developed, the sediments are filtered from the wine and the wine is bottled. But at a price: while the sparkling wine may be ready in as little as a month, it has neither the complexity nor the bubble quality of the more slowly made sparklers. In the United States, sparkling wine made in this way must be labeled "Bulk Process" or "Charmat Process."

Sparkling wines made in the traditional, time-consuming fashion may be labeled "Méthode Champenoise" or "Wine Fermented in this Bottle."

But read carefully. One sparkler labels itself "Wine Made in the Bottle." There's quite a difference in methodology here between "this" and "the." The latter is sparkling wine made in the transfer process, in which the second fermentation of the wine takes place in a bottle, but in which all the bottles of a particular batch—instead of being disgorged individually—are emptied into large tanks, under pressure. The sediments are filtered out, the wine is rebottled, corked, and shipped to market.

The different processes of making sparkling wine not only have an effect on the quality and complexity of the wine itself, but also on the quality of the bubbles. Filtered wines are not as complex as unfiltered ones: their bubbles are more sparingly distributed, and they do not last very long. But that doesn't really matter, since most wines made like that are drunk quickly anyway, at parties or weddings. More bubbly, anyone?

Hand-riddling is the process by which the champagne bottles are gradually rotated to collect the sediment in the neck of the bottle. (Courtesy Schramsberg Vineyards)

A candlelit banquet in the cask room of Merryvale Vineyards.

The tour of the winery is very good, and will teach you a lot about how sparkling wine is made, but perhaps best of all is the delightful bubbly you'll get to sip at the end of the tour. Tours and tasting at this especially charming winery are by appointment only. *1400 Schramsberg Road, Calistoga; (707) 942-4558.*

❖

After visiting Schramsberg you may either turn east on Dunaweal and make a circular route south along the Silverado Trail and west back to Rutherford; or you may continue north to Calistoga. (*See page 137 for Calistoga and north. See page 212 for Howell Mountain wineries.*)

■ SOUTH ON THE SILVERADO TRAIL

From CA 29/128 turn east on Dunaweal Lane, heading to the Silverado Trail, and look for tiny **Stonegate Winery,** founded by Jim and Barbara Spaulding in 1973. The wines, from grapes grown on Diamond Mountain, are consistently good, especially David Spaulding's cabernet sauvignon and merlot. The sauvignon blanc is also worth tasting. *1183 Dunaweal Lane; (707) 942-6500.*

Farther down the road are two of the splashiest wineries in the Napa Valley, both of which caused quite a stir when they were built.

Sterling Vineyards. When the winery opened in 1969, few enophiles expected the wines to be good—but they were, especially the reds. The original partners sold the winery to Coca Cola in 1977. The soft-drink company was not a good wine steward. But since 1983, when the winery was sold to Joseph E. Seagram & Sons, quality has been on the rise. Chardonnay and pinot noir are very good. They are made from Carneros grapes, grown in the renowned Winery Lake Vineyard, which Seagram bought from René di Rosa in 1986—amid the outcry of wine-makers who'd depended on those grapes for the excellence of their own wines. The cabernet and merlot are also good, but will benefit from bottle aging.

The winery, built in the stark white style of an Aegean monastery, sits atop a 300- foot-high knoll. You'll have to ride a tram to reach the top, and the fee you pay includes a wine tasting and is good for a discount on the first bottle of wine you buy. *1111 Dunaweal Lane; (707) 942-3344.*

Clos Pegase. Just after the valley had gotten used to the white monastery, art book publisher Jan Shrem raised everybody's blood pressure with a design for an Egyptian temple of a winery—across the street from Sterling. Clos Pegase opened in 1987, with modifications, say those who have seen the original design. The winery, designed by postmodernist architect Michael Graves, is outrageously individualistic. It is loaded, but not overloaded, with art objects Jan and Mitsuko Shrem have collected. Everybody's favorite seems to be a giant thumb by Cesar that rises out of a vineyard bordering on the winery. There are even art objects in the wine tunnels running deep into the hillside behind the winery.

What makes Clos Pegase so interesting is that all of this somewhat eccentric decor works. Jan Shrem wants people to feel the connection between wine and art, and he most certainly succeeds. Best of all, the wines are as interesting as the art and architecture, and they're getting better with every vintage. This is an especially interesting winery to visit. *1060 Dunaweal Lane; (707) 942-4981.*

Sterling Winery is reached via a cable car that carries visitors to the top of a hill on which the winery estate is perched.

Cuvaison Winery. Continue east on Dunaweal Lane to the Silverado Trail. Turn right (south) and look for the mission-style arches of Cuvaison Winery on the left. This small winery struggled after it was founded in 1969 as a tax write-off by two engineers. It was rescued in 1979 by Swiss investors (who own Tobler Chocolates, among other products). The new owners upgraded the facilities and bought estate vineyards in the Carneros, clear on the other end of the Napa Valley. But it seems to work, especially for cabernet sauvignon, which might seem strange when you consider that the Carneros is a cool growing region and cabernet likes warmth. But don't quibble. Enjoy the wine. *4550 Silverado Trail; (707) 942-6266.*

As you drive south on the Silverado trail, note a road cut on your left that's brightly banded in black, red, and whitish grey. Here you have a lesson in Napa Valley geology: black obsidian layered with red volcanic soil and volcanic ash.

Duckhorn Vineyards. Look closely to the west of the highway. The buildings are below the level of the road and easy to miss. Do as other pilgrims do: take off your hat and bow your head in homage to merlot. The winery also makes cabernet and sauvignon blanc; it's open regularly for sales; for tours and tasting by appointment. *1000 Lodi Lane, St. Helena; (707) 963-7108.*

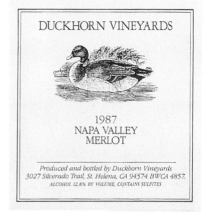

Joseph Phelps Vineyards. About four miles south of Duckhorn, after you pass the Pope Street bridge, look to the left for a green schoolhouse with white trim. The next road is the turnoff to Joseph Phelps. You need to turn left again at a big redwood gate in Spring Valley to reach the winery, which is up a slope to the north.

Phelps, a Colorado contractor, came to the Wine Country to build wineries for Pillsbury (the wineries which are now known as Rutherford Hill and Chateau Souverain). He fell in love with the area, bought the Connolly Hereford Ranch, and built himself a winery. That happened back in 1973; he didn't add a tasting room until 1995, just in time for that year's Napa Valley Wine Auction. As a builder, Phelps is tops, and the same can be said for Phelps as a vintner.

The winery attracted attention right away, especially the wines made by Walter Schug, who now has his own winery *(see page 148)*. Phelps's best wines in the past were rieslings; today they are reds: the superb Meritage blend called Insignia, the cabernet sauvignon, and the Rhone-style blends sold as Vin du Mistral and Le Mistral. Be sure to call ahead for an appointment. *200 Taplin Road, St. Helena; (707) 963-2745.*

Heitz Wine Cellars. Also in Spring Valley, to the south of Phelps, is the old Rossi stone winery now occupied by Heitz Wine Cellars. Joe Heitz opened his first winery in 1961, just south of St. Helena (it is now a tasting room), but bought the Spring Valley winery in 1964, after he outgrew the original space. Heitz also replanted the original vineyard almost exclusively with grignolino, an Italian grape of which he is uncommonly fond.

Heitz is one of Napa Valley's wine pioneers; successes with his powerful cabernet

Springtime brings lush green to the terraced vineyards.

sauvignon have spurred on others. But the wines have been a bit uneven in recent years. Taste carefully. Winery tours by appointment. The tasting room and sales office are open daily. *Tasting Room: 436 St. Helena Highway. Winery: 500 Taplin Road, St. Helena; (707) 963-3542.*

Return to the Silverado Trail and head south.

Rutherford Hill Winery. This winery (reached by turning west off the Silverado Trail on Rutherford Hill Road) began as the second home for Souverain, after Lee Stewart sold his pioneering Howell Mountain winery to a group of investors in 1970. The investors sold that winery to Tom Burgess *(see page 213)*, and built a new winery east of Rutherford named Souverain. In 1972, the investors sold the winery to

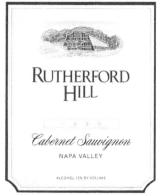

Pillsbury, who started building a second Souverain in the Alexander Valley (see Chateau Souverain below). Pillsbury realized in three short years it didn't have the proper mindset for running wineries and sold the Sonoma winery to a group of North Coast wine-grape growers (who, in turn, sold it to Nestlé's Wine World Estates) and the Napa winery to a group of local investors headed by Bill Jaeger and Charles Carpy. (According to historian Charles Sullivan, Pillsbury told the press the company "couldn't continue to operate Burger King and produce wine." What a lame excuse. Pillsbury could have taken the opposite tack and started selling cabernet to accompany whoppers at Burger King.) In 1997, Rutherford Hill was acquired by Paterno Imports of Chicago, which translates into a change of ownership, but not style, and brings a welcome infusion of money.

Rutherford Hill has one of the most extensive systems of wine caves of any California winery—nearly a mile of tunnels and passageways that were drilled by tunnel specialist Alf Burtleson, who used a special English drilling machine. Even with the mechanical help, it took almost a year and a half to drill the tunnels. Rutherford Hill may well become the leading quality producer of merlot in the United States. The winery also makes very good cabernet sauvignon and chardonnay. *200 Rutherford Hill Road, St. Helena; (707) 963-1871.*

Round Hill. Return to the Silverado Trail, turn left and immediately left again for Round Hill. Turn left again immediately, before the olive grove, and park in the small parking lot to the right. There's no tasting room, just a sales office.

Round Hill wines are not only good, but ounce for ounce a real bargain. It all started years ago, when Round Hill was located in an old stone winery off Lodi Lane and was primarily a negociant: that means it evaluated wines another winery had made, and if it liked them, sold it under its own label. Slowly, Round Hill evolved into a winery of its own. Today, it buys premium grapes from Napa Valley growers under long-term contract, which winemaker Mark Swain turns into first-rate wine. But the price structure has stayed the same. The 1989 and 1990 Quintessence, a red Meritage, can be rated among the best reds the Napa Valley produces. The winery's premium wines, now marketed under the Van Asperen label, has emerges as one of the Napa Valley's best high quality bargains.

The Gayot/Gault Millau guide likes this winery because the quality of the wines is sound and consistent. The authors go on to say, "These wines are priced modestly, and some of them—the Napa Valley Cabernet Sauvignon and the Napa Valley Zinfandel, for example—are quite high quality for their price." You can't ask more from a wine you can drink every day, year in, year out. *1680 Silverado Trail, St. Helena; (707) 963-5251.*

Mark Swain of Round Hill samples a new vintage.

The architecture of vineyard offices varies widely throughout the region. Pictured here are the wineries of Ehlers Lane (top), Opus One (above), and Sutter Home (right).

For **Chappellet Vineyards, Long Vineyards,** and **Nichelini Vineyards,** all located off CA 128 and east of the Silverado Trail, *see pages 215–217.*

Frog's Leap. The Napa Valley's newest "old" winery is reached by turning west on CA 128 back toward Rutherford (and after the first turn look for a large red barn in the vineyard to your right). While the wines of Frog's Leap are even better than they used to be, the winery itself is not where it used to be. After splitting up with partner Larry Turley, John and Julie Williams took their leaping frog label from the old frog farm north of St. Helena, where it was founded in 1981, south to Rutherford. In the summer of 1994, they bought the old red barn that served as the Adamson Winery from 1884 to 1896 (when phylloxera ate the vines) and later served as a storage shed. As soon as John and Julie Williams bought the property, plus a few acres of vines from old-time Napa Valley winegrower Chuck Carpy (of Freemark Abbey and Rutherford Hill fame), they started reconverting it into a winery, barely getting it ready for the 1994 vintage. Long-term plans include planting an orchard of fruit and nut trees, a second wine cellar, and a visitors center. Things are still a bit primitive, while construction continues, but don't let that discourage you. Everyone here seems to have a great sense of humor, the perfect antidote to wine snobbery. What do you expect of a winery whose motto is "Time is fun when you're having flies"? Great fun, great wine, and a delightful place to visit.

Frog's Leap (along with Cakebread, to the south) is a winery that should be on your must-see list, not only because the wines are great. They are great—especially the zinfandel, the sauvignon blanc, and the cabernet sauvignon. But more importantly, this is a winery on a human scale, a winery run by real people who will make you feel welcome and show you what the real Napa Valley wine scene is like, behind the glitzy fronts of showy fermentation palaces. Best of all, this is one winery that maintains a sense of humor, despite the hardships of making and marketing wine. Just listen to what John Williams has to say about his 1992 cabernet sauvignon: "It is an awesome responsibility making Napa Valley Cabernet. For many winemakers, it's the ultimate expression of our craft . . . our raison d'etre. I can't help but feel the weight of history and tradition upon my shoulders. I fully expect that St. Peter will ask me for a vertical of my Cabs at the Pearly Gates." He concludes with: "I like the '92 well enough that I'm hoping St. Peter will let me in!" St. Peter should, especially since the grapes used in Frog's Leap wines are organically grown.

On a more serious note, Williams dives into the discussion of whether Napa Valley chardonnay or sauvignon blanc is the better dinner wine:

> Quite frankly, we thought this poor-man's chardonnay thing was behind us. What we know is that sauvignon blanc has an ever-growing following not based on being a cheaper alternative to chardonnay, but rather on the fact that with a vast variety of food preparations a vivacious, freshly scented and crisp sauvignon blanc is a superb choice in white wine.

Call ahead as appointments are necessary to tour Frog's Leap and taste the wines. Be sure to ask for directions to the winery. To find the winery, look for a leaping frog weathervane atop a huge red barn. *8815 Conn Creek Road, Rutherford; (707) 963-4704 or (800) 959-4704.*

■ CALISTOGA

If, while driving north of St. Helena on CA 29, you decide to continue past Dunaweal Lane, you'll soon reach the small town of Calistoga. When you walk along Lincoln Avenue, Calistoga's main street, Mount St. Helena rises to the north, some 4,000 feet above the valley floor, with other tall mountains to the west and east. You might think you were high up in some Alpine valley, instead of a mere 365 feet above the level of the Napa River tidewater. The false-fronted shops, old hotels, and quaint stone buildings look like those of a cattle town tucked into a remote mountain valley, and you wouldn't be at all surprised to see a posse ride into town looking for a rustler or fugitive desperado. A hundred years ago, you wouldn't have been far off, for there were hold-ups of the stagecoach line that ran across the shoulder of Mount St. Helena to Clear Lake with the payroll for the quicksilver mines dotting the mountains. At one time, Calistoga even had a gold mine at the Palisades high above the town, but the town's real excitement was generated by water which spurted from natural hot springs.

Soda Springs, near Calistoga, became the region's most fashionable resort in the late 19th century. Victorian mansions once dotted the hillsides, accommodating tourists from San Francisco and elsewhere.

When Sam Brannan—Mormon missionary, San Francisco vigilante, entrepreneur, and vineyard developer—learned in 1859 that a place in the upper Napa Valley called Agua Caliente by the settlers did indeed have hot springs and even an "old faithful" geyser, he bought up 2,000 acres of prime property and laid out a resort. Planning to rival New York's famous Saratoga Hot Springs, which Brannan had visited on a proselytizing trip with Joseph Smith (founder of the Church of Jesus Christ of Latter-Day Saints), he built an elegant hotel, bathhouses, cottages, stables, an observatory, and a distillery (a questionable choice for a Mormon missionary). The distillery proved to be the only money maker in the place—its brandy was shipped as far as Europe.

The resort itself stayed unprofitable even after the railroad reached Calistoga in August of 1868. When the railroad too proved a loser, interest in the resort waned. Brannan left Calistoga in 1877, and the bank holding the mortgage sold the place to Leland Stanford, who intended to build his college here. But the college was built elsewhere, and Stanford sold his interest in 1919. Yet folks continued traveling to Calistoga to "take the waters." While the town never again achieved the status of a world-class resort, the springs supported a sprinkling of small hotels and bathhouses, built wherever a hot spring bubbled to the surface. Here you can still take soothing mud baths in a hot paste mixed from mineral water, peat, and volcanic ash, or you can submerge yourself in the naturally hot—and rather muddy —water of a whirlpool bath. You can finish up with a full-body massage. If the sulphurous waters emit a bit of a fire-and-brimstone aroma, don't let that disturb you. It's the price you pay for slipping back into the primal muck of the California Garden of Eden.

While Calistoga has remained more of a spa than wine town, its vineyards produce some of the Napa Valley's best wines. **Chateau Montelena,** renowned for its chardonnay and cabernet sauvignon, lies at the edge of town (*see page 201 for details.*) To the northwest, at the head of the valley, rises the steep mountain vineyards that grow Storybook Mountain's superb zinfandel. The **All Seasons Cafe,** on Lincoln, may well have the best list of local Napa Valley wines of any restaurant in the valley, besides serving great food. Several other restaurants in town, most notably **Wappo** and **Catahoula,** have also gained widespread fame for the quality of their cookery.

Despite its fame, Calistoga remains an understated sort of place—"Hometown U.S.A." in the Wine Country. You can tell that in the architecture along the quiet

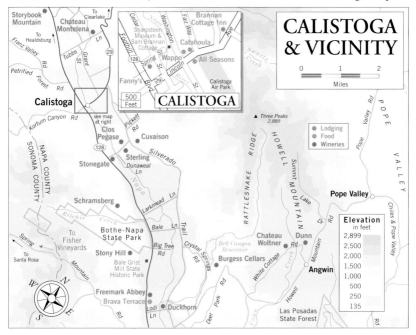

tree-shaded back streets where Calistogans live and where some run lovely bed-and-breakfasts. The Napa River flows right through town. You can walk across it at a ford and dangle your feet in its cold waters on a hot afternoon, but you'll be hard-pressed to find a sign directing you to those waters. Park at Pioneer Park on Cedar Street, just north of Lincoln, walk past the white gingerbread bandstand, and take the short trail down to the river. On the other bank the trail ends at the **Sharpsteen Museum** and **Sam Brannan Cottage,** sites you should not miss.

The museum was founded by Ben Sharpsteen, an award-winning Walt Disney animator, after Sharpsteen retired to Calistoga; the cottage is one of three in town to survive from Sam Brannan's day. It has been restored to its original appearance and now adjoins the museum. Sharpsteen also created detailed dioramas showing how the resort looked in its heyday, giving us glimpses of Calistoga's Chinatown and railroad days. After Sharpsteen took Walt Disney on a tour of the region, some of the more scenic parts of Calistoga and St. Helena ended up in the movie *Pollyanna* (1960)—as turn-of-the-century New England scenes. The Disney family has kept its interest in the Napa Valley: it now owns Silverado Vineyards just north of Napa.

Chateau Montelena has beautifully landscaped grounds, including garden islands set in a large pond. Picnic areas may be reserved in advance.

NAPA VALLEY WINE AUCTION

The Napa Valley Wine Auction is perhaps the most famous event in the Wine Country. It is avidly attended by everyone who wants to be seen, who cares about food, and who'll shell out lots of money to benefit charity while making off with some extraordinary bottles of wine.

Barrel Tasting. The Thursday afternoon barrel tasting is usually a "double barreled" event, held at one winery. The actual "barrel tasting" is largely of Napa red wines, and the event sometimes takes place in the winery's caves—a wonderful experience. Outside, at the Varietal Wine Pavilion, sparklers and white varietals are poured. Food purveyors are all lined up in booths close by, so you can taste and sample as you wander about.

Vintners' Dinners. On the first night of the auction, participating vintners (over 40 of them) give dinners at their wineries for the participants. Dinners range from country-style barbecues and dances to black-tie affairs. Chefs preparing the food in the past have included such well-known folks as Gary Danko, Nancy Oakes, George Morrone, Jeremiah Tower, Elka Gilmore, and Ben Davis.

Open Houses. On Friday afternoon, Napa Valley wineries hold special open houses for auction participants, with a series of lectures, comparative wine tastings, and barbecues.

Vintners' Ball. The Friday night Vintners' Ball, usually held at Meadowood Resort, boasts a spectacular dance—and of course dinner, prepared by a Bay Area star chef. Each course boasts a different Napa Valley wine chosen to complement the dish.

Buffet Luncheon/Auction. The next day, a buffet luncheon is jointly prepared by several Napa Valley restaurants. At the auction itself, wine lovers get their chance to bid—on some pretty pricey bottles. The most expensive bottle of wine has gone for over $105,000. (The auction may raise close to $2 million for local health services.)

Rustic Dinner. The close of the weekend is usually a casual, country-style feast, often with a Mediterranean accent (in keeping with Napa's culinary style). Chefs from the Culinary Institute of America's St. Helena campus help out, serving wonderful family-style dishes. It's always a great finale to the official part of the auction, but it never seems to mark the end of the weekend's food and wine indulgence. After all, you're in the Wine Country.

For information and reservations, call (800) 982-1371. A weekend package for two runs about $1,300. Profits benefit health-care facilities in the Napa Valley.

CARNEROS DISTRICT

. . . And, lastly, a man should not refuse a little wine when it is pressed upon him.
—*Yoshida Kenko, 1283–1350*

THE CARNEROS DISTRICT, AN AMERICAN VITICULTURAL APPELLATION established in 1983, stretches across the cool lower reaches of Sonoma and Napa counties. The region gets its name from its former use: *carneros* means sheep in Spanish and the slopes now covered with vines were once thought to be good for nothing but sheep pasture. The soils here are shallow, and water drains off quickly to marsh and slough.

To fully understand how different the Carneros region is from the other lands bordering San Francisco Bay, you should approach it from the water. From San Francisco travel north on US 101 to Novato and take the CA 37 turnoff to the east, which will take you along the upper reaches of northern San Francisco Bay, known here as San Pablo Bay. Seen across the shallow waters of San Pablo Bay on a cold, grey day, the Carneros region's flat marshes and low hills look very bleak, more like Scottish moor than a California shore. Even where the hills rise to meet the Sonoma and Mayacamas mountains, they look desolate, their grassy expanses interrupted only here and there by a copse of somber live oaks or by the bright green of a vineyard.

Vines grow slowly in the Carneros and yield few grapes. But the wine they make is very special. California's winegrowing pioneers recognized this in the mid-19th century and planted vast tracts of grapes. But because of the low yields, some of the land was allowed to revert to sheep pasture after phylloxera destroyed the vines in the 1890s. But the high reputation of the grapes survived the vineyards, and shortly after Repeal vines once again began to spread across the land. While most of the vineyards were owned by individual growers who grew other crops to minimize their economic risks, the Napa Valley's Louis M. Martini bought vineyards here in the 1940s. Sonoma wineries, too, expanded their grape plantings to the Carneros: Sebastiani at first, followed by Buena Vista and others.

The wines made from Carneros grapes are unique. Carneros grapes have better acids and more subtle fruit than grapes grown in the Wine Country's hot valleys— even warm-climate grapes like cabernet sauvignon and merlot ripen well in favored

Carneros locations. Yet zinfandel may not ripen at all, and chardonnay needs shelter. Surprisingly, the fickle pinot noir ripens well on exposed, windy slopes, making excellent wine of great complexity and depth. It and the chardonnay grapes grown here also make superb sparkling wine.

■ CARNEROS WINERIES

Viansa Winery & Italian Marketplace. If you enter the Carneros by turning north off CA 37 onto CA 121, this will be the first winery you encounter; it's on the right. Built in the style of a Tuscan country house, the winery overlooks the lowlands and marshes of lower Sonoma Creek and is protected from the winds by a low ridge. The winery is only a few years old but has deep roots: it was established by Sam Sebastiani, a scion of Sonoma's Sebastiani Vineyards, and his wife, Vicki, after the former left the family enterprise (the name is a contraction of Vicki and Sam). Even though Sam Sebastiani had gained experience at the family winery with traditional California grape varieties like barbera, cabernet sauvignon, zinfandel, and chardonnay, Viansa came into its own after the winery started exploring such Italian varietals as nebbiolo, sangiovese, and muscat canelli. There are also

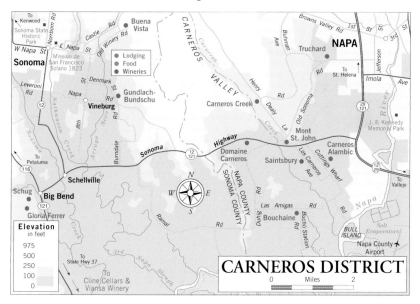

experimental plantings of vernaccia and malvasia. The Sebastianis believe in the marriage of food and wine—thus the "Italian Marketplace" in the name. The "marketplace" sells a wide variety of Italian-style food products as well as tasty dishes ranging from focaccia sandwiches to pasta salads to torta rustica (a sort of Italian quiche). Of course, visitors are encouraged to use the picnic area, which is shaded by olive trees and overlooks a restored wetland (administered by Ducks Unlimited) where more than sixty species of birds—including herons, egrets, ducks, and golden eagles—have been spotted, as well as turtles and river otters. Plan to spend some time at this winery, take the self-guided tour, relax, enjoy a picnic, take a walk but, above all, pick a sunny day—for it can be chilly even in the wind shade of the hill. *25200 Arnold Drive/CA 121, Sonoma; (707) 935-4700.*

Cline Cellars. You can really feel the famous Carneros winds at the next winery on your route: Cline Cellars started out in Contra Costa County's Oakley area, at the edge of the Sacramento River delta, where the Cline family raises old vines in very sandy soil. The soil is so sandy that the vineyards have never been devastated by phylloxera (the root louse does not like sand). Zinfandel and heat-loving Rhone varietals like marsanne, mourvèdre, and carignane thrive in this climate. Although the winery has moved to the Carneros and planted vineyards here, most of its grapes still come from Oakley. As you taste the wines you will encounter some unusual but very pleasing flavors. The marsanne tastes quite unlike any other California white, and the mourvèdre is quite different from the more familiar cabernet sauvignon. Be sure to taste the Cotes d'Oakley, a blend of red Rhone grapes, as well as the vin gris white, which is made with red mourvèdre grapes. There are also semillon and zinfandel for more traditional palates.

The place reeks with history—literally, since the warm springs on the property do have a bit of a non-vinous aroma. On July 4, 1823, Father Altimira founded Sonoma Mission in this very spot by planting a cross. When he returned a month later, he moved the mission to present-day Sonoma. If you wonder why the venerable padre had a change of heart, just stand still for a while and feel the wind. Then drive to Sonoma and feel the lack of wind. The fact that this farm was an ancient Indian village site has been commemorated by the construction of two willow-frame huts, which need only a covering of tule reeds to become habitable. An old bathhouse with graffiti dating back to 1877 shows that white settlers were just as fond of the warm springs as the native inhabitants were. Beyond the bathhouse, the

Viansa Winery was originally established by Sam and Vicki Sebastiani.

*Cline Cellars (above) resides on the site of the original Sonoma Mission, which was estab-
lished here in 1823, before being moved to its present location in the town of Sonoma.*

warm springs have been contained in a series of stone-walled ponds (to either side
of the 1850s clapboard farm house). They were built in the 1880s for raising carp.
They still hold a few fish, as well as turtles, but you are not allowed to angle. *24737
Arnold Drive/Highway 121, Sonoma; (707) 935-4310.*

Gloria Ferrer Champagne Caves. As you drive north from Cline, look for a winery
to your left up against the gentle slopes of the hills, a winery that looks sunny even
on a grey Carneros day. This is Gloria Ferrer Champagne Caves, built in 1982 by
the Spanish sparkling-wine maker Freixenet. The winery is named for the wife of
José Ferrer, the company president. The sparkling wines made here under the direction of winemaker Bob Iantosca are truly superb, but be sure to also taste the
chardonnay and pinot noir made by Iantosca. Both have that elusive Burgundian
quality California winemakers strive for but seldom achieve.

Sitting on the deck at Gloria Ferrer on a warm, sunny afternoon, sipping
sparkling wine as you look out over the vineyards and listen to the birds sing, is one
of the Wine Country's happiest experiences. *23555 Highway 121, Sonoma; (707)
996-7256.*

Gloria Ferrer Champagne Caves, where the sun seems always to be shining.

Schug Carneros Estate Winery. After leaving Gloria Ferrer, turn north on CA 121, then left on Bonneau Road, at Big Bend, to reach Schug Carneros. Walter Schug comes from a family which has made wine on the Rhine for a long time. After

studying winemaking at the German Wine Institute in Geisenheim, he came to Northern California in 1959. He became famous as winemaker for Joseph Phelps Vineyards. In 1980, he launched his Schug brand, while still working at Phelps, but left in 1983 to start a winery of his own. While he was best known at Phelps for cabernet sauvignon and riesling, Schug now concentrates on chardonnay and pinot noir. The winery provides a unique service. If you have a question about which wine to match to a certain food, call the winery's 800 number, and one of the Schug daughters will advise you on how to achieve the proper match. *602 Bonneau Road, Sonoma; (707) 939-9363 or (800) 966-9365.*

Domaine Carneros. After Big Bend, the Carneros Highway turns east, passing through a landscape of fields, pastures, and dairy farms before coming to the next winery, on the Napa side of the district. A large French chateau to the right side of the highway is Domaine Carneros, established in 1987 by the champagne house Taittinger along with a few American partners in response to the success achieved by Domaine Chandon, another French venture into California sparkling-wine making. The sparkling wines made here are very austere, the perfect accompaniment for fresh Tomales Bay or Point Reyes oysters, as well as for sturgeon caviar from farm-raised Sacramento Valley fish.

There's a reason why Domaine Carneros looks like an authentic French chateau: it is a copy of the Château de la Marquetterie, an 18th-century mansion owned by the Taittinger family in Champagne. *1240 Duhig Road, Napa; (707) 257-0101.*

Carneros Alambic Distillery. The sumptuous accoutrements of Domaine Carneros contrast with the workaday rustic look of Carneros Alambic Distillery. Established in 1982 by the French Cognac producer Remy Martin (originally in partnership with Jack Davies of the Napa Valley's Schramsberg Vineyards), the low, grey stone buildings of the distillery look like a French farm picked up bodily and dropped into the Carneros. You may sniff the brandy but not taste it (U.S. law prohibits the tasting of alcoholic spirits unless you buy a bottle). Visit the distillery, where large copper stills sparkle in a vast hall, but a working model in the reception room shows more clearly how brandy is made from wine. It is beautifully put together and is alone worth a visit. So is the aging room, where brandy slowly ages in small oak barrels, while the angels' share evaporates, leaving behind a more intense and concentrated liquor. A superb sound system fills the room with Gregorian chants. Relax, stand still, and listen—for a truly mystical experience. Cliff swallows love the stone walls of the distillery and build their jug-shaped nests under the eaves. Besides brandy made from wine, Carneros Alambic also distills an exquisite pear liqueur. *1250 Cutting Wharf Road, Napa; (707) 253-9095.*

■ UP THE OLD SONOMA ROAD

If you have some time to extend your visit, **Mont St. John Cellars** at the junction of CA 121 (Carneros Highway) and the Old Sonoma Road leading from Napa to Sonoma across the Carneros hills offers good value estate-grown chardonnay, muscat di canelli, gewürztraminer, Johannisberg riesling, and pinot noir from the Madonna Vineyard, which straddles the Napa/Sonoma County line along the west bank of Huichica Creek. Louis Bartolucci opened this winery in 1979, well ahead of the popularity the Carneros would achieve in the next decade. He brought a lot of local experience to his enterprise, since his family had farmed vineyards in the lower Napa Valley since the 1930s. *5400 Old Sonoma Road, Napa; (707) 255-8864.*

You will have to call ahead and make an appointment to visit **Saintsbury,** a small winery that has gained renown for the quality of its pinot noir. The quality of the wine makes Saintsbury well worth a visit. *1500 Los Carneros Avenue, Napa; (707) 252-0592.* To visit a truly pioneering winery, drop in at Francis Mahoney's **Carneros Creek Winery,** *1285 Dealy Lane, Napa; (707) 253-9463,* located a bit up hill, off Old Sonoma Road. While other wineries—most notably Louis M. Martini—established earlier Carneros vineyards, it was Mahoney's winery, opened in 1972,

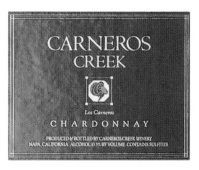

which proved that cool-climate pinot noir can be very complex indeed.

Not only do chardonnay and pinot noir grow well here, but merlot also reaches surprising complexity, as **Truchard Vineyards** has amply proved. This winery's pinot noir is also in a class by itself. Be sure to call ahead for an appointment at this small winery. *3234 Old Sonoma Road, Napa; (707) 253-7153.* **Bouchaine Vineyards,** on the south side of the Carneros Highway, is rather close to tidewater, lying between Carneros and Huichica creeks and the tidal sloughs of San Pablo Bay. But the alternately breezy and foggy weather has a special effect on the fermenting wine. Call ahead and make an appointment to taste the chardonnay and pinot noir, which are surprisingly Burgundian, as well as the gewürztraminer, which has a definite Alsatian character. *1075 Buchli Station Road, Napa; (707) 252-9065.*

■ CARNEROS WILDERNESS

Should you feel the need to take a break from all this serious wine-tasting, grab a picnic lunch and take Cuttings Wharf Road south to the Napa River, stop at the public boat ramp/fishing access floats, and dangle your feet in the river. If you have remembered to bring your fishing pole (and license), you might even catch a carp or two. Keep a lookout for white egrets, great blue herons, wood ducks, and other waterfowl. But beware: these waters are tricky and rise and fall with the tide. If the bleak marshes to the south look familiar, there's a reason: Francis Ford Coppola shot some of the Mekong Delta scenes for *Apocalypse Now* (1979) down here.

You can also relax by the river and hike through wildflower meadows and marshes in **J. F. Kennedy Park,** just south of Napa on CA 29. For a more rugged hike,

The Carneros region has some of the most beautiful vineyard scenery to be found anywhere in California.

climb the wooded knoll in **Westwood Hills Wilderness Park** on Browns Valley Road—a city park that is truly wild. Recent notices have warned against mountain lions, which have been spotted both in the park and in Browns Valley. Hikers are advised to "proceed with caution. Please avoid traveling alone and keep small children close." **Skyline Park** east of Napa (at the very end of Imola Avenue) is also wild, but has open meadows—which are garlanded with blue and white lupines, California poppies, and godetia in the spring.

SONOMA VALLEY

Rosalind: I pray you, do not fall in love with me,
For I am falser than vows made in wine:
Besides, I like you not. . . .
—Shakespeare, As You Like It

THE SONOMA VALLEY STARTS, like the Napa Valley, on the cool, windswept, and fogbound shores of the Carneros but, unlike the latter, it is open to the north as well, allowing cool marine air to funnel south from the Russian River Valley via the Santa Rosa Plain. Vines growing high up in the mountains get more sun and thus have more sugar in their grapes, but they are stressed by growing in poor rocky soils. Water runs off quickly, making for deep-rooted vines and intensely flavored grapes. One such district, Sonoma Mountain, produces such unique, complex reds that it has its own sub-appellation.

The town of Sonoma, the valley's cultural center, is not only the oldest town in the Wine Country but also the place where the first wine north of San Francisco was made.

■ TOWN OF SONOMA

While the small towns of the Wine Country share the same spirit, they differ widely in appearance. Like Healdsburg, Sonoma is built around a plaza, but the latter town is some 30 years older, having been founded in the early 1800s, when California was still part of Mexico.

The best way of approaching Sonoma is from the south, on Broadway (CA 12), a wide street which ends at the plaza (CA 12 turns left, towards Santa Rosa). This route was once not only part of the most important highway in California, but the end of the only overland route in California, El Camino Real, the king's highway.

During California's Spanish and Mexican periods, this highway ran past all of the missions: from San Diego de Alcala (1769), the first, to San Francisco Solano de Sonoma (1823), the twenty-first and last. North of San Rafael, El Camino Real

A view looking north up Sonoma Valley. In the foreground is Sonoma's town plaza.

passed over vast grasslands, past tule marshes and groves and groves of massive valley and live oaks. Farms and vineyards sprawl over the once-wild hills and valleys where deer, elk, and grizzly bears once roamed, but many of the tall oaks still stand—you can spot them here and there on the hills and in draws, and even along the highway.

The mission, most of which is restored, nevertheless looks very much the way it did more than 150 years ago, except that the large mission church and the plaza in front where El Camino ended are no more. Turning right on Napa Street and left on First Street East brings you to Spain Street, with the mission chapel on your right and the adobe barracks of Mariano Vallejo's Sonoma Fortress on your left. Continue on First for half a block and turn left. The large municipal parking lot here has unlimited free parking (you're limited to two hours on the plaza). North of here are **petonque courts** (for playing the French version of *bocce*) in Depot Park, and the **Depot Museum** with its local history exhibits.

Return to **the plaza,** where most of the local historical sites are clustered, as are the best restaurants and a number of interesting shops. It was here that American rebels proclaimed California's independence from Mexico on June 14, 1846

The adobe barracks of General Vallejo's Sonoma Fortress.

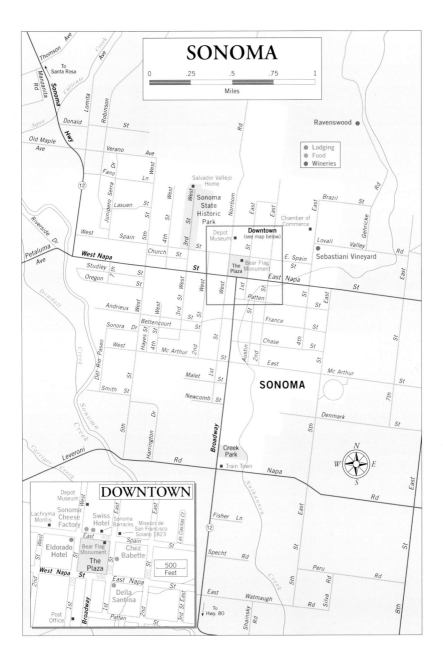

(which the Californios themselves had already done twice before, in 1831 and 1836). The rebels' Bear Flag flew over the plaza till the ninth of July, when the U.S. flag was raised here and Sonoma became an American garrison town.

Among the historic buildings surviving (all of which can be found along Spain Street, on the north side of the plaza) are the whitewashed adobe **padres' quarters** of the mission (after 1823); the **servants' quarters** of the mansion belonging to Gen. Mariano Vallejo (circa 1836); the **barracks** (built between 1836 and 1840); and the **mission chapel** (built by Vallejo in 1840). The **Blue Wing Inn,** built by Vallejo as a guesthouse, became a notorious saloon during gold rush days, with such diverse visitors as the scout Kit Carson, the bandit Joaquin Murrietta, and army officer Ulysses S. Grant. The **Toscano Hotel** dates from the 1850s, as does the nearby **Vasquez House,** which was built in 1855 by "Fighting" Joe Hooker, before he became a Civil War hero. It is now the home of the Sonoma League for Historic Preservation.

The **Sonoma Hotel** dates from the 1880s, but the third story was added and the building refurbished by Samuele Sebastiani in the 1920s. Rooms tend to be on the small side. Sebastiani, the founder of his family's wine dynasty, believed in sharing his wealth: he deserves credit for the elaborate—and aptly named—**Sebastiani Theatre** on the plaza's east side. He also built homes for his workers, donated a parochial school, built streets for the town, and contributed to many other civic projects. Sebastiani Vineyards is only four blocks east of the plaza. Besides taking a tour, tasting, and buying wine, you can picnic there.

The **Salvador Vallejo Adobe** on the west side of the plaza (home of Mariano's brother) dates from 1846; it was turned into the El Dorado hotel after the American occupation. With a second story added, the building saw a variety of different uses. It is once again a hotel—and a very comfortable one. Downstairs is a **Ristorante Piatti** (one of several in this chain), which serves some of the better Italian food around. The best rooms are behind the courtyard in back; breakfast in the courtyard is one of the highlights of a stay in Sonoma.

Sonoma is a town of courtyards. Several of the restaurants on or near the plaza are built around courtyards as are several shops, most notably those of **El Paseo** and **The Mercato.** You can spend a whole day enjoying the plaza: browse the excellent selection of old tomes at **Plaza Books,** taste local wines at **The Wine Exchange of Sonoma,** or pick up picnic fixings (for a picnic in the plaza or at a

The Sebastiani Building in the town of Sonoma houses a theater behind its Mission-style facade.

nearby Carneros or Sonoma Valley winery) at the **Sonoma French Bakery,** the **Vella Cheese Company** (home of the superb dry jack, truly a world-class cheese; one block east of the plaza on Second north of Spain), the **Sonoma Cheese Factory** (on the north side of the plaza; besides cheese, also a good selection of wines, breads, pickled olives, etc.). If you're planning to have a picnic-barbecue, stop at the **Sonoma Sausage Company** for great bratwurst and other sausages—or indulge in a ham or paté. *For more restaurants on or near the plaza, see pages 256–260.* And don't miss the galleries and gift shops nearby. Plan to spend a lot of time here before heading back out to tour wineries.

While Sonoma does have more than its share of historic adobes from the city's Mexican period, it is not at all a musty museum town, nor is the plaza a museum piece. The plaza is a place where people hang out, have lunchtime picnics on one of the many picnic tables, feed the ducks in the pond on the plaza's west side, or listen to musical performances at the small amphitheater. It has come a long way since being a dusty square where Vallejo drilled his troops and where locals butchered cattle. Today it is a grassy park, shaded by trees and brightened by roses. **City Hall,** a stone edifice erected in 1906, has four sides that are identical—so none of the merchants on the plaza would feel that city hall had turned its back to them.

The plaza is also the setting for several very folksy festivals, most notably the annual community **Ox Roast** and **Valley of the Moon Wine Festival.** Call the Sonoma Valley Visitors Bureau for dates; *(707) 996-1090.*

■ WINERIES IN TOWN

Sonoma vineyards were planted by the mission padres in the 1820s, almost as soon as they got the first adobe walls up. These came into the possession of Gen. Mariano Vallejo, and were later sold to an enterprising Italian immigrant named Samuele Sebastiani, who established a vineyard here in 1904.

Sebastiani Vineyards. The winery made only bulk wine until 1954, when Samuele's son August decided the wines were good enough to carry the family name on the label. He was right, of course. With name recognition came increased sales, and Sebastiani was soon by far the largest winery in Sonoma County. Sebastiani was among the pioneers planting grapes in the Carneros (in the Schellville area). The winery is well known for its hearty reds. Lately, traditional varieties like barbera, cabernet sauvignon, and zinfandel have been joined by such intriguing newcomers as cabernet franc, mourvèdre, and syrah (the true French Rhone variety, not the California premium grape known as petite sirah). Sebastiani has also produced a full range of white wines. Sebastiani's country wines are easy on the palate—and on the wallet. *389 Fourth St. East, Sonoma; (707) 938-5532.*

Buena Vista Carneros Estate. The old Buena Vista winery, founded by Hungarian adventurer Agoston Haraszthy in 1857, suffered heavy losses when phylloxera devastated its vineyards, then had a second blow when the great 1906 earthquake collapsed its cellars and destroyed the stored wine. The winery lay idle until the 1940s, when Frank Bartholomew, a UPI war correspondent, bought the old edifice, reopened the tunnels, and replanted the vineyards. When Bartholomew sold the

winery to Young's Market of Los Angeles in 1968, he kept the vineyards, forcing the new owners to look for vineyard land elsewhere. They found it in the budding Carneros district of southern Sonoma and Napa counties—hence the new name. The winery was purchased in 1979 by the German firm A. Racke, which proved to be a boon for its further development. The wines are well made and pleasant to drink, although they rarely achieve greatness, with perhaps the exception of the Carneros cabernet sauvignon. The Carneros production facility is closed to the public, but the old Sonoma winery has a

Samuele Sebastiani, founder of Sebastiani Vineyards, ran the enterprise from 1874 until his death in 1944. (Courtesy Sebastiani Vineyards)

tasting room and a shaded courtyard perfect for picnicking and for watching performances of Shakespeare plays. An especially nice place to visit. *18000 Old Winery Road, Sonoma; (707) 252-7117.*

Gundlach-Bundschu. Like many wineries in Northern California, Gundlach-Bundschu, established in 1858 as California Bonded Winery No. 64, closed its doors during Prohibition. But the property did not change hands. Since Jim Bundschu replanted the family's Rhinefarm Vineyard (one of the oldest in California) and reopened the winery in 1973, the place has been known mostly for the high quality of its red wines, while great-great-grandfather Jacob Gundlach had gained fame for his high-quality whites.

The place looks a bit like an overgrown gun bunker, but don't let that scare you away. The looks relate to the history of the place. By the time Bundschu got around to rebuilding the winery, only three walls of the original building still stood, and the aging tunnels had to be redug almost from scratch, thanks to earthquakes and neglect. But now everything works again—splendidly. Bundschu also has imbued the winery with a sense of fun. You're bound to hear jazz, pop music, or rock-and-roll over the sound system as you walk into the tasting room, instead of the classical "muzak" permeating the air at more staid establishments. Be sure to taste the Rhinefarm merlot, the cabernet sauvignon, and the zinfandel. There's

The 1871 harvest at Buena Vista was caught on film by Eadweard Muybridge, who was famous for his "body in motion" photography. (Courtesy Buena Vista Carneros Estate)

also a riesling made from the Kleinberger clone introduced by Jacob. *2000 Denmark Street off Napa Road, Sonoma; (707) 938-5277.* A short, breathtaking hike up the hill takes you to a viewpoint from which you can overlook much of the lower valley and the Carneros. You'll most likely notice lots of Sonomans picnicking: this is one of their favorite hangouts.

Ravenswood. This winery building looks even more like a hillside bunker than does the one at Gundlach-Bundschu. You almost get the feeling these Sonomans are digging in to ward off a threatened invasion from Napa, on the other side of the ridge. Ravenswood was established in 1976 in the Russian River Valley, where winemaker Joel Peterson worked with the late Joseph Swan. It later moved to a shack at the

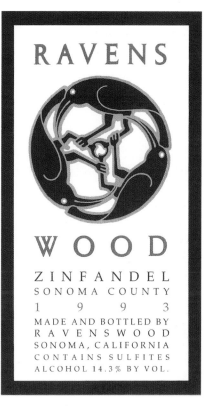

edge of the Sangiacomo vineyard in the Carneros, and moved uphill into the former premises of the Haywood Winery in 1991, after the latter was bought by Buena Vista and shut down (its name survives on a Buena Vista label).

To reach Ravenswood, go north on Fourth Street, past the Sebastiani Winery, to Lovall Valley Road, then turn left on Gehricke Road and wind your way up into the mountains. Chances are you'll be following zinfandel pilgrims en route to their mecca, for Ravenswood is adored by many for its zinfandel. Be sure to try the other wines as well, especially the merlot. To complement the wines, there's a barbecue in the vineyards—chicken and ribs—weekends from May through September. *18701 Gehricke Road, Sonoma; (707) 938-1960.*

■ NORTH OF TOWN: SONOMA VALLEY

The Sonoma Valley Highway, CA 12, runs north from Sonoma through an eclectic clutter of strip malls, tract homes, and small towns with a hangdog look. After the valley opens up, oaks and stone fences, rather than stucco and clapboard, dominate the landscape. Look for the sign directing you to B. R. Cohn Winery.

B. R. Cohn Winery. This is a delightful place, a family farm that has not succumbed to chateau-mania and preserves the old look of the California countryside with its whitewashed cottages, vineyards, and olive grove. Bruce Cohn, best known as manager of the musical Doobie Brothers, grew up on a Sonoma County dairy goat farm and, as he says it, never lost his rural roots. In 1984, he bought Olive Hill Farm and turned it into a winery. When he discovered a grove of rare picheline olive trees on the property, he started making olive oil too, and became a double winner: the oil is as good as the wines. Both the oil and the cabernet sauvignon made from Olive Hill plantings are world class. The winery asks you to call ahead to make an appointment for tastings, but chances are it will be open as you pass by. Feel free to drop in for a chat with Bruce's brother Marty, who runs the operation. And don't taste just the cabernet; try the chardonnay too.

An especially nice place to visit. *15140 Sonoma Highway, Glen Ellen; (707) 938-4064.*

■ GLEN ELLEN

Glen Ellen, nine miles up Sonoma Creek from Sonoma, seems almost out of place in the valley. Tucked among the trees of a narrow canyon, it looks more like a town of the Mother Lode gold country in the Sierra foothills than a settlement of the Coast Range wine country. Its main street—which runs past houses climbing a steep mountainside, the brick Chauvet Hotel (abandoned) and the wood-balconied Poppe Store, and several up-to-date shops and restaurants in old buildings—is narrow and crooked. Two tree-lined creeks, the Sonoma and the Calabazas, merge in the center of town, just above the bridge, which puts a further kink in the road by crossing Sonoma Creek at right angles. Sonoma Mountain rises west of the creek, with much of its eastern flank covered by the forests of **Jack London's Beauty Ranch**—which London's wife Charmian operated as a dude

An olive oil festival at B. R. Cohn Winery.

JACK LONDON ON GLEN ELLEN

Jack London State Park is a place of beauty, just like the almost mystic locale described below. Billy and Saxon, hero and heroine of London's novel, end their peregrination, which has taken them from Oakland south to Carmel and north to Oregon.

*T*hey came to the rim of a deep canyon that seemed to penetrate to the heart of Sonoma Mountain. Again, with no word spoken, merely from watching Saxon, Billy stopped the wagon. The canyon was wildly beautiful. Tall redwoods lined its entire length. . . . They dropped down into the Canyon, the . . . . The air was aromatic with laurel. Wild grape-vines bridged the stream from tree to tree. Oaks of many sorts were veiled in lacy Spanish moss. Ferns and brakes grew lush beside the stream.

"I've got a hunch," said Billy.

"Let me say it first," Saxon begged.

He waited, his eyes on her face as she gazed about her in rapture.

"We've found our valley," she whispered.

—Jack London, *Valley of the Moon*, 1913

ranch after the writer's untimely death. The ranch is now a state park, which contains the ruin of Jack London's **Wolf House** and the cottage where he wrote many of his stories; there are also an artificial lake and an elaborate pigsty known as the "Pig Palace." The **House of Happy Walls**, built by his widow after London's death, contains London memorabilia. London's grave is nearby, in a grove of ancient oaks. You can hike a three-mile trail to the top of Sonoma Mountain, or you can sign up with the **Sonoma Cattle Company** for a guided trail ride; for reservations and information call *(707) 996-8566.*

Wine has been part of Glen Ellen since the 1840s, when Joshua Chauvet's sawmill (built by Mariano Vallejo) and his flour mill both proved to be unprofitable. After carrying his millstones all the way from France, Chauvet first tried starting a flour mill in Oakland, but soon moved to the gold country. He ran his Glen Ellen mill for only 18 months before he ran out of grain. But he must have liked the place anyway, for he abandoned his millstones, planted grapes, and built a winery and distillery—the first such operations in the valley. The winery machinery was powered by steam; the boilers were fueled with wood from local oak trees. Chauvet built a three-story stone winery in 1881. This was sold to the Pagani family in 1913, who tore down the old building and replaced it with a concrete structure. The winery made some 50,000 gallons a year, which were sold in four-packs of gallon bottles. When a customer finished the wine, he or she washed out the bottles and returned to the winery for a refill. The winery was shut down in 1954, when Charles Pagani died.

But the Paganis hung on longer farther north in the Sonoma Valley, where they operated another winery. That winery was sold to the Martin Lee family in 1970 and is now known as the **Kenwood Vineyards** *(see page 170)*. It is noteworthy that this winery has acquired the sole rights to grapes from Jack London's old vineyard (in the Sonoma Mountain Appellation, above the fog belt of the Sonoma Valley).

Other valley farmers followed Chauvet's example, and soon many raised grapes besides the more traditional cattle. Wine was even made during Prohibition, when the locals took a liberal view of the 200 gallons each family was allowed to produce for personal consumption. Local resort owner Henry Garric quipped:

The local oak trees were used for both firewood and cooperage.

If you ran a resort or restaurant, you had to serve wine. So you probably made a little more wine than if you were making it for your own use. . . . It was common to have a little fermentation tank that I estimate held almost 200 gallons, and people had about 10 or 12 fifty-gallon barrels that they put the wine into after it got through fermenting. As I recall, law enforcement people didn't bother anybody; they knew it was mostly for family use.

Today, Glen Ellen and Kenwood have several excellent resorts and restaurants. When you check into one of the utterly comfortable local lodging places, the **Gaige House** or the **Kenwood Inn,** you're following in the footsteps of the countless visitors who traveled to this sunny region to give their congested lungs a much deserved rest from San Francisco's foggy air. Dine at the **Glen Ellen Inn** or the **Kenwood Restaurant.** But whatever you do, be sure to stop at the **Jack London Bookstore** at the southern edge of Glen Ellen. Owner Jack Kingman knows a lot about Jack London, and the book store has several works hard to find elsewhere. Best of all, it has an excellent selection of books on local history and wine, as well

The bucolic setting of the Kenwood Inn makes it a favorite layover for many visitors to the valley.

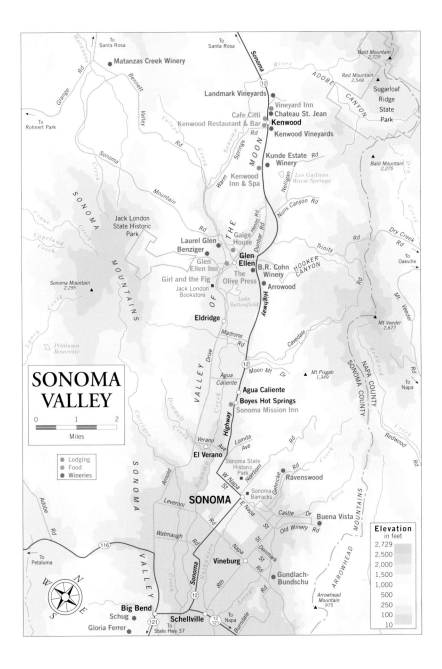

as rare volumes on a variety of subjects. Stock up on picnic fare and wine at the **Village Market** across the street from the Chauvet Hotel.

Benziger Family Winery. After selling off its Glen Ellen label to a bulk wine producer, this family winery has been making serious wine from the estate vineyards surrounding the winery. This is a fun—and educational place to visit. A trolley takes visitors through the vineyards, and signs explain grape varieties and what's going on in the vineyards. Bring a picnic. *1883 London Ranch Road, Glen Ellen; 707-935-3000 (call for directions).*

Matanzas Creek Winery is reached from Glen Ellen via Bennett Valley Road. This is a lovely spot to visit. Not only does the building jut dramatically from the hillside, but the winery gardens are planted with more varieties of lavender than you've ever met. When the lavender blooms in summer and autumn, it's truly a feast for the senses. *6097 Bennett Valley Road; (707) 528-6464.*

North of Glen Ellen, Arnold Drive, the road running parallel to CA 12 on the west side of the Sonoma Valley, merges with the Sonoma Valley Highway.

■ WINERIES OF THE KENWOOD DISTRICT

Kunde Estate Winery. The first thing you note here is a sort of rustic purity. Everything is almost uncannily tidy, from the square barn that serves as winery to the crush pad and the stainless steel tanks out back. You'd think the place was a large working model of a winery. Even the vineyards that surround the winery and climb up the hillside to the east look well-manicured. A rock-walled road leads to a wooden door built into the side of the hill. The door opens to tunnels dug into the hillside—the caves where the wine ages in small oak

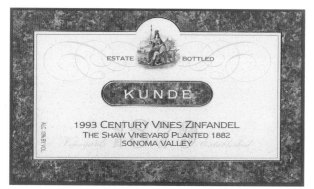

The red soils of the Kunde Estate Winery produce some of the finest zinfandel in the region.

barrels at a perfect and even temperature. You can take a tour of those cool caves and absorb their timelessness through the aromas of aging wine and oak.

As growers, the Kundes go back five generations, starting with Louis Kunde, who bought Wildwood Vineyards in 1904. The family continued making wine during Prohibition (no one says whether this was sacramental or under-the-counter wine) but stopped making wine in 1942, when the eldest son went off to war. The family returned to winemaking in 1990, but even now they use only 50 percent of the grapes they grow; the remainder is sold to other wineries—who prize them highly. The tasting room tells you right away that this is a serious winery, where the wine counts more than the frills. All of the Kunde wines are estate grown and well worth tasting, even the generic blend of cabernet sauvignon and zinfandel sold as "Bob's Red." The 1993 Century Vines Zinfandel—made from vines growing in the Kundes' 1883 zinfandel vineyard—is well worth searching for (in case you can't buy it at the winery). The chardonnay and merlot are also very good. Considering how long it took the Kundes to get back into the business of winemaking, their achievements are astounding. This winery is definitely worth a special journey. *10155 Sonoma Highway, Kenwood; (707) 833-5501.*

Kenwood Vineyards. A short stretch up the Sonoma Valley Highway, on the same side of the valley, you come to Kenwood Vineyards. Back in California's Tortilla Flat days, when wine was sold by the barrel instead of the bottle, and when you could bring your gallon jugs to a winery to have them filled with rustic quaffing wine, this winery was owned by the Pagani brothers. When the Lee family and friends bought out the Paganis in 1970, the wines were upgraded to the sipping variety, but even now Kenwood still makes some good basic red wine, as well as its more showy cabernet sauvignons and zinfandels. The best of these come from Jack London's old vineyard on Sonoma Mountain (Kenwood has an exclusive lease). But what the wine connoisseurs keep coming back for is Kenwood's crisp sauvignon blanc.

The old Pagani barns have been turned into a high-tech winery with a tasting room and a rather extensive gift shop. The place is particularly pretty in spring and early summer when the long driveway is lined with blooming wildflowers. *9592 Sonoma Highway, Kenwood; (707) 833-5891.*

Chateau St. Jean. Far off to the right, at the foot of the mountain, are the grandiose grounds of Chateau St. Jean, an old country estate once owned by a

A classic Wine Country vista of manicured vineyards and wooded hills.

family of Midwestern industrialists and expanded when it was turned into a winery in 1973. A couple of ponds in the shape of Lakes Michigan and Huron speak of this past ownership. One of this winery's nicest features is the view over the vineyards you get from the tower. The wines are good, but they lost some of their sparkle after winemaker Dick Arrowood left in the 1980s to open his own winery. Chateau St. Jean has recently been acquired by the Beringer group. Taste the chardonnay and fumé blanc. *8555 Sonoma Highway, Kenwood; (707) 833-4134.*

Landmark Vineyards. Turn into Adobe Canyon Road and then left at the first driveway to reach this winery. It was founded in 1974 in Windsor, north of Santa Rosa, but moved to its present location in 1990 to escape encroaching subdivisions. Besides wanting to taste its wines, you might want to stop here to take a close look at the building, which is a faithful reconstruction of a mission-period rancho—up to the shingle roof (a feature introduced to Northern California by George Yount, who earned himself Napa Valley's Caymus Rancho by splitting shingles for the mission padres and rancheros at Sonoma). Landmark is best known for its Overlook and Damaris Reserve chardonnays, but the winery

Tasting wine.

released its first-ever red wine, a pinot noir, early in 1996. This wine is available only from the tasting room. *101 Adobe Canyon Road, Kenwood; (707) 833-0053 or (800) 452-6365.*

❖

Two small Glen Ellen wineries make wines of such a high quality that they must be mentioned here. Dick Arrowood made great wine when he was the winemaker at Chateau St. Jean up until 1985, and he continues making great wine at his own place, **Arrowood Vineyards & Winery.** The tasting room is open daily. Try the cabernet sauvignon and the zinfandel. *14347 Sonoma Highway; (707) 938-5170.*

Patrick Campbell of **Laurel Glen Vineyard,** near Glen Ellen, has made only reds for the last 15 years in his tiny Sonoma Mountain vineyard. Production is small, the wines are incredibly rich and supple—what else can we say. This winery is not open to the public; but call to sign up for their mailing list. *(707) 526-3914.*

❖

A few miles beyond Landmark Vineyards, the subdivisions take over. You can continue straight on CA 12 through Santa Rosa to US 101 and the northern Sonoma wine country described in the next chapter, or you can turn right on the Calistoga Road and head for the northern Napa Valley.

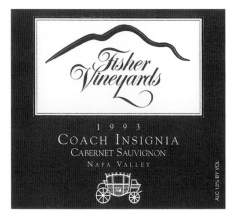

Fisher Winery. If you do take the mountain road described above, call ahead for an appointment and directions to this family winery. Tucked away in the woods, it is one of the most beautiful wineries in California, especially when the roses and wildflowers bloom at the same time. Watch for wild turkeys on the narrow road to the winery. The view from the vineyard, across the hills and dales, makes you realize how beautiful the Wine Country really is. Fisher produces exceptional cabernet sauvignon and merlot: big, complex, yet silky smooth. This is a very private winery, and there is just a tiny sign. *Appointment necessary. 6200 St. Helena Road, Santa Rosa; (707) 539-7511.*

NORTHERN SONOMA COUNTY

*For they wished to fill the winepress of eloquence
not with the tendrils of mere words but with the
rich grape juice of good sense.*
— *St. Jerome,* A.D. *342–420*

HEALDSBURG IS THE CENTER, THE BEATING heart of a vast, rapidly expanding agricultural region. Three of Sonoma County's viticultural appellations meet, virtually, in the center of town. Vineyards start at the edge of town and seem to run on forever: northwest into the **Dry Creek Valley**, southeast along the lower course of the **Russian River**, and east and north up and down the **Alexander Valley.** The more than 70 wineries in this area are embraced by lovely countryside. Add fine picnic sites and delis where the bread is fresh-baked and the olives and cheeses local, and you have the makings of a wine tourist's day in Eden *(see page 239 for picnic ideas).*

If you're driving north from San Francisco on US 101, you may wish to begin your touring with the Russian River appellation. To do this, turn west at Cotati on CA 116, the Gravenstein Highway (named for the apple which is the region's most famous product); or stay on US 101 through Santa Rosa, then turn west on River Road. To begin with the Dry Creek or Alexander Valley appellations, head straight north to Healdsburg.

■ RUSSIAN RIVER APPELLATION

The Russian River has a unique climate, ideally suited to the growing of premium grapes. Because of its low elevation, sea fogs push far inland to cool the land, yet they dissipate often enough during summer to give the grapes enough sun to ripen properly. As importantly, the river, as it cut its way downwards through strata of rocks, deposited a deep layer of gravel that in parts of the valley goes down 60 to 70 feet. This forces the roots of grapevines to grow farther down in search of water and nutrients. In the process, the roots nourish the plants with a multitude of trace minerals that add complexity to the flavor of their grapes. In California as in France, such gravelly soils produce some of the world's greatest wines.

Map of the Russian River Region.

■ RUSSIAN RIVER SPARKLERS

Iron Horse Vineyards. The sparkling wines made at Iron Horse smoothed the way of *glasnost* when American presidents served them at the White House and in foreign capitals. Ronald Reagan served Iron Horse sparkling wines at his summit meetings with Mikhail Gorbachev; George Bush took some to Moscow for the signing of the START treaty. Bill Clinton and Al Gore drank a bottle at their election night victory party. Iron Horse also makes excellent chardonnay and, from time to time, a nice pinot noir. Cabernet sauvignon is made from Alexander Valley vineyards owned by winemaker Forrest Tancer.

Despite its fame, Iron Horse has avoided pretense and grandeur. The winery buildings are of the simple Sonoma red-

ESTATE   BOTTLED

IRON HORSE™
BRUT LD
SPARKLING WINE, SONOMA COUNTY GREEN VALLEY

ALC. 12.5% VOL.   NET VOL. 750 ML.

1989

Iron Horse is best known for its sparkling wine. It also produces an excellent chardonnay, shown above.

wood barn style, but an access road lined with palms, olive trees, vast flower beds, and acres of fruit orchards and vegetable gardens make this a beautiful place indeed. In 1995, Tancer released his first "late disgorged" sparkling wine, a very complex, deeply flavored sparkler with a long, rich finish. Tancer also added to the complexity of his sauvignon blanc by blending in a little viognier, and he made sangiovese in the "super Tuscan-style" by rounding it out with a touch of cabernet sauvignon. Iron Horse is a beautiful place to visit. Open by appointment. *9786 Ross Station Road (west off the Gravenstein Highway), Sebastopol; (707) 887-1507.*

The wines of two small producers in this area, whose wineries are not open to the public, are worth searching for in specialty shops. They are **Rutz Cellars Winery and Cave** which makes a splendid pinot noir (with that elusive Burgundian nose), and **Kistler Vineyards** which is known for its fine chardonnay and pinot noir.

❖

Return to the Gravenstein Highway. If you are driving to Healdsburg, turn right, then take Guerneville Road east to Santa Rosa and turn north on US 101 to

Healdsburg. If you're continuing on to Guerneville, turn left. Applewood is on your right as you emerge from narrow Pocket Canyon a short stretch above the Russian River Bridge.

A few miles east on River Road takes you to **Korbel Champagne Cellars.** When the Korbel brothers, who had left their native Bohemia to escape political repression, logged the redwood forests of the Russian River, they began planting crops among the stumps. After trying tobacco and other crops first, they found that grapes grew best. So in 1882 they established a winery and began making "champagne." Korbel passed into the hands of the Heck family (which originally came from the Alsace region) in 1954.

The word "champagne" in the winery's name and on its labels is a popular misnomer. Champagne is made only in the French region of that name; everything else is sparkling wine. (Unless you approve of the tendency of the English language to absorb brand names as generic terms, and you're willing to apply that rationale to products named for regions.) The French, however, take the different rules of their language to heart, and the Champenois have tried to stop English-speakers from misusing their name for more than a hundred years—just as the Bourguignons have tried to get us to stop using designations like "Burgundy" and "Chablis." Perhaps we'll stop when the French start making money by labeling their bulk wines "Napa" and "Sonoma." That said, the sparkling wine/champagne made by Korbel is quite good and reasonably priced. The "Natural" is best.

The winery is a visitor's delight, with its 19th-century buildings (including a tower in which brandy was made), a deli and microbrewery, and extensive rose gardens in the beautifully landscaped grounds. The tour—by many considered the best in Sonoma County—will give you a very good idea of how sparkling wine is made. It includes a display of wine memorabilia and old photographs. *13250 River Road, Guerneville; (707) 887-2294.*

■ WESTSIDE ROAD WINERIES

From Korbel turn left (east) on River Road. Look for the turnoff to Westside Road on the left (if you cross the Russian River, you've gone too far; the turnoff is just before the river). Slow down, and enjoy the scenery of vineyards alternating with woods and meadows as you follow this meandering road into Healdsburg. There

Korbel's winery tour is one of the region's best.

Canoeing on the Russian River

are a lot more wineries along this road than we have space to mention. If you have time, stop at as many as you can—they all make good wine.

Porter Creek Vineyards. You'll have to look closely to see the sign, set just after a sharp bend in a wooded part of the road. If there weren't an inviting sign out front, you might never take this place for a winery. It's a very small family farm that also happens to make very good wine. All the grapes are estate grown. Compare the hillside pinot noir with the creekside pinot noir to taste which one you prefer. The chardonnay is made from hillside grapes only and has a very Burgundian character. *8735 Westside Road, Healdsburg; (707) 433-6321.*

Davis Bynum Winery. From the road, Bynum looks more like a summer retreat in the woods than a serious winery, but once you've made it past the white entrance cottages and tasted the wines, you'll agree that this winery's reputation is well deserved. The winery was founded by Davis Bynum in 1965 in an Albany (California) storefront and moved to its present location in 1973. Bynum was the first to make pinot noir exclusively from Russian River grapes and has championed local grapes ever since. Quality has kept up with the expansion of production. In addition to the pinot noir, be sure to taste the merlot, the zinfandel, the fumé blanc, and the gewürztraminer. *8075 Westside Road, Healdsburg; (707) 433-5852.*

Rochioli Vineyards & Winery. Return to Westside Road and turn left. As you see the triple-turreted hop kiln of the namesake winery loom up ahead of you (see below), look for the small parking lot on your right. The Rochiolis became wine-growers in 1933, when they took over vineyards planted in the 19th century and planted new vines of their own on gravelly bench lands above the Russian River. After decades of selling their grapes to local wineries, the Rochiolis started making their own wine in 1982. Production is small, but the wines are worth stopping for. Considering their background in farming, it is not surprising that Joe and Tom Rochioli believe in letting the vineyard determine the quality of the wine (of course, they know they have just the right vineyard for this). Because of the cool growing conditions, the flavors of their pinot noir, cabernet sauvignon, chardonnay, and sauvignon blanc (from old vines) are intense and complex. The tasting room patio, shaded by roses, is a great place for sipping wine and enjoying the view across the Russian River vineyards. *6192 Westside Road, Healdsburg; (707) 433-2305.*

Hop Kiln Winery. One driveway up the road from Rochioli is this small winery. A unique feature of Hop Kiln is that it was built in and around a historic hop kiln without destroying any of the kiln's equipment. Thus, you'll find wine stored in the old ovens (kept cool by their thick stone walls), with strange pipes and rail car tracks running through it all. The wines are mostly

estate-grown and include such rare varietals as valdiguié. Your best bet for a picnic on the winery's beautiful and sunny grounds is a wine appropriately called "Marty Griffin's Big Red." *6050 Westside Road, Healdsburg; (707) 433-6491.*

■ EAST OF THE RIVER

Four wineries on the east side of the river deserve attention. At **Mark West Estate,** Kerry Damskey, formerly of the Gauer Estate Winery, makes the wine. The winery borders on Mark West Creek and has a beautiful picnic area, plus a deli where you can stock up on food to enjoy with your wine. *7010 Trenton-Healdsburg Road, Forestville; (707) 544-4813.*

Sonoma-Cutrer. Founded in 1973 by Brice Cutrer Jones, a former Vietnam War fighter pilot, this winery is open to the public by appointment only, but it's well worth your time to call and plan for a tour. The winery makes chardonnay only, from three renowned Sonoma County vineyards: Les Pierres, Russian River Ranches, and Cutrer Vineyard. The ultra-modern winery's other attraction comes as a bit of a surprise: professional croquet grounds. Here the winery hosts two annual events, the World Croquet Championship held in May and the ACA-US open in September. Chardonnay and croquet! Quel mariage! *4401 Slusser Road, Windsor; (707) 528-1181.*

Alderbrook. On Westside Road just south of Healdsburg is a small winery surrounded by acres of vines. It makes splendid sauvignon blanc from estate-grown grapes, a food wine that goes better with many dishes than does chardonnay. Alderbrook has also released small quantities of an incredibly rich, sweet, but well-balanced semillon. *2306 Magnolia Drive, Healdsburg; (707) 433-9154.*

Foppiano Vineyards. One of the oldest Russian River wineries, dating all the way back to 1896. The winery made primarily bulk wine until 1970, but in recent years its varietals, most notably petite sirah (from old vines) and cabernet sauvignon, have shown that Foppiano can produce wines of high quality. The zinfandel is a good, everyday drinking wine in the Italian country-wine tradition. *12707 Old Redwood Highway, Healdsburg; (707) 433-7272.*

J Wine Company. It makes for interesting comparisons when you have two wineries owned by different members of the same family, not only in the same county, but in the same appellation. Quite frankly, we find Judy Jordan's sparkling wine outfit a lot more interesting than the "restaurant wines" produced at Jordan winery by her father, Tom. In 1997, "J" moved to the former Piper Sonoma facility south of Healdsburg. Tours and tastings are offered. *11447 Old Redwood Highway, Healdsburg, (707) 431-5400.*

■ HEALDSBURG

The heady aroma of southern magnolias drifts through the open windows as you park your car in a shady spot on the Healdsburg plaza on a hot summer afternoon. If the scent of magnolias seems incongruous with grapes, look around the other trees which make the plaza such a shady spot. The magnolias grow next to tall Canary Island date palms, which rise beside California redwoods towering over beds of roses. But you will find no grapevines growing among the flowers of the plaza. If the nearby vineyards are a hurricane of activity, the plaza is the eye of the storm,

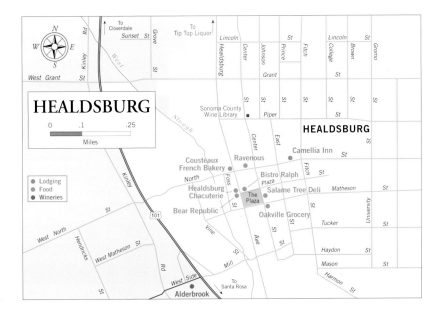

a center of repose, the poetic heart of a hard-working farm town. It's almost other-worldly. A sign in the window of a plaza bookstore sets the tone. "Shoplifting is bad for your karma," it admonishes.

The plaza is a bit unusual, even in California, where some of the older towns, most notably San Juan Bautista and Sonoma, were laid out with Hispanic-style plazas by their Mexican founders. Healdsburg, on the other hand, may be the only town with a plaza laid out by an American. Harmon Heald founded Healdsburg in 1852 as a trading post. When he planned the townsite, he donated the plaza to the city in perpetuity, with the catch that it could be used for recreational activities only. While that clause may not preclude building a municipal water slide in this popular spot, the city fathers wisely decided to keep the plaza as a tree-shaded park. This is a thoroughly wholesome plaza, without the panhandlers and other dubious characters infesting big city squares. After all, this is small-town America at its best. Healdsburg resident Millie Howie says it's "straight out of a Norman Rockwell painting." She's right. The flower beds are free of weeds, the bandstand always looks freshly painted, and the businesses lining the plaza are dressed up in style.

It's this wholesomeness which makes Healdsburg such an appealing place to live in and to visit. Locals don't mind gathering here, day or night. While the plaza does attract its share of visitors, it's mainly a local hangout, where Healdsburg residents enjoy free summer concerts, eat at the restaurants (more than a dozen restaurants are in easy walking distance from the plaza), or go to the movies.

What gives Healdsburg—and the other small towns of the Wine Country—their special character is that they offer both residents and visitors more things to do, without being tourist traps. The Healdsburg plaza has plenty of shops—bakeries, clothiers, antique emporiums, bookstores, and toy shops, to keep the most discriminating visitor happy. But as you wander about the perimeters of the plaza, you'll notice that the locals shop here too.

One new place that's very popular with Healdsburg area winemakers is the **Oakville Grocery** in the renovated former city hall (not to be confused with the Oakville Grocery in Napa, though it has the same owner). This luxury deli (with patio dining) has a great selection of local wines, breads, cheeses, olive oils, et. al. A take-out counter dispenses big sandwiches, hearty soup, and other fare. It's a great place for a quick lunch or for stocking up on picnic fare. *124 Matheson Street, (707) 433-3200.*

A most enjoyable way of catching the Healdsburg spirit is to go to the plaza early in the morning, before the sun bears down. Get a pastry and a cup of coffee at the **Downtown Bakery & Creamery** and sit in the plaza—in the shade in summer or on a sunny bench during the rest of the year. Listen to the rustling of the palm fronds and the chattering of birds as they perform their morning chores (the wilted leaf skirts, the hollows above the stubs of broken-off leaves, even the crowns of palms make perfect nesting and roosting places). After a Sunday breakfast, you might just hang out in the plaza and listen to one of the popular concerts. The music varies each week, from jazz to Sousa marches, and from Cajun, bluegrass, and Gaelic folk songs to Broadway melodies. Or you might want to go window shopping at galleries or hang out all morning at **Toyon Book Store**. And on Saturday mornings in the center of town, local producers of cheese, olives and olive oils, and the freshest of vegetables gather at the open-air **Farmers Market** to sell their wares and talk to buyers.

The small town of Healdsburg features a number of antique stores around its charming central square. Nearby are bakeries and wine stores, a bookstore, and a farmers market.

Healdsburg is a very active community, with what seems like a different public event every weekend. One of the best of these is the **Russian River Wine Festival** held in the plaza in late May. You can browse artists' booths, taste local foods, sip wines from more than 40 wineries, and generally have a good time. In summer, you can head for **Memorial Beach Park** on the Russian River and swim in the pool created behind a seasonal dam (Memorial Day to Labor Day) or rent a canoe and drift downstream. You can visit the Healdsburg Museum or learn more about local wines at the superb Wine Library located in the Healdsburg Regional Library at Piper and Center streets.

You don't even have to leave town to sample local wines. Outlets for **Kendall-Jackson** and **Windsor Vineyards** are on the plaza. **Tip Top Liquor Warehouse** near the corner of Dry Creek Road and Healdsburg Avenue has a superb selection of local wines, including the excellent and hard-to-find **Bannister** chardonnay and zinfandel. If you cannot find the wine you seek, call winemaker Marty Bannister

One way to search out wineries in northern Sonoma is with this mural map in downtown Geyserville, just north of Healdsburg.

directly at *(707) 433-6402,* and ask to be put on the mailing list. She makes only a few hundred cases of each varietal, and the wines have been known to sell out quickly. For picnic fixings try the **Salame Tree** at 304 Center Street.

❖

Seghesio Vineyards & Winery. Founded in 1895 when Italian immigrant Edoardo Seghesio and his wife, Angela, planted vineyards; they added a winery in 1902. For years, the winery sold its wine in bulk to other wineries, including Paul Masson and Gallo, but began bottling wines under its own name in 1980. The majority of the grapes used by Seghesio are estate-grown, on vineyards in the Alexander, Dry Creek, and Russian River valleys. Even though winemaker Ted Seghesio prefers his wines to be immediately drinkable, they have surprising depth and aging potential. The winery does not take in drop-in visitors but you might want to search for their wines in local shops. Be sure to try the reserve zinfandel and the sangiovese.

Simi Winery. Located at the northern edge of Healdsburg, this winery was founded in 1876 by the Simi brothers, recently Italian emigrés. They originally named the winery Montepulciano, which proved too much of a tongue twister for local non-Italians. But they left up the old sign even after they changed the winery's name to their more easily pronounceable last name. The winery had its ups and downs, until 1981 when it was bought by French investors Möet-Hennessy-Louis Vuitton. Zelma Long, who became winemaker in 1979, stayed on and has since turned Simi into a financial and critical success.

Simi has also pioneered the matching of food and wine, and enlightens the public through educational brochures, programs, and dinners. Are you curious about what wine to serve with asparagus? Call Simi.

This winery looks mostly to the Alexander and Russian River valleys for its grapes. While about half the production has been chardonnay, sauvignon blanc has shown well lately, as has Simi's Alexander Valley cabernet sauvignon. Simi gives a very informative tour and has a very knowledgeable tasting room staff. *16275 Healdsburg Avenue, Healdsburg; (707) 433-6981.*

■ DRY CREEK VALLEY

From Simi Winery or the plaza area, take Healdsburg Avenue to Dry Creek Road and turn west. Almost as soon as you pass under the US 101 freeway bridge, you'll feel like you've slipped back in time. Although the Dry Creek Valley has become renowned for its wines, it has preserved a rustic simplicity rarely found in California today. The road, brightened by wildflower-strewn shoulders in spring and early summer, offers tantalizing views of vineyards as it skirts a steep hillside on the east side of the narrow valley. The valley's well-drained, gravelly floor is planted with chardonnay grapes to the south, where an occasional sea fog creeping in from the Russian River cools the vineyards, and with sauvignon blanc in the warmer

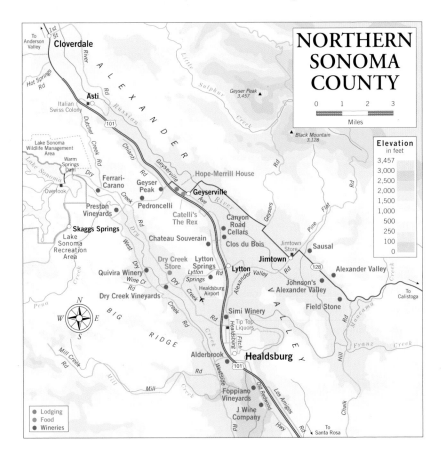

NORTHERN SONOMA COUNTY

The Dry Creek Valley's gravelly soil has become renowned for producing quality zinfandels.

vineyards of the northern valley. The red, decomposed soils of the bench lands bring out the best in zinfandel—the grape for which Dry Creek has become famous. But they also produce great cabernet sauvignon, as Ernest and Julio Gallo have discovered at their Frei Brothers Winery. And they seem well suited to Rhone varieties like cinsault, mourvèdre, and marsanne, which need lots of heat to ripen properly.

Grapes like this valley so well that they grow wild by the side of the road—not just the native slip-skin grapes, but vinifera grapes which have spread beyond the confinement of the vineyards and grow wild in roadside thickets, the way blackberries sprawl elsewhere in the West. The course of Dry Creek is marked by the dense riparian forest crowding its banks. Beyond the valley, the Coast Range rises in a series of foothills and mountains. Between here and the coast the land is mostly oak and scrub wilderness where loggers and ranchers, not farmers, eke out a living.

If you've forgotten to stock up on picnic fare before leaving Healdsburg, drop in at the **Dry Creek Store,** a rustic emporium on Dry Creek Road just past Lambert Bridge Road. To the right, not open to the public, lie some of the Gallo family's vast vineyard holdings.

Dry Creek Vineyard. A left turn at Lambert Bridge Road brings you to the Dry Creek Vineyard, often touted as the first local winery opened since Prohibition. The historical record shows that that's not exactly true, but Dry Creek's founder David Stare has been a pioneer in putting the valley's wines onto the enological map. The winery offers the usual assortment of wines, from big reds to light and fruity whites, but it stands out for its sauvignon (fumé) blanc and zinfandel. The winery has a delightful picnic area brightened by flowers, and is a perfect place to hang out on a hot summer's day. *3770 Lambert Bridge Road, Healdsburg; (707) 433-1000.*

Continue west on Lambert Bridge Road, then turn right (north) at West Dry Creek Road. This narrow lane is the quintessential Wine Country road. It doesn't get prettier (or more rustic) than this. Watch for speeding cars and leisurely bicyclists—especially around sharp curves. This road winds about so much as it hugs the western slopes of the valley that it forces you to slow down. Relax. Enjoy the flowers, look for quail crossing the road, watch the hawks and ravens soar overhead. After passing several vineyards on your right you'll see an attractive wood and cinder-block barn that turns out be **Quivira Vineyards.** Dry Creek viticulturists, with an exception or two, like to keep their facilities understated and express their exuberance through their wines, not their architecture. The winery is best known for its sauvignon blanc and zinfandel, but it also produces an excellent blend of red varietals called Dry Creek Cuvée. *4900 West Dry Creek Road, Healdsburg; (707) 431-8333.*

❖

Preston Vineyards. Return to West Dry Creek Road and head north. Follow the lane past its junction with Yoakim Bridge Road (ignore the "dead end road" sign) and look for the Preston Vineyards sign on the right. Take this even narrower lane along the bank of Peña Creek to the winery. The tasting room is on the west side of the large fruit-drying barn that's been converted into the winery. All Preston wines are estate-grown—and an eclectic bunch they are. They include such rarities as cinsault, marsanne, mourvèdre, and viognier, which Preston uses in varying proportions to make two interesting Rhone-style blends: Faux, a red; and Le Petit Faux, a rosé. The winery also bottles marsanne, syrah, and viognier, as well as more traditional varietals. As with other Dry Creek wineries, the zinfandel and sauvignon

blanc are standouts. A Cuvée de Fumé blend is tops. But the real surprise was the 1993 barbera, which is much richer and complex than wines usually made from that grape.

Preston has also planted some 150 olive trees imported from Italy, with varietal names like leccino, casaliva, and grignano. So far, the trees have been too young to bear commercial quantities of oil. But who knows, in a few years you may be able to buy estate-grown olive oil at the winery as well.

Recommended for its charm, beautiful surroundings, and homespun feel. Stroll in the gardens, or sit on the back porch and sip wine and listen to the birds. *9282 West Dry Creek Road, Healdsburg; (707) 433-3372.*

❖

On your way back, turn east (left) on Yoakim Bridge Road. If you are visiting between June and Labor Day, be sure to stop at **Dry Creek Peach & Produce,** the farm stand by the side of the road, for tree-ripened peaches, nectarines, and apricots, or other locally grown fruits like apples, plums, and melons, or those most elusive of delicacies, vine-ripened red and yellow tomatoes.

Ferrari-Carano. From Yoakim Bridge Road turn left on Dry Creek Road. This winery has undergone a bit of change since it was founded in 1981 by Don and Rhonda Carano. The latest addition is the Villa Fiore, a pink confection of a hospitality center that's visible for quite a distance across the valley. The wines are a bit less opulent in style, although the chardonnay and fumé blanc are as big as they come. Besides their Dry Creek vineyards, the Caranos own vineyards in the Alexander and Knight's valleys, as well as in the Napa part of the Carneros. Since

winemaker George Bursick believes in blending, it's tough to figure out where exactly the grapes for a wine labeled "Sonoma County" come from. A zinfandel made from Dry Creek grapes is excellent; a cabernet/sangiovese blend named Siena shows promise. The wine shop in the villa carries an assortment of goods, from wines to specialty foods and garden tools to clothing (there's even a dressing room). *8761 Dry Creek Road, Healdsburg; (707) 433-6700.*

Pedroncelli Winery. From Ferrari-Carano turn right on Dry Creek Road and left onto Canyon Road. Look for a mix of farm buildings on the left, and you'll see a winery that wasn't planned but "happened," as witnessed by the eclectic array of buildings. It all started in 1927, when John Pedroncelli bought 90 acres of grapes with an existing winery on the property. He sold grapes till Prohibition ended, then started making wine. The operation was very simple, as Jack Florence Sr. tells in *A Noble Heritage: The Wines and Vineyards of Dry Creek Valley.*

By about 1935 Pedroncelli had a label and customers were coming by to fill their gallon jugs. The winery kept a spigot on one barrel to facilitate their customers' request for a fill-up. The wines of all operating wineries were basically the same, a red and a white.

The tasting rooms at Quivira Vineyards (left), and a view from the Villa Fiore terrace (above).

In 1963, sons James and John took over, and began increasing production and started a varietal program. The wines have steadily improved in quality while prices have remained low. The Pedroncelli pinot noir is surprisingly good; their cabernet and zinfandel are among the best the region produces. There's a picnic area and bocce court outside the tasting room—the perfect place for sipping the winery's refreshing chenin blanc. *1220 Canyon Road, Geyserville; (707) 857-3531.*

❖

You can continue on Canyon Road to US 101 and then drive south to Healdsburg. Just west of the freeway at Lytton Springs Road is **Lytton Springs Winery.** It offers tastings of zinfandel from old vines, as well as a few wines made by its parent company, Ridge Vineyards. *(707) 433-7721.*

Nalle Winery is not open to the public, but you can find Nalle's superb zinfandels in local shops and on the wine lists of Healdsburg restaurants. The **E. & J. Gallo Winery** makes wine from local grapes at the **Frei Brothers Winery,** bought by the Gallo brothers in 1976. This winery is quite definitely not open to the public. It is a culmination of a program started by the Gallos in the 1950s, when they

Sea fog occasionally spills over into northern Sonoma County from the Russian River Valley.

began steering Napa and Sonoma county growers away from cheap bulk grapes and encouraged them to plant premium varietals by paying top price for them. This, more than anything else, prepared the way for the great winery boom that was to come. Had no premium grapes been available no premium wine could have been made. The Gallos' Dry Creek venture is an attempt to go beyond the pop wines which made the Gallos rich and to instead make serious wine that can compete with the best. If recent tastings are any indication, they are succeeding. Their Sonoma County cabernet is especially fine, and even the "Hearty Burgundy" has improved tremendously since being made from north coast grapes.

■ ALEXANDER VALLEY

This appellation covers both sides of the upper Russian River Valley from Chalk Hill east of Healdsburg to the Mendocino county line north of Cloverdale. Its landscape varies from flat bottomlands—the drop in elevation at river level is only 50 feet from the upper to the lower part of the valley—to hills over 1,500 feet high, with small side valleys that are very hot. It is warmer than the Russian River appellation. Sea fogs only occasionally drift in from the Santa Rosa Plain, and while they cool the land, they burn off more quickly than they do on the lower river. Climatically and geologically the valley is so diverse that it may take centuries to figure out what grows best where. Soils include loam, gravelly loam, and gravelly sandy loam, as well as well-drained gravel flats near the river. But because a mere dozen years ago the valley was mostly planted to walnuts, pears, prunes, and bulk grapes—except for the sections left in scrub and pasture—one might argue that experimentation has hardly begun. So far, chardonnay, sauvignon blanc, and cabernet sauvignon seem to do well in places, while zinfandel may actually get too ripe. Italian grapes like sangiovese or the Rhone varietals, which do so well in the Dry Creek Valley, may make great wines in the warmer parts of the Alexander Valley. Stay posted for a decade or two. This valley is full of surprises.

■ LOWER ALEXANDER VALLEY

To reach the lower Alexander Valley from Healdsburg, drive north on Healdsburg Avenue and stay to the right when it splits into Lytton Station Road and Alexander Valley Road. At Jimtown, CA 128 comes in from the left. Continue straight on CA 128. The **Jimtown Store** on your left has great espresso and a good selection of deli items. It gives you another chance to stock up on bread and cheese for a picnic, if you've neglected to do so in Healdsburg. Or indulge in a gourmet sandwich. Have either wrapped up and take them to your next winery's vine-shaded picnic patio.

Sausal Winery. Located a couple of miles up the road from Jimtown, Sausal makes a zinfandel that gets better by the vintage. It's a beautiful place shaded by ancient oaks and is fun to visit. Sausal makes an excellent cabernet and truly outstanding zinfandel. The best comes from vines more than a hundred years old. Buy a bottle, grab a table on the patio, and enjoy your lunch and the view of vines stretching all the way to the hills. Watch ravens and turkey vultures and an occasional hawk soar overhead. Sniff the air. If the wind is right, the breeze carries a heady aroma of grapes and wild laurel. *7370 Highway 128, Healdsburg; (707) 433-2285.*

Alexander Valley Vineyards. Just up the road, off a long driveway leading left, is this 1841 homestead of Cyrus Alexander, for whom the valley is named. The winery itself, however, is new. It was built in 1975 by the current owners, the Wetzel family, with adobe blocks and weathered wood to make it look older than it is. It works. To lend veracity to the history angle, you can wander up a grassy hill behind the winery to the cemetery of Cyrus Alexander and his family. *Sic transit gloria mundi,* and all that. But enough of gloomy reflections. *Carpe diem.* Grab a bottle of the winery's splendid proprietary zinfandel called Sin Zin and head for the picnic tables. Or go for the cabernet—it's very good. *8644 Highway 128, Healdsburg; (707) 433-7209.*

Johnson's Alexander Valley. On the other side of the highway, look for a small winery run by a family of grape growers specializing in rustic wines—made in a barn with state-of-the-art winemaking equipment—and in sophisticated pipe organs from the golden age of movie theaters. There's a 1924 theater pipe organ in perfect condition, so don't be surprised if you're greeted by a blast of music. But don't get too distracted to taste their zinfandel: you must try it. *8333 Highway 128, Healdsburg; (707) 433-2319.*

Field Stone Winery & Vineyards. A few miles up the road to your right, the highway takes a turn to the left, and you'll come to the entrance gate. This winery takes its name from the field stones which came from the hill and now cover the winery's facade. When Wallace Johnson built his winery in 1977, he did not dig tunnels into the hillside to create aging cellars; he dug a ditch across the crown of a hill. Then he built the cellars in the trench and put the excavated soil back on top. The stones dug up in the process went into the facade. Wallace Johnson (who, incidentally, invented a mechanical grape harvester) passed away in 1979, but his family continues operating the winery. You should stop here and taste the cabernet sauvignon and petite sirah, as well as the sauvignon blanc. *10075 CA Highway 128, Healdsburg; (707) 433-7266.*

■ UPPER ALEXANDER VALLEY

As you head north from Healdsburg on US 101, the west side of the road contains a stretch where wineries of the Dry Creek and Alexander Valley appellations appear to mingle. That's because the dividing line runs along Dry Creek Ridge, and wineries in the canyons are closer to the Russian River than to Dry Creek. Thus you can make this a trip where you visit wineries from both appellations, say, Pedroncelli

Chateau Souverain, a well-known restaurant and winery in the Alexander Valley.

and Geyser Peak (the former is on Canyon Road, the latter just north of its junction with US 101), or Lytton Springs and Chateau Souverain.

Chateau Souverain. If there's one success story that's turned sour it has to be the old Souverain (see the earlier history of the label under Rutherford Hill above). When it was built in 1972, Souverain was intended to be Pillsbury's Sonoma County winery under that conglomerate's short and ill-fated foray into the wine business. No expenses were spared in putting up an imposing structure that looks like a very elegant cross between a French chateau and Sonoma County hop kilns. It is a beautiful winery, and one wishes it had been blessed with better luck. At first, Pillsbury couldn't decide what to call it: it was first called Ville Fontaine while under construction, had its name changed to Chateau Souverain before the 1973 vintage, and was renamed Souverain of Alexander Valley shortly after the 1974 crush. By 1976, Pillsbury had sold both the Napa and Sonoma Souverains. Wine World Estates, the winery's most recent owner, changed the name back to Chateau Souverain. A bit confusing? You might say so. The latest installment in this enological soap opera came late in 1995, when Wine World Estates was sold to new investors. Let's hope the new owners will keep the winery on a track to excellence. If you have not yet visited this beautiful winery, you might want to do so soon: who knows what lies in its future? There's a cafe—open on weekends only—that used to be a full-service restaurant, open all week long. Nevertheless, the food is still very good (be sure to make a reservation), and the wines are superb. *400 Souverain Road off Independence Lane, Geyserville; (707) 433-8281.*

The Geyser Peak Winery. Faring better is the Geyser Peak Winery. Built in 1882, it too had its ups and downs. It went through its corporate phase after the Jos. Schlitz Brewing Co. bought it: they're the ones who upgraded the buildings and added garden terraces—but they also brought us wine in a box. Just before the venerable old place slipped into bulk wine oblivion the way the Italian Swiss Colony did, Geyser Peak was rescued by Santa Rosa developer Henry Trione and his sons in 1982. Ever since that takeover, the wines have improved steadily and can once again be considered premium wines. The winemaker, Daryl Groom, learned his trade in Australia. Thus it should come as no surprise to find a "shiraz" (syrah) among Geyser Peak's offerings. But the zinfandel, merlot, and cabernet are excellent, too. A Meritage called Reserve Alexandre is, despite the pretentious misspelling of the late Cyrus Alexander's name (the pioneer who gave the valley its name), a wine of great depth and beauty. It is a blend of the five Bordeaux varieties: cabernet sauvignon, cabernet franc, merlot, malbec, and petit verdot. *22281 Chianti Road, Geyserville; (707) 857-WINE or (800) 945-4447.*

Geyser Peak also owns the old Nervo Winery on the floor of the Alexander Valley, now called **Canyon Road Cellars.** It's a great place for picking up inexpensive quaffing wines, and it's very popular. *19550 Geyserville Avenue, Geyserville; (707) 857-3417.*

Finish up this excursion with a visit to the new tasting room at **Clos du Bois.** This winery is now owned by a large spirits conglomerate, but its wines are still good; the top-of-the-line Marlstone Bordeaux blend has been superb in past years. *19410 Geyserville Avenue, Geyserville; (707) 857-1651.*

Double back to CA 128 to reach the lower half of the Alexander Valley, or spend the night in Geyserville, or return to Healdsburg to start out again the next morning, well rested and refreshed.

Geyser Peak Winery at the turn of the 19th century. (Sonoma County Library)

COUNTRY ROADS

A Book of Verses underneath the Bough,
A Jug of Wine, a Loaf of Bread and Thou
Beside me singing in the Wilderness
Oh, Wilderness were paradise enow!

—Edward Fitzgerald, The Rubaiyat of Omar Khayyam

WHAT COULD BE MORE ROMANTIC than driving through rolling hills and peaceful valleys along a Wine Country back road, where oak forests, vineyards, and wildflower meadows are still largely undisturbed by the hectic pace of our times? Here 20th-century progress can be detected in the high quality of the roads' pavement—which makes travel a lot more pleasant than it was in the age of dirt and gravel thoroughfares. Good pavement doesn't mean you have to speed along these roads—though many of the natives do. (Watch out for the Daytona wannabes who will pass across a double yellow line, before a blind curve, uphill.) Don't be in a hurry. Pull over to let hotrodders pass. Relax. Back roads should be savored. Be patient with lumbering pieces of farm machinery and with the occasional herd of cattle slowly mooing down the road. And watch out for cowboys on horseback. Never honk at them: you might spook the horse. Besides, if you speed on these narrow, winding roads, you will miss the sights: strange rock formations by the side of the road, uncommon trees like tanbark oak or cypress, wildflowers, and wildlife.

Look for wildlife in unexpected places. Deer, for example, have a way of popping up behind blind curves, and hawks and eagles, in pursuit of prey, will skim across the road at breakneck speed. But not all large birds are eagles: the ones with dingy brown-black plumage and bare heads are turkey vultures. They live on carrion and are Nature's way of disposing of reckless drivers' roadkill.

While traveling on these back roads, give yourself time to stop now and then. Turn off your car's engine, listen to the song of birds, and inhale the restorative aromas of meadow grass, roadside flowers, laurel, and pine. Savor the cool freshness rising from a purling creek, or feel the heat radiating from sun-warmed rocks. Here—only steps from the pavement—you can step into a landscape that seems to have changed little since time began.

Several of these back roads allow access to creeks and rivers—though the trail leading to water may be steep. Beware of poison oak,

Paintbrush (Castilleja affinis)
Blooms from May to August.

Deer are a common sight and hazard along the Wine Country's back roads. (Photo by John Doerper)

rattlesnakes, and "No Trespassing" signs. The latter are sometimes accompanied by angry locals waving shotguns. Wherever you tread, step lightly. Stay on established trails and do not trample fragile vegetation. And never pick wildflowers. Leave them for bees, hummingbirds, and the next wayfarer to enjoy.

These Wine Country back roads do not idly wind across the landscape. They actually take you places: across the Vaca Hills, over the Mayacamas and Sonoma mountains, to the sea. When planning your Wine Country trip, you might include one or more of them—to drive from the Sonoma to the Napa Valley, to extend your trip with a scenic detour, or just to relax from the sometimes hectic pace of the winery-tour circuit. Following are some of our favorites.

Lupine (Lupinus)
Blooms throughout spring, but is most spectacular in May.

■ Mount St. Helena–Pope Valley Loop

This day trip curves from CA 128 around Calistoga before taking you over the flanks of Mount St. Helena to Middletown in time for lunch (or to a shaded glade for a picnic). It continues down Butts Canyon Road through the Guenoc and Pope valleys before returning to the Napa Valley via Chiles Valley Road. Allow a whole day, so you'll have time for both a hike on Mount St. Helena in the morning and a stop at a backcountry winery in the afternoon. *(Refer to map on page 9.)*

As you're driving north on CA 29, that highway turns right in Calistoga onto Lincoln Avenue, towards downtown, Mount St. Helena, and Clear Lake. It ceases to be a wine road, while CA 128, with which it has co-mingled since Rutherford, goes on to become one of only two wine roads shared by both Napa and Sonoma counties. Before leaving Napa County, CA 128 skirts Storybook Mountain Vineyards.

Storybook Mountain Vineyards. The vineyard here is among the most dramatic in the wine country: vines rise steeply from the winery in theatrical tiers. You hardly know there's a winery, it's so small, tucked into the rock face of the mountain. Zinfandel is king of the mountain at Storybook, and those produced by Jerry (Dr. J. Bernard) and Sigrid Seps are truly royal wines—deeply red in color, full-flavored, richly complex, with a unique, peppery spiciness that is so distinct, there's talk of cloning a special Storybook Mountain zinfandel grape. These wines are well-structured and age beautifully. The winery itself goes back to 1888, when Jacob Grimm, a gentleman farmer from San Francisco, had Chinese workmen dig three deep hillside tunnels for aging the wine of the winery and distillery he built on the site. Storybook's tasting room may well be the most romantic one in the Napa Valley: a vaulted cavern connecting two of the tunnels. The tunnels are among the best preserved in California, perhaps because they are fronted by a facade of solid concrete—an uncommon building material at the time they were built. Storybook is one of the most charming wineries to visit in the Wine Country, but visitors must call in advance to make an appointment. *3835 CA 128, Calistoga; (707) 942-5310.*

Returning on CA 128 to Calistoga, turn left at **Tubbs Lane** (shortly after you pass the turnoff to Petrified Forest Road). Soon a tall, exotically rustic gate rises on the left: the entrance to the Napa Valley's very own Old Faithful Geyser. After paying a modest entrance fee, you follow the signs to the geyser and wait. While the geyser erupts faithfully, it pauses some 40 to 50 minutes between blasts (there's a picnic area to make the wait more pleasant). You most likely just missed the last one. But, whoosh! Here it goes! A column of 350-degree water shoots 60 feet into the air, like wine from an overheated champagne bottle. Poof. It's gone. But it was worth waiting for, if only because this is one of only three "faithful," that is, predictably erupting, geysers in the world—and this one is much less crowded than Yellowstone's. **Old Faithful Geyser of California,** *1299 Tubbs Lane, Calistoga; (707) 942-6463.*

Seeing all that water popping into the sky like champagne is bound to make you thirsty. Fortunately, there's a winery just up the road.

Chateau Montelena. To some extent, Chateau Montelena is a curiosity: a French chateau of hewn gray stone rising above an artificial lake where swans glide among islands topped by Chinese pavilions. But the architectural eclecticism makes perfect sense when you consider that the chateau was built by California senator Alfred L. Tubbs in 1882, at the height of the California wine boom brought on when the phylloxera root louse sucked France's vines dry. The lake and the chinoiserie (Chinese frills) were added in the 1950s by a Chinese engineer who made a lot of money building the Manchurian Railroad. (The Napa Valley has ever appealed to the international set.)

The property had fallen on hard times by the early 1970s, when Los Angeles attorney Jim Barrett bought it and hired Miljenko "Mike" Grgich as winemaker for the restored winery. Hiring Grgich proved to be a stroke of genius: the 1973 chardonnay took first place in 1976, in the famous "Judgment of Paris" tasting of top French and Californian wines. Mike Grgich has since left to open his own winery, but the Chateau Montelena wines, now made by Bo Barrett, are still world-class. Be sure to taste the chardonnay, the estate-grown cabernet sauvignon, and the zinfandel.

The island pavilions, incidentally, are the winery's "picnic area." But you'll have to call ahead and make a reservation. There's a long waiting list: in 1995, the wait was half a year or more in part because the islands were featured on San Francisco Bay Area television. *1429 Tubbs Lane, Calistoga; (707) 942-5105.*

❖

Turn left as you leave the winery. You'll soon come to a T-intersection. This is CA 29. Turn left (watch for downhill traffic, which may be going faster than you think!) towards Mount St. Helena. The road climbs steeply and becomes a nightmare of curves and switchbacks. But it's splendidly scenic. The landscape has changed little since Scottish writer Robert Louis Stevenson passed through the region in 1880. He writes in *Silverado Squatters*:

> *V*ineyards and deep meadows, islanded and framed with thicket, gave place more and more as we ascended to woods of oak and madrona, dotted with enormous pines. It was these pines, as they shot above the lower wood, that produced the pencilling of single trees I had so often remarked from the valle . . . . The oak is no baby; even the madrona, upon these spurs of Mount Saint Helena, comes to a fine bulk and ranks with forest trees; but the pines look down upon the rest for underwood. As Mount St. Helena among her foot-hills, so these dark giants out-top their fellow vegetables. Alas! if they had left the redwoods, the pines, in turn, would have been dwarfed. But the redwoods, fallen from their high estate, are serving as family bedsteads, or yet more humbly as field fences, along all Napa Valley.

❖

Drive slowly as you ascend Mount St. Helena, at 4,344 feet the tallest peak in the Bay Area, so you can note the changing vegetation and the variety of rock formations. At the 2,250-foot level, the highway crosses a broad saddle. Here are two parking areas, one to either side of the road. Trails lead from the parking lot into the countryside *(see page 206)*.

The northern descent of Mount St. Helena is not as steep as the ascent, because the mountain is actually a long, undulating ridge with a steep southern face. Besides, when you left Calistoga, at an elevation of a mere 365 feet, you rose almost 2,000 feet to the saddle, but you're dropping less than 900 feet, because Middletown in Lake County, your next destination, is at an altitude of about 1,300 feet.

Middletown, in the heart of the Loconomi Valley, home of Coyote in the myths of local Indians, got its name because it lies exactly midway between Lower Lake and Calistoga.

Blue iris (Iris douglasiana)
Blooms from late February to May.

Hiking on Mount St. Helena is just one of the recreational opportunities available to visitors in the Wine Country.

Continue north on CA 29. At the end of town, where the pioneer cemetery lies, turn right into Butts Canyon Road. This quiet drive winds through a pastoral valley surrounded by high hills. The white plumes rising in the hills to the west are steam plumes from volcanic fumaroles, which operate in principle much like a geyser, except that the water turns to steam before it reaches the surface.

Drive carefully on this road and watch your speed—there are some nasty right-angle turns which are hard to see until you're almost on them. After a few miles, the scenery changes. Conical volcanic hills, with grassy slopes and toupee-like arboreous crowns, rise from the valley floor and blue-green serpentine rocks crop up in low ridges. When you come to Guenoc Lake, slow down. You may see ducks, geese, and swans here, in season, and perhaps a blue heron or one of the resident bald eagles. Black beef cattle graze in the pastures; as do, on occasion, black wild boars, which abound in this valley.

Mariposa lily (Calochortus)
Blooms from May to early summer.

Guenoc Winery. Look for the sign on the left and drive up the rocky road to this hilltop winery. It's in the building that looks like a large barn. The tasting room entrance is to the right. Of the different wines made by Guenoc, you may want to sample the Genevieve Magoon reserve chardonnay as well as the red and white Meritage wines ("Meritage" is a blend of wine from several harmonious Bordeaux varieties—a winemaker's quest for the perfect wine). And don't miss the view across the vineyards. The white manor in the distance, half hidden by huge valley oaks, is the house where British actress Lillie Langtry stayed when she owned Guenoc Ranch in the late 19th century (though the appearance of the house has been much changed). Her profile graces the winery's label.

Look up toward the top of the ridges to your right. You should be able to see a vineyard. Grapes were first planted here in 1854, when stagecoaches ran from St. Helena across the ridges separating the Guenoc and Napa valleys. Today, the forest has reclaimed the once-cultivated land, but you can still tell the course of the old road by the moss-covered stone walls along its margins. Here and there in the woods you'll discover the ruin of an abandoned winery, and you may stumble over an ancient vine maintaining itself among the oaks, laurels, and pines. As you drive south from Guenoc on Butts Canyon Road, the valley narrows dramatically and becomes densely overgrown with oaks, laurels, cypresses, gray pines, and chaparral scrub. Drive carefully and look for animals on and along the road. If you're lucky, you'll see a deer or wild boar foraging among the trees, or a coyote stalking a wily quail. After a few miles of winding about, the road enters a large, grassy glen: you have arrived in the Pope Valley. For more than a hundred years, some of Napa County's best grapes have been grown here and in neighboring, slightly higher, Chiles Valley—the reason both are included in the Napa Valley Appellation. But you'll see few grapes on this tour—most of the vineyards are to the south and east. *21000 Butts Canyon Road, Middletown, Lake County; (707) 987-2385.*

❖

Pope Valley has preserved its rustic charm. Aside from the road and a few automobiles and telephone poles, you'll encounter few signs of 20th-century civilization here. But the valley has its oddities as well, as you'll notice right away when you reach "Hubcap City," a ranch where almost every fence post and tree has been decorated with hubcaps. Litto, the old man who collected these caps, has passed away, and his daughter discourages the trading the old man was so fond of, but you can still stop and look.

The Pope Valley grasslands are studded with great oaks—some of them among the most magnificent of their kind in the state. In spring, the meadows are bright with wildflowers. A side road to the east takes you to Lake Berryessa. A road to the west leads to **Aetna Springs Cellars** which makes cabernet from local grapes, as well as some chardonnay. There's also a nine-hole golf course. *7227 Pope Valley Road; (707) 965-2675.*

At the Pope Valley gas station and store, stay to the left and continue on Pope Valley Road (which now becomes Chiles Valley/Pope Valley Road and turns into Chiles Valley Road after the Lower Chiles Valley turn-off). This will take you past vineyards to the tree-shaded canyon of Chiles Creek—which can be pleasantly cool on a hot summer afternoon—and to Lake Hennessey. The **Green & Red Vineyard** makes a splendid zinfandel from its steep, 16-acre hillside vineyard, which is hidden away in Chiles Canyon. *3208 Chiles Valley/Pope Valley Road; (707) 965-2346.* It is open by appointment only. Take a side trip up Lower Chiles Valley Road,

---

STEINBECK ON CALIFORNIA WEATHER

What John Steinbeck wrote about dry years in the Salinas Valley applies equally well to the Napa and Sonoma valleys.

*I*n the winter of wet years the streams ran full-freshet, and they swelled the river until it sometimes raged and boiled, bank full, and then it was a destroyer. The river tore the edges of the farm lands and washed whole acres down; it toppled barns and houses into itself, to go floating and bobbing away. It trapped cows and pigs and sheep and drowned them in its muddy brown water and carried them to the sea. Then when the late spring came, the river drew in from its edges and the sand banks appeared. And in the summer the river didn't at all run above ground. . . .

There were dry years too . . . The water came in a thirty-year cycle. There would be five or six wet and wonderful years when there might be nineteen to twenty-five inches of rain, and the land would shout with grass. Then would come six or seven pretty good years of twelve to sixteen inches of rain. And then the dry years would come, and sometimes there would be only seven or eight inches of rain. The land dried up. . . . And it never failed that during the dry years the people forgot about the rich years, and during the wet years they lost all memory of the dry years. It was always that way.

—John Steinbeck, *East of Eden*, 1952

which skirts a hillside and gives you some nice views of vines, pastures, and wooded hills, and follow it to Rustridge Winery. This winery doubles as a bed-and-breakfast, and triples as a thoroughbred horse breeding ranch. There are miles of trails, but you'll have to bring your own horse if you want to ride. **Rustridge Ranch, Vineyard, and Winery,** *2910 Lower Chiles Valley Road; (707) 965-9353.*

❖

At the end of the road, turn right on Chiles Valley/Pope Valley Road, then left at Pope Valley onto Howell Mountain Road to reach the Napa Valley near St. Helena.

■ TRAIL UP MOUNT ST. HELENA

To reach the trail up Mount St. Helena, drive up CA 29 *(see page 202)* to the mountain's saddle and park in one of the two parking areas. The trail starting at the eastern parking area leads to the Palisades—a series of steep-sided cliffs of volcanic origin—and into very scenic backcountry. A grassy flat above the western parking spot on the road up Mount St. Helena was the site of a tollhouse used in the days

Pope and Guenoc valleys are the driest of the appellations in the Wine Country. Above, the vineyards of Guenoc, in Lake County, are pictured. Orville Magoon, right, is Guenoc's owner.

when the highway was a toll road frequented by stagecoaches, miners, and high-waymen.

Look for stairs on the west side of the meadow: they mark **the start of the trail** which leads to the abandoned shaft of the Silverado Mine and to the site of the cabin occupied by Robert Louis Stevenson and his bride Fanny Osbourne in the summer of 1880. A monument, carved in the shape of an open book from Scottish granite, commemorates Stevenson's stay. The trail continues uphill from the small wooded flat to connect with the fire road that runs all the way to the top of the mountain. Look for the mouth of the Silverado Mine high in the hillside, above a skirt of reddish cinnabar rock tailings.

The mine had been abandoned by the time Stevenson arrived, but the highway was busier than ever with travelers and with the folk who preyed on them. Stevenson commented that "we are here in a land of stage drivers and highwaymen: a land in that sense, like England a hundred years ago . . . . Only a few years ago, the Lakeport stage was robbed a mile or two from Calistoga." He adds that "The cultus of the highwayman always flourishes highest where there are thieves on the road, and where the guard travels armed, and the stage is not only a link between country and city, and the vehicle of news, but has a faint warfaring aroma, like a man who should be a brother to a soldier."

❖

But now you're on your way. A raven glides past on stiff wings, half-shrouded by the swirling mists of an errant cloud. Clouds wrap the top of 4,344-foot-high Mount St. Helena in a veil of ambiguity; they soften the outlines of rocky cliffs and obscure the scraggly trees clinging to the weathered stones. As you climb the lower slopes, you note curiously eroded knobs of hard volcanic rock. These outcroppings, known locally by names like Turks Head, Bubble Rock, or Goat Roost Rock, seem to be sitting upright on their haunches like trolls. (They look asleep, but who knows, they may be patrolling the mountain at night, when no humans are about.)

As you near the top a miracle happens. A ray of sun cleaves the clouds; the wind pushes them apart. Suddenly, to the south, the Napa Valley stretches from the foot of the mountains to the salt marshes of San Pablo Bay; to the west, the sun illuminates the hills and vales of Sonoma County. North and east of the mountain, valleys and mountains stretch to distant horizons.

From the top of Mount St. Helena, the Wine Country stretches out below in an almost rhythmic pattern of narrow valleys and mountain ranges. These extend in a

At 4,344 feet, Mount St. Helena is the region's highest peak.

northwest to southeasterly direction, because they were formed by subsidiary faults of the great San Andreas, which has pushed and pulled this land for millions of years. The rocks on top of Mount St. Helena were spewed into the air from the mouth of a nearby volcanic vent along with quantities of volcanic ash. These rocks, and the sedimentary bedrock beneath, eroded to form soil. Mixed with volcanic ash, the soil washed down into the valleys, forming the perfect growing medium for grapevines.

Much of the land below is covered by dense grasslands, brushwood, and forests, but erosional gullies and slipped slopes are also visible. Like glacial cirques, they are marked by semicircular scars. Wine Country soils become waterlogged if the wet season brings heavy rains: they sag, slump, and begin to slide downhill. But much of the land has been stable for centuries, as forests of large oak trees and Douglas firs attest.

On warm days, sea fogs creep through the Golden Gate and fill the valleys below Mount St. Helena like a diaphanous tide, blotting out the sun and cooling the land with white billows that hide all but the highest ridges and peaks. (If you're on top when this happens prepare for a chilly hike back to the parking area, even though up here, above the fog, the air stays warm.) If a vineyard below is shielded by a low ridge from the full impact of these fogs, it may be able to produce cabernet sauvignon grapes; if it sits right in the path of sea breezes and fogs, it may only be able to ripen pinot noir and chardonnay grapes.

Early pioneers remember much open grassland in the wine regions. It was a landscape cultivated by the native Wappo, who, in order to increase their food supply—acorns from the numerous oaks—regularly burned off the underbrush in controlled burns. This is also true for other parts of the Wine Country where the "native" oak–grassland is quite definitely a man-made landscape created over hundreds of years. To the pioneers, of course, this was the land as they first saw it, a veritable Garden of Eden with flowery meadows and wooded glens. The laurel, live oaks, buckeyes, manzanitas, alders, willows, and the ash (plus "occasional giant madronas" described by an early citizen) still thrive below you, as do the cypresses and sugar pines on Mount St. Helena.

And within those woodlands and fields still live a marvelous variety of animals. The grizzly bears noted by pioneers are no more. But black bears still survive in hidden nooks—on the north side of Mount St. Helena and in the wild mountains separating Napa and Sonoma counties from Lake County, for instance.

Other denizens of the wild which wait in the woods just beyond the vineyards include deer, coyotes, bobcats, cougars, quail, rabbits, skunks, and rattlesnakes. Beware the rattlesnake! Rattlers are generally shy and will try to get out of your way, since they recognize humans as non-prey. Get out of their way, too. Chances are you will never see wild boars or wild turkeys (both species were introduced). Then again, a flock of wild turkeys may come sailing across the road, or you may spot a herd of wild boars grazing out in the open, among black cattle. The Mayacamas Mountains and the hills bordering the Dry Creek Valley are good places to look for them, if you're curious.

If, from the top of Mount St. Helena, a grand view unfolds, so does the impression that the rugged Wine Country mountains hide valleys that should be traversed and explored on foot. Much of this land is privately owned, but parts can be explored from **Bothe-Napa State Park** or the Sonoma Valley's **Sugarloaf Ridge State Park.** Just north of Calistoga, **Oat Hill Trail** also takes you into the backcountry.

BOTTLED POETRY

During Robert Louis Stevenson's honeymoon in the Wine Country, he spent many evenings with pioneer Jacob Schram who entertained Stevenson in his wine caves at Schramsberg vineyards on Diamond Mountain.

*W*ine in California is still in the experimental stage; and when you taste a vintage, grave economical questions are involved. The beginning of vine-planting is like the beginning of mining for the precious metals: the wine grower also "prospects." One corner of land is tried with one kind of grape after another. This is a failure; that is better; a third best. So, bit by bit, they grope about for their Clos Vougeot and Lafite. Those lodes and pockets of earth, more precious than the precious ores, that yield inimitable fragrance of soft fire; whose virtuous Bonanzas, where the soil has sublimated under sun and stars to something finer, and the wine is bottled poetry: these still lie undiscovered; chaparral conceals, thicket embowers them. . . .

—Robert Louis Stevenson, *Silverado Squatters,* 1883

A lone oak against the evening sky.

As you wander along these trails, you may see long vines of native grapes draping oak trees. And you may ask yourself: how did they get up there? Grapes do not sprout in tree forks and then send tendrils down; they only grow from the ground up. There's only one way they could have gotten up that high: they must have grown up with the oaks. Since some of these oaks are several hundred years old, so are the grape vines. Who knows, some of those vines were probably around when Sir Francis Drake landed on the California coast in 1578.

■ HOWELL MOUNTAIN AND LAKE BERRYESSA

This trip will take you from the Napa Valley over Howell Mountain to Pope Valley, Lake Berryessa, Chiles Valley, Sage Canyon, and Lake Hennessey. En route you will drive through forests of native pines and oaks and see—in season—meadows and cliffs covered with wildflowers. You can stroll along the shores of Lake Berryessa, and you may visit several backcountry wineries. Allow half a day if you're pressed for time, a whole day if you're not. Be sure to bring a picnic luncheon to enjoy at the Nichelini picnic area or on the lakeshore.

Sticky monkeyflower (Mimulus aurantiacus)
Blooms from May to August.

A perfect vineyard.

❖

In the Napa Valley, turn right off CA 29 north of St. Helena onto Deer Park Road. Cross the valley floor and the Silverado Trail at the blinking red light, then climb to the forested heights of Howell Mountain, a grape-growing area that is quite a bit cooler than the Napa Valley floor and is distinct enough with its austere soils and cold nights to have its own appellation. As you ascend the mountain, look for Burgess Cellars on the left. *(Refer to map on page 99.)*

Burgess Cellars. This old stone winery may be difficult to find because it is a real cliffhanger, hugging the steep western flank of Howell Mountain. A handsome new sign is clearly visible but be careful when you turn left across the road. Downhill traffic usually travels at high speed and the turn is complicated. It's worth the trouble. The winery was built in 1875 by Carlo Rossini, a Swiss winemaker. It became Lee Stewart's original Souverain Cellars in 1942, and shared in the post-Prohibition Napa Valley wine resurrection. Tom

Shooting star (Dodecatheon)
Blooms in early spring.

Burgess bought it in 1972—just in time to share in another wine renaissance. Since then, the winery has made superb zinfandel, cabernet sauvignon, and chardonnay. The wines became less tannic and more elegant in the mid-1980s, but that did not diminish their aging capability. A mature Burgess red is truly a great experience. *Tours by appointment only. 1108 Deer Park Road; (707) 963-4766.*

Chateau Woltner. After visiting Burgess, turn left, uphill. At the intersection with Howell Mountain Road turn left into White Cottage Road, which curves around the top of Howell Mountain and brings you to Chateau Woltner.

This winery, set in a sere glen atop Howell Mountain, is unabashedly, rustically French, without frills. There's nothing glamorous about old-fashioned Burgundian wineries, and there's nothing glamorous about Chateau Woltner—an austere old stone building of simple design erected by French vintners in 1886—nothing but the excellence of its chardonnay. It's worth visiting for the building alone with its honey-colored stone walls and huge wooden trusses inside the cellar.

The winery's stone cellars lie west of the road (look for tall, columnar cypresses); the vines grow in the rocky soils just to the east. The winery is owned by Francis and Françoise DeWavrin-Woltner, former owners of the very prestigious Chateau La Mission Haut Brion in Bordeaux, who acquired the old stone winery in 1980. Breaking with family tradition, they decided to make only chardonnay here—wine from a Burgundian rather than Bordelais grape.

The winery was built by two French vintners, Jean Adolphe Brun and Jean Chaix, who named it the Howell Mountain Winery. Later owners made wine here until Prohibition, and bulk wine was made here until 1946. After that the winery lay idle until the Woltners resurrected it and the vineyards. They have succeeded in imbuing it with the serene spirit of the French countryside. Sitting at a table just outside the old stone arch leading to the cellars and sipping the incomparable chardonnay is an experience not to be missed. The wines are great. Drinking them outside—in the mountain air (you're at about 1,600 feet elevation) below the vineyards that grew the grapes and just feet from the barrels they were fermented and aged in—makes them even more special. And they are special indeed: the rather snooty André Gayot/Gault Millau *Guide to the Best Wineries of North America* raves, "the quality of the Chardonnay made here equals that of the best Chards produced in America or anywhere else for that matter. Indeed, Woltner wines are comparable to the top white Burgundies they so much resemble," and concludes that

"Woltner's Titus and Frédérique Vineyard chardonnays are about as good as it gets in North America." True. To visit, you must make an appointment. *150 South White Cottage Road; (707) 963-1744.*

❖

Farther east on White Cottage Road is the unmarked driveway of **Dunn Vineyards.** Here Randy Dunn, who gained his reputation as winemaker for Caymus, proves that cabernet sauvignon made from estate-grown Howell Mountain grapes can be great indeed. Because this winery is so small—and sells out its annual bottling right at release—the winery is not open to the public.

White Cottage Road ends at Howell Mountain Road. Turn left. Drive carefully. The road is very steep (up to 10 percent grade), with many switchbacks. It runs through beautiful forests of tanbark and black oak (their acorns were important foods of local Wappo Indians), ponderosa pine, and Douglas fir before reaching Pope Valley at a very rustic barn, gas station, and country store. (Ask to see the rattlesnakes kept in a barrel.)

Follow the road as it curves to the right and becomes Chiles Valley/Pope Valley Road; then look for Pope Canyon Road on your left. Follow this scenic road to the northwest shore of Lake Berryessa. The submerged canyon where Pope Creek enters the lake is a favorite local swimming hole. Turn right onto the Berryessa-Knoxville Road. Much of Lake Berryessa's west shore is included in vast Oak Shores Park, a pleasant region of grassy glens and wooded draws. If you're lucky, you'll see deer, raccoon, fox, or coyote by the lakeshore. Or perhaps you'll spot a heron standing in the shallows, waiting for a fish, frog, or muskrat to swim by. Wild boar live in the densely forested mountains west of the lake.

❖

You'll reach CA 128 at Turtle Rock, at the northern end of Capell Valley. Turn left towards Rutherford. This scenic road takes you first into **Chiles Valley,** one of the region's oldest grape-growing regions. You'll be driving through vineyards, but there's no winery here. You'll encounter your first winery after the road leaves Chiles Valley and plunges into rock-walled **Sage Canyon.**

Nichelini Winery. This family-owned winery clings to a steep embankment where the road skirts a cliff, and is the sort of rustic country place you wish your family owned. The buildings are old and sit, very scenic, by the edge of the road. There is a pretty picnic area here—a lovely place to wile away an afternoon with a bottle of

The Napa and Sonoma valleys have experienced a building and population boom over the past two decades. Above is an intersection in 1978 . . .

wine, a loaf of bread, a book of verse—and a thou sitting underneath a bough. Be sure to taste the zinfandel and the sauvignon vert. The latter grape was once commonly planted in California but has lately fallen out of favor. Nichelini is the last winery to make a varietal wine from this grape. It is crisp and very refreshing. Due to the location, parking is very limited. The winery is open on weekends only. *2970 Sage Canyon Road; (707) 963-0717.*

❖

Sage Canyon opens to Lake Hennessey. CA 128 skirts the southern shore of the lake which has several public access areas, as well as public restrooms, and soon reaches the Napa Valley where Conn Creek crosses under the Silverado Trail. CA 128 becomes one of the Wine Country's main roads here; it resumes its back-road status north of Cloverdale *(see page 217).*

Several wineries which are open by appointment only are on Pritchard Hill south of Lake Hennessey. You'll have to call ahead not only for an appointment, but for directions as well, since even the mailboxes are unmarked. **Chappellet Vineyard,** *1581 Sage Canyon Road; (707) 963-7136,* produces superb chardonnay,

Wild mustard (Brassica campestris) Blooms in early spring.

. . . and again in 1995. Does this mean pinot will supplant chardonnay as the region's most popular varietal?

merlot, and cabernet sauvignon, as well as excellent sauvignon blanc. **Long Vineyards,** *1535 Sage Canyon Road; (707) 963-2496,* makes only 3,000 cases of estategrown chardonnay, white riesling, sauvignon blanc, and cabernet sauvignon—though very little of the latter is made.

From Lake Hennessey take CA 128 west to the Napa Valley.

■ ANDERSON VALLEY IN MENDOCINO COUNTY

North of Healdsburg, US 101 reaches the small town of Cloverdale. Just north of town, CA 128 heads west to the wine-growing region of the Anderson Valley, and on through Boonville to Philo, the vineyards, and the redwoods of the lower Navarro River.

From Cloverdale, CA 128 climbs steeply in serried switchbacks through an eclectic mixture of chaparral and oak forest. Look for spice bush growing by the side of the road. The leaves of this dark green shrub release a pleasantly spicy aroma when crushed, and the maroon,

Blue dicks or wild hyacinth (Brodiaea pulchella)
Blooms from March to May.

thick-petaled flowers (which appear between April and August) grow into unique, urn-shaped woody capsules that may be up to two inches long. As the road rises, it follows a creek bed. This is Dry Creek, which runs south from Yorkville to Sonoma Lake and through the renowned grape-growing valley that has taken its name, until it merges with the Russian River at Healdsburg. West of the mountain crest, as you slowly drop down into the Anderson Valley, you'll soon feel that the road gyrates as much as the turkey vultures riding thermals high in the sky. After traversing seemingly endless stretches of blue oak savannah and sheep pasture, you finally reach a valley floor green with pastures and apple orchards.

The highway follows Rancheria Creek into **Boonville**, a small farming town that was once so isolated, residents invented a lingo of their own, known as Boontling. Few traces of this unique language survive, except in the names of a coffee shop known as Horn of Zeese ("cup of coffee"), and a phone booth called Buckey Walter. Boonville is a lot less isolated these days, thanks largely to a steady stream of Bay Area weekenders passing through town en route to the Mendocino Coast (by far the quickest way to go).

But Anderson Valley wineries have also played a role in ending this self-imposed isolation, as did a now defunct restaurant called the New Boonville Hotel which attracted a lot of attention in the mid-1980s among Bay Area gourmets. And all because Charlene Rollins, the chef, had a special knack for dealing with local meats and produce, much of which was produced in the restaurant's extensive garden— resembling a small farm. The place proved unprofitable, however, and the owners caused quite a scandal by fleeing their creditors, first to France, then to Oregon, where they opened the much-acclaimed New Sammy's Cowboy Bistro in Talent, a few miles north of Ashland.

The Boonville restaurant, renamed the **Boonville Hotel and Restaurant,** is now run by John Schmitt, whose cooking has an even more loyal following than that of the previous owners. The hotel is also living up to its name by having rooms for rent. *(707) 895-2210.*

What's surprising for a town as small as Boonville, however, is that it has not just one good restaurant, but two. The **Buckhorn Saloon** sits across the highway from the hotel, atop its own brewery, the **Anderson Valley Brewing Company.** The food here is as good as the beer. Boonville's other claims to fame are the annual **Apple Show** and **Sheep Dog Trials** held in October.

❖

Northwest of Boonville, the highway cuts through a low ridge, which is just high enough to impede the sea fogs creeping up the Navarro River. North of here the land is much cooler than the southern valley—making it perfect for redwoods, apples, and grapes. The Anderson Valley's best vineyards lie between Philo and Navarro, near the redwoods. Philo, where Rancheria, Anderson, and Indian creeks merge to form the Navarro River, has long been the center of an apple-growing region—primarily of Gravensteins, which need a cool climate to give their best.

Bob Thompson writes in *The Wine Atlas of California and the Pacific Northwest* that grapes were first planted in the Anderson Valley about a hundred years ago, high on the ridges, by primarily Italian grape growers, or by farmers making wine for home use. Zinfandel found a unique home here. To quote Thompson: "At their best they are like none other from the variety: dark, lean, firm, balanced, and intensely berry-like in flavor." But these plantings were only known to the few. While some winegrowers, like Ukiah's Parducci family, slowly expanded their Anderson Valley holdings over the years, the valley's wine boom dates only from the early 1970s, when Tony Husch of Husch Vineyards and Ted Bennett of **Navarro Vineyards**, *5601 CA 128, Philo; (707) 895-3686,* planted gewürztraminer vines in what they considered to be the perfect climate for this finicky Alsatian grape—the cool part of the Anderson Valley. But he found that chardonnay and pinot noir grew even better here—and sold better. He also believes these two make a great sparkling wine. John **Scharffenberger** firmly placed the Anderson Valley among America's top producers in 1981, and so impressed the French with his bubbly that the champagne producer **Roederer** moved in next door in 1982, instead of settling in the Napa Valley as other French wine entrepreneurs had done. In 1989, Scharffenberger sold a controlling interest in his winery to another French champagne maker, the house of Pommery. Today, the sparklers of these neighboring wineries consistently rank among the top half dozen produced in North America.

The success of the sparkling wines called attention to the excellence of other Anderson Valley wines. One you don't want to miss is **Husch Vineyards**, *4400 CA 128, Philo; (707) 895-3216.* It's family-owned—albeit not by its founders but by the Oswalds, who bought the winery from Tony Husch in 1979. The estate-grown gewürztraminer is about as good as it gets anywhere, and the pinot noir has a distinctly Burgundian structure—as well as that elusive aroma and flavor. Gewürztraminer is also the show wine at Navarro Vineyards and is well worth seeking out.

HUSCH
ESTATE BOTTLED

1994
ANDERSON VALLEY
GEWURZTRAMINER

GROWN, PRODUCED AND BOTTLED BY THE H.A. OSWALD FAMILY
PHILO, CA, ALCOHOL 13.0% BY VOLUME, RESIDUAL SUGAR 0.8%

But don't let that tempt you into neglecting the chardonnay, which is also excellent. **Handley Cellars**, too, produces a splendid chardonnay from Anderson Valley grapes, a delightful sauvignon blanc, and some very good sparkling wines, *3151 CA 128; (707) 895-3876.*

While there are no wineries further downstream than Navarro, the **Floodgate Store & Grill** makes for a great highway luncheon stop. By now, you're quite close to the magnificent giants of **Navarro River State Park**. Its cool glades are perfect for a post-prandial stroll which will put you in the mood for an afternoon of wine tasting.

If you're visiting in summer or fall, be sure to stock up at one of the many fruit stands along the highway. They offer ample proof that the grapes have not driven out the apples. **Gowan's Oak Tree** is still the best. Besides freshly picked apples, you can buy refreshing apple cider and other fruits and vegetables in season.

❖

You can leave the Anderson Valley by several different routes. Continuing north on CA 128 through the redwoods, the road eventually arrives at the mouth of the Navarro River and the Pacific Ocean. Here you can turn south on CA 1, the Pacific Coast Highway, toward Elk, Stewart's Point, and the Sea Ranch or north toward Mendocino and Fort Bragg. If you're planning to head south along the coast, you can also take a very scenic "cut-off" that's not for the faint of heart, since the road is narrow and winding: Mountain View Road from Boonville across the convoluted ridges of the Coast Range will bring you to the coast, and CA 1, somewhat south of Manchester. From here you can continue south on the coast highway, or you can turn inland at one of many

Columbine (Aquilegia formosa)
Blooms from late spring to summer.

Grafting a new varietal onto a vine.

roads—none of which are easy to drive. From Stewart's Point a road takes you to Sonoma County's Dry Creek Valley. An easier, albeit still winding road, CA 253, leads from Boonville north to US 101 and Ukiah.

■ BACKROAD INTO NAPA FROM POINTS NORTH

This trip follows CA 128 from Interstate 505 through Putah Creek Canyon, past Lake Berryessa through Capell Valley and Sage Canyon to the Napa Valley.

You feel smug and perhaps a little self-satisfied as you hum along with the mariachi music playing on the car radio. You've just had a very tasty (and inexpensive) lunch at a taco wagon, one of the food vans catering to farm workers with freshly made tacos and fruit juices. You watched as the woman behind the counter patted out tortillas from balls of masa dough, popped them on a griddle for an instant and topped them with spicy shredded pork, lettuce, tomato, and a slice of lemon. Sitting in the shade of an ancient olive tree, eating your tacos, sipping watermelon juice, and listening to Mexican music blaring from the taco wagon's radio, you

Grass nut or ithuriel's spear (Brodiaea laxa)
Blooms from April to June.

began to relax and feel good. You reflected on the morning, driving drearily flat stretches of Interstate 5, and you needed this break before tackling the winding mountain road leading to the valleys of the Wine Country.

From Winters, CA 128 runs straight to the west between fruit orchards, away from the level fecundity of the Central Valley to the soft billows of the Vaca Hills. The hills glow with a pale straw color in the autumn sun—the hue of the dead wild oat culms and leaves that dress their sinuous flanks. But the hills don't stay soft for long. You round a curve and enter Putah Creek Canyon, which cuts through the hills like a jagged scar gouged into soft flesh. Jagged ridges loom ahead, marking the breaking point where the shales and sandstones of the Great Valley formation floor fractured as they were thrust skyward and set on edge by the tectonic forces of continent building. The poor, gravelly soils of these hills, and of the valleys they encompass, may appear sere in the dry season, but they nonetheless grow some of the best and most complex fruits known to man: wine grapes.

❖

The vegetation changes as the road enters the hills. Along Putah Creek, the bright green foliage of Fremont cottonwoods contrasts with the grey-green leaves of streamside willows. The hills are broken by rocky cliffs and crags, and their steep slopes are studded with somber blue oaks and patches of chaparral scrub. Off to the right you pass deep thickets of trees with large, dark green, deeply lobed leaves. These are mission figs, introduced to California by Spanish padres but since taken to the wild. They may be found growing wild in most of the mountain valleys, as well as on the Napa Valley floor and along the levees of the great rivers, the Sacramento and the San Joaquin. Oaks, their thick trunks and stout branches contorted in the arrested motion of a dryadic dance, grow on grassy slopes which in spring and early summer are speckled blue with brodiaeas and lupines, purple with pentstemon, and pink with godetias and clarkias. As summer and fall pass, the redbud's magenta flowers grow into purplish seed pods, and the buckeye loses its leaves altogether. By late fall, the buckeye reveals its gnarled grey trunk and by the baseball-sized seeds suspended from the ends of naked branches. This canyon, now almost devoid of human habitation, must have been densely settled in prehistoric times, for the tops of many of the flat rocks near the creek are still marked with rounded depressions where Wintun Indians ground acorns into meal.

❖

The road winds in a great switchback from the creek to the top of **Monticello Dam**. The dam gets its name from the town of Monticello, center of the idyllic Berryessa Valley, which was drowned when the dam impounded the waters of Putah Creek. This valley, one of the most fertile in Napa County, was settled by Mexican rancheros in the 1840s, carved up into smaller ranches and farms in the 1860s, and cleared of all signs of civilization in the mid-20th century to make room for the lake. The small town of Monticello (whence the dam and the road leading from Napa east into the hills get their name) and surrounding ranches and farms were leveled, but the stone bridge over Putah Creek, the longest such structure in Napa County, still stands beneath the waters. Be sure to stop at the dam. This concrete bastion closes off the narrowest part of the canyon, where giant slabs of sandstone stand on edge. Cliff swallows build their jug-shaped nests on these rock walls, and wildflowers grow in their moist cracks.

Just beyond the dam gapes a huge concrete siphon, the lake's overflow, which is known locally as the "**Glory Hole**." It is truly a scary sight when the lake is full and water flows down the siphon, as though a maelstrom had opened in the waters and was about to suck down not only the excess runoff, but the surrounding mountains and trees as well. But chances are you will find the "hole" high and dry—the lake has not overflowed for some 18 years. Not because of lack of rainfall (though the region experienced two droughts during this period) but because Solano County farmers, who hold the rights to the lake's waters, use too much of it to irrigate their fields. In fact, the farmers have started a water fight that affects every tributary of the lake, all the way to the distant headwaters of Putah Creek, in Lake County.

❖

Lake Berryessa is some 26 miles long (six miles longer than the valley that bore its name) and all of its western shore is public property, though some of this is leased out to resorts. There are several access places in the next couple of miles, between the dam and Markley Canyon resort, but the trails are rocky and steep. In spring, shooting stars and delicate maidenhair ferns grow in the shade of hillside shrubs.

As you leave the lake on Steele Canyon Road—aptly named "Cardiac Hill" by cyclists—the aromas of laurel, ceanothus, and yerba santa waft through the air. The latter is a tall herb whose sticky leaves were much used by California's native and pioneer Hispanic populations to make a soothing tea said to heal all sorts of ailments, from upset stomachs to the common cold. The road descends in a series

The California golden poppy is the state flower and blooms from early spring through June.

of switchbacks to the narrow, pastoral valley of upper Wragg Creek. In spring, the meadows along the road are covered with golden poppies, cream and yellow buttercups, baby-blue-eyes, and other wildflowers. Long, pale shrouds of sheet lichen bedeck the oaks. These move in the slightest breeze and, at night, appear like ghosts ready to pounce on the unwary traveler.

❖

When you see a huge volcanic monolith, Raney Rock, looming ahead, you have to make a choice. You can turn right into Capell Valley and follow CA 128 to Rutherford, or you can continue south on CA 121, the Monticello Road, to the city of Napa. The place where CA 128 meets CA 121 is known as **Moskowite Corner.** There's a store-cafe-saloon northeast of the intersection, and a gas station. A road leads north to Lake Berryessa's Steele Canyon resort area.

Capell Valley is a place of pastures and small ranches in the rain shadow of Atlas Peak. Here and there outcroppings of serpentine, a slick greenish-blue rock scraped off the deep-sea ocean floor by tectonic forces, push through the soil. You might want to stop and touch a polished piece of this alien rock and feel how smooth, almost greasy, it feels. It's as close as most of

Larkspur (Delphinium)
Blooms from March through May.

us will ever get to the deep-sea floor. (Never mind that you're some 600 feet above sea level.) Before years of oxidation, serpentinic soils are notoriously sterile, and only a few plants—most notably gray pine and leather oak—can grow in them. You'll notice the change right away, because the vegetation changes drastically from lush green to stunted chaparral. Roadsides in this area are a good place to see clarkias and godetias in spring.

CA 128 winds through Chiles Valley and Sage Canyon and along the south shore of Lake Hennessey before taking you to the Napa Valley at the Silverado Trail and, after a few more turns and twists, to CA 29 in Rutherford. From here it runs north on CA 29 to Calistoga, before once again heading off on its own to the northwest, through the Mayacamas Range to Knights Valley and the Alexander Valley, before crossing the Coast Range north of Cloverdale and traversing Anderson Valley on its way to the Pacific Ocean.

WINE COUNTRY GENTRY

*F*ather now thinks of us as landed gentry. One day he was enjoying the shade of his garden after lunch, lying on a chaise lounge with his loyal dog, Max, at his feet. He was wearing a Sea Island cotton shirt with a discreet "B" monogrammed on the pocket, beige pants, his silver Iron Horse belt, and cowboy boots. I said, "Daddy, you look like a Ralph Lauren ad." I meant it as a compliment, but he was miffed. "Ralph Lauren is just an imitation of people like us," he said.

—Joy Sterling, *Cultivated Life: A Year in a California Vineyard,* 1991

Baby blue eyes (Nemophila menziesii)
Blooms from February to June.

FOOD AND WINE

Wel loved he garleek, oynons, and lekes!
And for to drynken strong wyn, reed as blood.
. . . .
And when that he wel drunken hadde the wyn,
Then wolde he speke no word but Latyn.

—*Geoffrey Chaucer, The Friar's Tale, ca. 1343–1400*

WHEN SPANISH PADRES RODE NORTH FROM MEXICO in the 18th century to establish a chain of missions in California, they brought with them an ancient tradition of food and wine. The padres—and the Mexican soldiers and settlers who accompanied them—felt at home in northern California because the Mediterranean climate of the region was congenial to their way of life. The grains, vegetables, and fruits they were accustomed to—corn, chiles, tomatoes, beans, squash, eggplants, figs, and olives—grew well here. Cattle and sheep multiplied on the dryland pastures. The padres planted wine grapes not only because the ritual of the Catholic Mass required wine, but because they themselves, as sons of a Mediterranean culture, enjoyed a little wine with their meals. Grapes thrived in the newly planted vineyards, and soon the missions had surplus wine to distill into *aguardiente* (a coarse brandy) or to sell to soldiers and settlers.

William Heath Davis, son of a prominent Honolulu ship owner, wrote in *Sixty Years in California*, an account of rancho days of the 1830s, that the tables of the rancheros were "frugally furnished." The food consisted mainly of "good beef broiled on an iron rod, or steaks with onions, also mutton, chicken, eggs."

Tortillas, sometimes made with yeast (like Mediterranean flatbreads) served as bread. Beans were a staple dish. Davis does not seem to have taken to the way the Californios seasoned their food, finding their meat stews too highly seasoned with red pepper. He calls the people sober, sometimes drinking "California wine, but not to excess."

Bostonian Henry Richard Dana, who spent 1834 on the California coast as a common sailor, wrote in *Two Years Before the Mast* about thriving on a diet of fresh fried beefsteaks three times a day, for breakfast, lunch, and dinner. The beef was augmented by nothing but tea and hard bread, yet every man was perfectly healthy—not a mean achievement when many ships' crews still succumbed to scurvy.

Matters hadn't changed much by 1846, when Walter Colton became American consular agent in Monterey (and was elected alcalde of that city under Mexican rule). He commented on the eating habits of the Californios in *Three Years in California:* "The only meat consumed here to any extent is beef. It is beef for breakfast, beef for dinner and beef for supper. A pig is quite a rarity; and as for chickens, they are reserved for the sick."

■ SETTLERS AND THE FOOD THEY ATE

While the Mexicans established ranchos in inland northern California, Russian fur traders had settled on the Sonoma coast, at Fort Ross and Bodega Bay. Their eating had nothing Mediterranean about it, but with its reliance on pork and cabbage was much like the native food of the Yankee traders who visited the coast. Seaman and fur trader Peter Corny, who visited the Russian establishment at Fort Ross in the early 1800s, commented on the Russian farm at Bodega Bay (in *Voyages in the North Pacific*) as "growing excellent wheat, potatoes, hemp and all kinds of vegetables." He claims to have seen a radish weighing 28 pounds, "and much thicker than a man's thigh, and quite good all through without being the least spongy."

The Russians also had a large stock of cattle, sheep, and pigs. The Russian influence did not linger, except that Russian farmers had shown that northern European produce would grow as well in the Wine Country as Mediterranean fruits and vegetables. It is quite possible that the most lasting impact the Russians have had on the region is through their pigs. Escaping to the wilderness of the oak-covered slopes, they became the ancestors of the wild "Russian boars" found in the mountains of the Wine Country today.

Unlike the Russians, non-Hispanic immigrants to northern California at first adopted the local eating customs. Thus a Christmas dinner served at Sutter's Fort in nearby Sacramento in 1845 included appetizers of dried fruits, nuts, raisins, *panocha* (a sugar concoction), sweetmeats, chile peppers, unbolted wheat bread, and, served with each course, salt, pepper, and jerky. The first course consisted of beef soup, the second course was roast beef, the third, beef pie, the fourth, fried beef. All came with the same garnish of *frijoles* (Mexican beans), red pepper, and garlic. Dessert was a Mexican-style plum pudding made with beef tallow, wild grapes, chile, and black pepper. We did not learn whether wine accompanied the meal, but we do know that Sutter was among those who experimented with making wine from native grapes.

■ THE YANKEES ARE COMING

The food and wine tradition started by the padres has stayed with us in California, though it was shortly pushed into the background when the gold rush brought Yankees from the East Coast and farmers from the Midwest, who were more likely to make corn into pone than tortillas. Yet there were popular Mexican restaurants in San Francisco by the late 1800s. But what the nouveau-riche miners and business hankered for most was the elegance of French food, and French restaurants sprang up everywhere.

Returning 24 years later, in August of 1859, to the already well-established city of San Francisco, Dana, by then a respected author and lawyer, commented on the difference between the rancho days and the new era: "It is generally noticeable that European continental fashions prevail generally in this city—French cooking, lunch at noon, and dinner at the end of the day, with café noir after meals." Dana claimed that some of the dinners he enjoyed in San Francisco were "as sumptuous and as good, in dishes and wine, as I have found in Paris."

■ ARRIVAL OF THE ITALIANS

A convivial Mediterranean food culture, mostly Northern Italian, was superimposed on the French food culture of San Francisco in the 1880s—at about the same time Italians began to settle in the Wine Country. At one of the city's Italian opera houses, La Moderna, wine was all but legal tender, as were food items like a brace of wild duck. Wrote one observer: "two friends of mine . . . in exchange for a fifty-pound rock cod, got box tickets for an entire run of Verdi." The Italians knew a good thing when they saw it, put down roots, and thrived on locally produced foods and wines central to their culture. In no time at all, San Francisco Italians had a disproportionate influence on the way San Francisco perceived food—perhaps because they seemed to enjoy eating so much, and San Franciscans have never

Freshly baked bread at the St. Helena farmers market, held
Friday mornings in Crane Park behind the high school.

been known to forego pleasurable experiences. Grapes, figs, pomegranates, oranges, lemons, beans, artichokes, and other Mediterranean fruits and vegetables grew well here. The Italians, more than anyone else, continued the tradition of simple, tasty foods and wines served together during meals. They also raised olives and made olive oil at a time when hardly anybody else in California seemed interested. Most importantly, they kept the wine industry alive during Prohibition, since they simply could not imagine having a meal without wine.

❖

When Italian chef Joseph Coppa opened a restaurant where wine was unlabeled and free with dinner, it quickly turned into the Bohemian hangout, where Gelett Burgess and other founders of *The Lark,* a San Francisco literary journal, congregated. Coppa fell victim to the earthquake but food and wine in San Francisco did not. Before Prohibition in 1918, most of the Wine Country's wine was bottled in San Francisco. During Prohibition, the city took the bulk of the Wine Country's grapes for "home winemaking." After Repeal in 1933, San Franciscans were among the first to drink California wine—with plenty of advice on how to improve the product.

Harvest day, late 19th century.

A grape harvest of an early vintage.

■ CULINARY DARK AGES

In 1935, native San Franciscan Alice B. Toklas, who had lived in France since before World War I, accompanied her companion Gertrude Stein (who grew up in Oakland) on a lecture tour through the United States. Stein's main concern was food. "Would it be to her taste?" Toklas wrote in *The Alice B. Toklas Cookbook*. As it turned out, the two expatriates ate very well, especially after they reached California. In Monterey they ate abalone for the first time and found it delicious. They appreciated the simple preparation—in a cream sauce in its shell, lightly browned with bread crumbs without cheese. Toklas said, "Abalone has a delicate flavor of its own and requires no barbecue or barbarous adjunct." (Today, abalone is one of the special dishes of the Sonoma Wine Country.) In San Francisco, Toklas and Stein:

> . . . *I*ndulged in gastronomic orgies—sand dabs meuniére, rainbow trout in aspic, grilled soft-shell crabs, paupiettes of roast fillets of pork, eggs Rossini and tarte Chambord. The tarte Chambord had been a specialty of one of the three great French bakers before the San Francisco fire. To my surprise in Paris no one had heard of it.

Toklas does not discuss California wine—not even when she and Stein drive to the Wine Country: "At Fisherman's Wharf we waited for two enormous crabs to be cooked in cauldrons on the side-walk, and they were still quite warm when we ate them at lunch in Napa County." It's not surprising, of course, that wine was not mentioned: the trip took place two years after Repeal, when California wineries were just beginning the struggle to reestablish themselves as premium producers. And local wine was shipped out in barrels, and rarely sold by the bottle in small-town grocery stores.

❖

Even during pioneer days, city folk had easy access to an abundance of local and imported foods. But life was much simpler on Wine Country farms. Living on a ranch outside Healdsburg, old-timer Fritz Kennedy recalls in *I Remember . . . Healdsburg*:

> *We* had everything on the ranch. It was completely self-sufficient. We had prunes, grapes, berries, a large garden, every fruit tree and animals galore—pigs, cattle, sheep, horses, rabbits, turkeys, chickens, ducks, geese and even pigeons. Of course we had a smoke-house and brooder house too. Any time of the year my mother could gather food and feed us and guests. . . . My dad used to haul our grapes to the Red Winery which was . . . the third largest winery in the state.

It seems that the American farms of the period were just as independent in matters of food as the mission ranchos had been earlier in the century. Even large winery estates, like that of the de Latours, who owned Beaulieu, had extensive kitchen gardens and orchards for supplying the kitchen.

Latin-Mediterranean tradition in California was never as "pure" as Mediterranean cooking in the Old Country. Other influences, first from southern China, then (in the second half of the 20th century) from Thailand and other southeast Asian countries, had an impact because many of the tropical and sub-tropical ingredients used in these cuisines adapted well to California, and many of California's Mediterranean ingredients—like peppers and eggplants—were shared by cooks from both cultures. Rice had been carried from East Asia to the Mediterranean by medieval traders, and now California became a preeminent rice growing region; thus rice was integrated most naturally into the local cuisine.

Vegetables have always flourished in the region's valleys.

At the end of the 1945 United Nations Conference in San Francisco, 350 Latin-American delegates and their wives were invited to the Sonoma Wine Country at the request of Mrs. Oliver Grant, representative of the San Francisco branch of the Pan-American League. After welcoming speeches in the Sonoma Plaza, the delegation moved to the Sebastiani winery, where (according to novelist Gertrude Atherton) "canapés and rare California wines were served, unlimited cigars given to the men, and lovely corsages to the ladies. In small groups the entire party was taken through the winery and presented with especially labeled bottles of finest sauterne and Burgundy."

After that the delegates headed for the Jack London Ranch which for the occasion was guarded by "jeeps with antiaircraft guns [which] had been stationed at various spots on the hillside surrounding the ranch." Here they were served quite a meal. The silver had been borrowed from the Memorial Opera House Conference canteen, "the women of Sonoma had sent their finest linen, and the Sonoma Chamber of Commerce had furnished the cooks and the food, built the tables and the huge barbecue pit. The luncheon consisted of a fruit cup, barbecued chicken, vegetables, salads, ice cream, coffee, milk, red and white wines and beer."

■ MEDITERRANEAN RENAISSANCE

Restaurant food in the California Wine Country did not change significantly until the 1960s, when the back-to-the-land movement permanently changed the way Californians looked at food. People who had been perfectly happy subsisting on hamburgers and fried chicken rediscovered local foods—preferably organically grown. Because of California's unique climate, these proved to be Mediterranean, and cooking styles adapted to make the most of these fresh ingredients. The movement found its high priestess in Alice Waters, who by her own confession read *Larousse Gastronomique* and decided California food was Provençal by nature, if not outright Mediterranean. She opened a restaurant to spread the gospel, and the rest is history. The cooking styles pioneered in Waters's Berkeley restaurant, Chez Panisse, were admired and replicated throughout the Wine Country, in part because so many chefs who'd been trained in Waters's kitchens later opened restaurants of their own.

Most importantly, the locally produced foods which inspired the chefs turned them toward a Mediterranean style of cooking. The wines changed from the predominantly sweet styles that were in vogue until the 1960s, and were hard to match to any food, to the dry wines we are so familiar with now. The wines changed again, but this time in harmony with food. As Wine Country food became more hearty, "earthy," in a Mediterranean fashion, so did the wines. They became heartier to match the food—that is, wineries increasingly produced Rhone blends instead of cabernet; marsanne and viognier instead of riesling or chenin blanc; sangiovese instead of gamay.

The new Wine Country cookery is more down to earth than the style the French call "haute cuisine," yet it has too many fancy touches and complex flavors to be classified as "bourgeois." Perhaps this is what makes it so "Tuscan," since Tuscan cookery is a style based on simplicity as well as on perfectly fresh ingredients at their peak of flavor. A good example of this evolution is Philippe Jeaunty, chef at Yountville's Domaine Chandon restaurant, who was trained in France in the classical tradition but has changed to a sunnier style under the influence of northern California food products.

Domaine Chandon began a new trend in 1977 by opening a restaurant in its winery. But other chefs had flocked to the Napa Valley before, to explore wineries as well as local foods. Some of these chefs, with national or international reputations, were invited by wineries like Robert Mondavi or Beringer to cook meals for special occasions, to teach classes, or to lecture on food and wine.

The most prominent chef who decided to stay was French-trained cooking teacher Madeleine Kamman, who has written several books and has a PBS cooking show. After settling in the Napa Valley in the late 1980s, she opened a School for American Chefs at Beringer Vineyards, where she teaches her students the importance of working with the foods the land produces and of matching those foods to local wines. Kamman links California's Wine Country cooking to Mediterranean styles, because of its climate and food products. Her classes start with a lecture on climate and a tour of vineyards, where students literally grasp the soil and study the vines, and stress the importance of food and wine harmonies throughout each course. Through her students and their happy dining-room customers, Kamman has done more than anyone else to spread the Napa Valley's reputation as one of the nation's top food and wine regions. Her courses predate, by almost a decade, the classes taught at the new Culinary Institute of America campus that opened in St. Helena's old Greystone Winery building in the fall of 1995.

Kamman emphasizes "simple" cooking, without fancy touches that do nothing to improve a dish. With that approach, she has put her finger right on the pulse of Wine Country cooking trends. Simple foods not only go well with wine, they go with a variety of different wines. Yet this simplicity does not translate into dull or simple-minded food. Our cooks have become more accomplished over the years, as they learned about the complexities of local foods and wines. By relying on the best and freshest of local products, cooks—whether they work in a home kitchen or in a restaurant—do not have to overly season their dishes to give them flavor but can let the natural savor of the ingredients speak for themselves.

Some restaurant chefs create their own, high-quality ingredients, as for example Michael Chiarello of St. Helena's Tra Vigne restaurant, who produces his own Italian-style cheeses, sausages, and prosciutto from local raw materials. Others, like Fred Halpert of the Napa Valley's Brava Terrace restaurant, grow fresh herbs in the restaurant garden or, like Mark Dierkhising at Calistoga's All Seasons Restaurant and Wine Shop, contract with specialty produce growers for the best and most flavorful vegetables.

■ COOKING WITH WINE

The flavors of herbs and vegetables are tremendously important in Wine Country cookery—as any Provençal or Tuscan chef will affirm—for they enhance the savor of fish, fowl, and meat. Whether they are parsley or thyme, celery, onions, or carrots, they give structure to stocks and sauces and bring out hidden flavor nuances. With their help, a very simply constructed dish can have very complex layers of flavors—if it contains the proper and properly matched seasoning herbs and vegetables. These help match it not just to one wine, but to several different wines, allowing, for example, zinfandel or merlot to go with lamb, whether it be rack of lamb with cilantro pesto, or just plain lamb chops.

You can determine, to some extent, what wine will go with a certain dish by cooking it in a particular wine or by making adjustments to the stock. If beef, for example, is stewed in chicken stock instead of a deeply flavored beef stock, it may go well with a rich chardonnay or sauvignon blanc. Alsatians traditionally accompany beef with a glass of dry riesling or even gewürztraminer. Oysters—whether raw or cooked—are enhanced by crisp, bone-dry white wines, whether those be chardonnays, rieslings, or sauvignon blancs. Salmon cooked in pinot noir can be accompanied by that red wine.

If you use a little cabernet or merlot in making a chocolate cake, you will be surprised how well such a tannic red goes with chocolate. Almost any dessert is enhanced by being cooked in a full-flavored, sweet dessert riesling or sauternes-style semillon or sauvignon blanc. Pears and sweet riesling are a particularly satisfying match. Vegetables benefit, too, from a touch of wine. Wine—either red or white—does marvels for stir-fried chicken, helping to give flavor to as well as tenderizing chicken or turkey breast. In other words, wine used in cooking is as versatile as your culinary imagination allows you to be. But whether or not you use wine in cooking a dish, keep in mind that the traditional matchings—red wine with red meats, white wine with fish, fowl, or white meats—work very well with French wines but do not fully explore the versatility of California wines.

■ MATCHING FOOD AND WINE

In California Wine Country cooking, merlot or cabernet sauvignon may accompany rare-grilled ahi or yellowfin tuna, steaks of oak-grilled beef or venison, or be reserved for the cheese course. Duck, in different preparations, is often served with

The pleasures of a cozy fire, fine food, and an excellent wine!

merlot, especially in Sonoma County, where duck and merlot are becoming a classic match. But duck also goes well with zinfandel, which is a truly adaptable wine. Wineries have served their zinfandel with spit-roasted wild boar, with grilled beef marinated in ginger wine sauce, with sausages, with a simple dish of arugula, pears, and cheese, with ripe tomatoes, fresh mozzarella, and basil (which Italians accompany with Chianti), and with duck salad.

Cabernet sauvignon may accompany a variety of beef dishes, or be served with veal, and even with roasted or grilled pigeons. But, more often than not, in these less-meat days, it may be served with the cheese course. Pinot noir is sometimes matched to suckling pig, to fresh ahi tuna, and to lamb. It is a versatile wine, for it holds up to grilled salmon, can bring out the flavor nuances of duck burgers (topped with red pepper mayonnaise), and stand up to a soba noodle and seafood salad. It also goes well with grilled chicken—as do riesling and chardonnay.

In the Wine Country, chardonnay is often served with seafood, but it has been matched to chilled lemon cucumber soup, to stuffed breast of veal with salsa verde, to Sonoma County cheeses and figs, to sushi, and to won ton crab sandwiches. But another wine that goes even better with crab and other seafoods is sauvignon blanc (as well as its bone-dry incarnation, fumé blanc). Sauvignon blanc, straight or blended with semillon in the Bordeaux fashion, can enhance crab cakes with a sundried tomato and cilantro aioli, salmon cakes with tomatillo salsa, and has even held up to glazed pork loin with chorizo and pine nut stuffing (though the latter dish had a choice of zinfandel as an alternate wine selection). Sauvignon blanc is the Wine Country's best white food wine, far better than chardonnay, since its multiple, complex flavors go well with almost any food from plain goat cheese to coulibiac of salmon or beef stew. Zinfandel is the Wine Country's most versatile—and thus most successful—red food wine.

Other successful food and wine match-ups include a mousse of Sonoma foie gras with a rosé, blue corn cakes with Sonoma jack cheese and tobiko caviar with a blanc de blancs bubbly, smoked salmon and golden caviar cake, also with a sparkling wine, as well as saltimbocca and sangiovese, which works as well in Sonoma County as it does in Tuscany. Gewürztraminer, such as the one produced by Husch Vineyards in Anderson Valley, makes a fine complement to spicy oriental foods such as Thai cuisine.

■ LA VITA RUSTICANA: PICNICS

I cooked hotdogs on freshly cut and sharpened sticks over the coals of a big wood fire, and heated a can of beans and a can of cheese macaroni in the redhot hollows, and drank my newly bought wine, and exulted in one of the most pleasant nights of my life.

—*Jack Kerouac*

You don't have to cook a fancy meal or go to a restaurant to experience the joys of the Wine Country's foods and wines, however. Enjoying wine with a simple meal of bread, cheese, and dry sausage—under sunny skies—is an old tradition. M. F. K. Fisher recalled in "Wine Is Life," an introductory essay she wrote for *The Book of California Wine,* how, as a child, she drove to small wineries with her father:

> The ranchers always seemed glad when we drove up their roads in our open Model-T. The women would put tumblers and a long loaf of their last baking, and cheese or a dry sausage, on the kitchen table or under the grape arbor out back. When the men came with two or three bottles from the old barn or hillside cellar where the casks were stored, they would eat and try the wines and talk.

You can have a similar experience at wineries that have picnic areas where you can sit down for a comfortable meal of wine with food. Some wineries have their own well-stocked delis, like Viansa in the Carneros (Tuscan specialties and sangiovese), Buena Vista in Sonoma (Carneros cabernet sauvignon with bread and cheese), and V. Sattui in the Napa Valley (cabernet sauvignon, bread, and cheese). Or, you can also stock up at a Wine Country delicatessen for your picnic, drive to a winery for a bottle of wine, settle in the shade of a tree and enjoy your meal. (Etiquette requires that if you use a winery's picnic grounds, you must buy their wine.) Following are a few suggestions for al fresco dining.

Zinfandel Lane Picnic. In the lower Napa Valley, the Oakville Grocery has the widest selection of foods; *7856 St. Helena Highway, Oakville.* Drive to **Raymond Winery**, buy a bottle of their wine (as is required and polite) and enjoy their picnic area. As you drive down Zinfandel Lane, make a mental note to expand your experience of zinfandel by trying the deep, complex, and very elegant zins produced by **Robert Biale Vineyards**. At this time there is no tasting room, but to get on the mailing list call 707-257-7555 .

Eating al fresco *at Vichon winery, a popular picnic spot.*

Napa Valley Views Picnic. For picnic supplies, drop in at the venerable Napa Valley Olive Oil Mfg. Co. at Charter Oak and Allison avenues in St. Helena (a few blocks east of CA 29) for bread, cheese, dry salami, and great olives (or try the splendid new Dean & DeLuca store on Highway 29 a mile and a half south of downtown). Then drive to Rutherford Hill Winery (take Allison to Pope Street, turn right on the Silverado Trail, left at Rutherford Hill) and enjoy the views across the Napa Valley from the shade of the olive grove while sipping a glass of merlot.

Sage Canyon Picnic. On a weekend, you might want to drive up CA 128 past Lake Hennessey to Nichelini Winery in Sage Canyon, buy a bottle of crisp sauvignon vert, and enjoy it with your food in the idyllic picnic area.

Trail or Mountain Picnic. In the northern Napa Valley, the Palisades Market in downtown Calistoga has the best selection of picnic supplies. Hike out of town on the Oat Hill Trail for a picnic in the hills, drive to the trail head on Mount St. Helena, or reserve a picnic island with Chinese pavilion at Chateau Montelena and enjoy the winery's lovely cabernet sauvignon with your meal (you'll need to make reservations at least two months ahead of time).

Picnicking at Chateau St. Jean.

Alexander Valley Picnic. Drive east on CA 128 to the Alexander Valley, buy a bottle of zinfandel at Sausal Winery, and picnic on the winery's vine-shaded patio.

Sonoma Picnic. In Sonoma, stock up on everything at the Sonoma Cheese Factory at the north side of the plaza, then head for Gundlach-Bundschu Winery, one of Sonoma's favorite picnic places. Or drive up the valley to Chateau St. Jean to picnic on the lawn, accompanied by a bottle of chardonnay.

Russian River Picnic. In Healdsburg, buy your picnic bread at the Downtown Bakery and Creamery and get the toppings a few steps away at the Salame Tree Deli. Then drive on Westside Road into the Russian River Valley to picnic at Rochioli Vineyards with a bottle of sauvignon blanc or pinot noir. The Hop Kiln Winery next door also has a picnic ground, but the views across the Russian River Valley vineyards are a lot better at Rochioli.

Dry Creek Picnic. In the Dry Creek Valley, stop at the Dry Creek Store for picnic supplies or sandwiches (if you eat small portions, one sandwich is enough for two), then take the short dogleg up Lambert Bridge Road to Dry Creek Vineyard where you can picnic under shady trees with a bottle of chenin blanc or zinfandel.

■ SONOMA COUNTY FOOD

■ CHEESES

Several excellent cheeses are made here. Petaluma's **Bellwether Farms** is the only sheep dairy in California. On the farm, a 34-acre sheep ranch near Valley Ford in coastal Sonoma County, Cindy Callahan and her son, Liam, make some very tasty sheep-milk cheeses. Currently, these include a Tuscan-style pecorino—which comes in plain, smoked, and peppercorn-laced versions—and a small quantity of roblar and ricotta. Callahan studied cheesemaking at Washington State University and in Tuscany. Had she gone to Roquefort too, even more exciting things might be happening. Bellwether Farms cheeses are served by San Francisco Bay Area restaurants and can be found at several farmers markets: Marin (Thursdays), St. Helena (Fridays), and San Francisco Ferry Plaza (Saturdays). For information about the cheeses, contact Cindy Callahan at *Bellwether Farms, 9999 Valley Ford Road, Petaluma; (707) 763-0993.*

An elegant luncheon at Auberge du Soleil on a terrace overlooking the Napa Valley. (Kerrick James)

Redwood Hill Farm of Sebastopol makes a traditional chevre from goats' milk, a goats' milk feta, and a goats' milk yogurt. There's nothing very distinctive about these cheeses, but Redwood Hill also sells a sharp and a smoked goats' milk cheddar—made by another Sonoma County cheesemaker—that's very special and goes beautifully with aged Sonoma County red wines.

Bodega Goat Cheese makes Peruvian-style goat cheeses from the milk of Sonoma County goats: queso fresco, a feta-style cheese, queso crema, a cream cheese with a lot more flavor than the run-of-the-mill chevre, as well as a ricotta-style queso ranchero, a rennetless cheese that comes in six (!) flavors—plain, basil, green onion, cilantro, jalapeño, and dill. (For information, contact Javier and Patty Salmon in Bodega; *(707) 876-3483.)*

■ VEGETABLES

Mediterranean vegetables on sale at local farmers markets include an incredibly varied array of greens, eggplants, and peppers. At the height of the tomato season, this delectable fruit—vine-ripened, of course—comes in a number of incarnations: slicer, cherry, currant, ruffled, round, pear-shaped; red, orange, yellow—and green. These are not the kind of unripe tomato you'd use to make a dish of fried green tomatoes. These green globes are ripe, with all the flavor of the fully mature fruit. **The Farmery,** which provides some of these tomatoes, also grows pink, white, black, and purple tomatoes. Look for their produce in your market and if this really intrigues you, contact Leonard Diggs at The Farmery, Inc.; *875 River Road, Fulton, (707) 546-3276.*

■ OLIVE OILS

Olives were first brought to California by Spanish padres in the 18th century and planted around their missions. Since then, California olive oil has been made from "cooking oil" olives like the mission or manzanilla. But California is about to undergo an olive oil revolution. Among the fine locally produced olive oils are the oil made from Provençal picholine olives by **B. R. Cohn Winery** in the Sonoma Valley, as well as the experimental 1994 Dry Creek Valley extra virgin olive oil from Toscana Sonoma, Inc., sold under the name **DaVero**. Starting in 1990, Toscana has imported some 3,000 Italian olive trees of the varieties that have made olive oil

The production of gourmet olive oils in Napa Valley has been keeping pace with wine production in recent years.

Ridgley Evers and Colleen McGlyn (above) of Toscana Sonoma proudly display a bottle of their DaVero olive oil.

from Lucca justly famous: leccino, frantoio, maurino, and pendolino. Initial pressings from the as yet very young trees show promise. While the oil does not yet have the depth and complex structure of its Italian model, it's quite definitely on the way. Toscana is not alone in its exploration of oil produced by high- quality olive trees.

The Olive Press is an olive oil shop with an olive press. Not only does it offer a great variety of locally produced olive oils for sale, but the shop organizes several community olive pressings each fall (for a small charge). People from as far away as San Jose have brought their olives for pressing. A local innkeeper who participated was able to harvest only 18 olives from his tree, but they were pressed just the same as the bigger lots. *14301 Arnold Drive, Glen Ellen, 707-939-8900.*

Farther north in the Dry Creek Valley, Lou Preston at **Preston Vineyards** is experimenting with plantings of imported trees, and Michael **Schlumberger,** southeast of Preston, has olive groves as well. Across the ridge to the east, Tom Jordan at **Jordan Winery** has planted some 1,500 Italian olive trees in the hills south of his Alexander Valley winery; and **Trentadue** is also growing olives.

Finger-food at an olive oil tasting at B. R. Cohn Winery.

■ FARMS TO VISIT

Many farms welcome travelers, allowing them to experience the bounty firsthand. You can get a map listing more than a hundred specialty producers and their specialties by sending a self-addressed, stamped envelope with 55¢ postage to *Sonoma County Farm Trails, P.O. Box 6032, Santa Rosa, CA 95406*, or pick up this map free at any Sonoma County Chamber of Commerce or Visitors Center. To learn about what products are in season and which farms carry them, call the Visitors Information Center at *(707) 523-8075* on a touchtone phone, enter 1058, and listen to the message.

GRATON

Walker Apples
Lee & Shirley Walker
P.O. Box 220
(707) 823-4310
At the end of a half-mile scenic dirt road; 23 varieties of apples. Their motto: "Try before you buy." Open daily August to November.

HEALDSBURG

Westside Farms
Pam & Ron Kaiser
7097 Westside Rd.
(707) 431-1432
This is the place the locals swear by: perfect produce, fresh and dried flowers, and pumpkins in October. There are also farm animals for children to pet and hay rides during the annual October celebration. Also open to the public in June for self-serve berry picking.

Dry Creek Peach & Produce
2179 Yoakim Bridge Rd.
(707) 433-7016
Tree-ripened peaches, nectarines, and apricots. Apples, plums, melons, strawberries, white corn, red and yellow tomatoes, sweet onions, and more. June—Labor Day: Open Tuesday—Sunday.

SEBASTOPOL

Foxglove Farm
5280 Gravenstein Hwy. North
(707) 887-2759
Organically grown vegetables and fruits, including sweet corn, green beans, tomatoes, basil, squash, figs, Gravenstein and other apples. Victorian gifts and country crafts. July to October: open Thursday to Tuesday; November to last week before Christmas: open Thursday to Sunday; closed January to June.

Luther Burbank's "Gold Ridge" Experiment Farm
Western Sonoma County Historical Society
7781 Bodega Ave.
(707) 829-6711
Docent or self-guided tours of the farm and cottage. Sales of Burbank's plant and fruit creations. Open April to October by appointment.

SANTA ROSA

Joe Matos Cheese Factory
Joe & Mary Matos
3669 Llano Rd.
(707) 584-5283
Joe Matos produces a splendid Portuguese Queso São Jorge at his rustic farm hidden at the end of a country lane. This semisoft cheese is made from raw, cultured milk and aged for 60 days. It comes in wheels. Open all year, daily.

Mom's Head Gardens
Vivien Hill Grove & Karen Brocco
4153 Langner Ave.
(707) 585-8575

Registered organic nursery specializing in medicinal herbs from folklore. Over 150 varieties. Herb garden. April to October: open Thursday and Friday afternoons, but call ahead.

Willie Bird Turkeys
5350 Highway 12
(707) 545-2832
If you're tired of supermarket turkey, this is the place for you. Pick your turkey fresh, ground, or smoked, as sausage or steak. Open all year, Monday through Saturday.

A favorite summer outing: visiting the farm. (Library of Congress)

RESTAURANTS

And we meet, with champagne and a chicken, at last.
—Lady Margaret Wortley Montagu, 1689–1744

WINE COUNTRY DINING DID NOT BECOME a world-class experience until 1977, when Domaine Chandon opened a restaurant in its new sparkling wine facility in Yountville. Auberge de Soleil followed, with the inspired cooking of the late, and much lamented, Masa Kobayashi, and other restaurants followed in its wake, most notably: Mustard's Grill, Trilogy, Terra, All Seasons Cafe, Brava Terrace, and The French Laundry. At first, Sonoma County lagged behind Napa, but soon caught up, with places like John Ash & Co., and the restaurant at Chateau Souverain. Today, dining in the Wine Country is more exciting than ever, with many different restaurants and types of cuisine to choose and pick from. Almost every Wine Country town, small or large, has at least one decent Mexican or Asian (more often than not, Thai) restaurant to choose from, as well as an assortment of steak houses and hamburger places. Here are some restaurants I have enjoyed over the years, with a star [★] marking the ones I've enjoyed the most:

> *P*rices per person, without wine or tip:
> $ = less than $10; $$ = $10–$20; $$$ = $20–$30; $$$$ = over $30

■ NAPA VALLEY

★ **Alexis Baking Company.** 1517 Third St., Napa; (707) 258-1827 $
You don't go to this downtown neighborhood cafe for the atmosphere, but for great hamburgers, sandwiches, tacos, and pasta salads. The "ABC" is very popular with locals, though one friend complains she can never go there for lunch because she runs into so many friends she ends up talking instead of eating.

★ **All Seasons Cafe & Wine Shop.** 1400 Lincoln Ave., Calistoga; (707) 942-9111 $$
If there is a perfect Wine Country cafe where visitors mingle with winemakers over tasty food and local wines, this cafe/wine shop is it. The freshest of local food products are used in these dishes, yet meals are quite inexpensive. You can accompany your soups, salads, pastas, pizzas, or sandwiches with wines from

one of the region's most complete wine lists. If you're not sure about which wine to enjoy with your dinner, this is the place for you: the menu is built around wine recommendations. You can also buy a special bottle at the wine shop and, for a corkage fee, pour it at your table.

☆ **Ana's Cantina.** 1205 Main St. (CA 29), St. Helena; (707) 963-4921 **$**
Beer, rather than wine, is the beverage of choice at this Mexican cantina in downtown St. Helena on a sweltering summer evening. But it's a place where locals hang out, obeying the old saying that "it takes a lot of beer to make good wine." The food is simple Mexican *campesino* fare, but the burritos, tacos, and enchiladas are uncommonly tasty.

Auberge du Soleil. 180 Rutherford Hill Rd., St. Helena; (707) 963-1211 **$$$$**
An elegant restaurant in an spiffy hillside resort that sometimes achieves the greatness it was once known for. Dishes have recently ranged from cioppino to Dungeness crab toast, from shaved Smithfield ham with corn pudding to grilled New Zealand venison rack with sweet potato rosti and Oregon huckleberries. But never mind the food; the view is as great as ever. *(Photo page 243)*

Bistro Don Giovanni. 4110 St. Helena Hwy., Napa; (707) 224-3300 **$$**
This California-Italian-style bistro-trattoria near La Residence *(see page 264)* has some of the best California-Italian food in the valley, with such delights as

BISTRO DON GIOVANNI

Mediterranean chicken salad (grilled chicken breast, spinach, romaine, avocado, and sweet pepper relish with Roquefort vinaigrette), warm calamari, or spaghetti and clams. There's also braised lamb shank with Tuscan white beans, house-made ravioli, and pizza, plus other pastas and specials.

☆ **Brava Terrace.** 3010 St. Helena Hwy. N., St. Helena; (707) 963-9300 **$$$**
Chef/owner Fred Halpert trained in Provence, and you can most certainly taste the Mediterranean sun in his exuberant dishes, which make creative use of the best and freshest of local ingredients and are seasoned with herbs from the restaurant's garden. In summer, you

BRAVA TERRACE

can dine outside on the restaurant's shady patio; in winter you can snuggle up to the fireplace. Great food and attentive service make this one of the Wine Country's great restaurants.

Catahoula Restaurant & Saloon. 1457 Lincoln Ave., Calistoga; (707) 942-2275 **$$$**
Chef Jan Birnbaum cooks unabashedly Louisiana-style food that tastes great but does not go well with the local wines, unless you're willing to settle for generic red or white. The restaurant has been billed as a refuge from wine snobs.

Celadon. 1040 Main St., Suite 104, Napa; (707) 254-9690 **$$$**
This small, intimate restaurant is tucked into a quiet downtown nook above Napa Creek near its junction with the Napa River. (Enter the parking area from Pearl Street and take the foot bridge across the creek to the restaurant.) The food, flawless California cuisine with Asian touches is produced in an amazingly tiny kitchen. Locals love the frog legs. Be sure to make reservations as the restaurant is very popular.

Compadres Mexican Bar & Grill. 6539 Washington St., Yountville; (707) 944-2406 **$$**
This is a simple restaurant with good Mexican food and great margaritas. Highlights of the menu include seafood tacos, green corn tamales, and carnitas. One word of caution: If you're dining outside and the oranges on the trees in the garden are ripe, beware. Squirrels have been known to toss the fruit at unsuspecting diners.

The Diner. 6476 Washington St., Yountville; (707) 944-2626 **$$**
Legendary for serving great breakfasts.

✿ **Domaine Chandon.** One California Drive, Yountville; (707) 944-2892 **$$$$**
It may seem impossible for a restaurant to start with perfection and maintain its high level of quality for two decades, but that's what the restaurant at Domaine Chandon did, with Philippe Jeanty in the kitchen. A new chef, Robert Curry, known for his interesting approach to modern French cooking took over the kitchen in 1997. We expect him to maintain the high standards established by Jeanty. Time—and tasting—will tell. In the meantime, settle down, and enjoy the food with L'Etoile, the winery's premium bubbly. In warm weather you can dine outside on the terrace and enjoy the birds singing in the oak trees. The

DOMAINE CHANDON

restaurant's service is impeccable, and the wine list is among the region's best.

French Laundry Restaurant. 6640 Washington St., Yountville; (707) 944-2380 $$$$

Chef/owner Thomas Keller has brought French food back to a valley increasingly dominated by sunnier fare. Set in an old stone house with a courtyard in the center, the French Laundry was described in the *New York Times* "Critic's Notebook" as "the most exciting place to eat in the United States."

Gillwoods. 1313 Main St., St. Helena; (707) 963-1788 $

This plain, storefront restaurant proves that you can eat well—and very cheaply—even in the heart of St. Helena, which is perhaps why locals like to hang out here. The food is basic American fare: pancakes, scrambles, omelets, and other egg dishes for breakfast, burgers and sandwiches for lunch, the same for dinner, except for specials. There's a limited wine list. But it's all very well prepared and proves that plain American cooking can hold its own even in the heart of the wine country.

Gordon's Cafe and Wine Bar. 6770 Washington St., Yountville; (707) 944-8246 $ -$$

This pleasant, very relaxed restaurant/ gourmet food and wine shop occupies the 1876 Yountville General Store, a clapboard building that has aged gracefully. The shop and restaurant occupy a large room, with a serving bar off to the side. Breakfast and lunch daily; dinner Friday evenings only. The menu includes such delectable breakfast items as housemade granola and freshly baked muffins and scones. For lunch you can pick from an assortment of salads and sandwiches. Dinners include such fare as wild mushroom ragout, roast pork loin, grilled swordfish, and fresh Dungeness crab.

The Grill at Meadowood. 900 Meadowood Lane, St. Helena; (707) 963-3646 $–$$

In decor, this bright cafe epitomizes the understated elegance of Meadowood Resort. The food has a vaguely California-French tenor, and dishes tend to be on the light side. A separate spa menu is available from which you can diet on such sumptuous fare as lamb chops, potatoes, and green beans with mustard-herb juice or steamed clams and mussels with peppers, white wine, garlic, and herbs, and still stay below 400 calories. Every afternoon, an English tea is served on the terrace with house-made scones and finger sandwiches. At night, the **Restaurant at Meadowood** above the grill serves sumptuous four-course dinners, with four choices per course. Service at Meadowood is about as good as it gets. The bar serves great martinis.

★ **Mustard's Grill.** 7399 St. Helena Hwy., Yountville; (707) 944-2424 $$$

This busy—often noisy—restaurant serves American comfort food with a California twist or two from its big open

MUSTARD'S GRILL

kitchen. The dishes are country fare: grilled rabbit, tender pork chops, mesquite-grilled seafood and duck, as well as very good salads and soups. The food is very popular because it's basically a form of mom's homecooking raised to the level of haute cuisine. The international wine list groups wines by variety rather than country of origin. Service is fast and efficient. Best of all, while everyone always seems to be rushing about, no one ever rushes you. Be sure to make reservations or you may have a long wait.

Old Adobe Bar & Grille. 376 Soscol Ave., Napa; (707) 255-4310 $$$
This is not the Napa Valley's greatest food, but its unique historical setting in Napa's oldest adobe, dating from the 1840s, is of interest.

Pairs Parkside Cafe. 1420 Main St., St. Helena; (707) 963-7566 $$-$$$
This small cafe, run by two CIA (Culinary Institute of America) graduates, has captured the heart of the locals because it's rarely crowded and the food is very good. Their style is "Cal-Asian" and the selection is eclectic: try such delicacies as vegetable spring rolls, fried calamari with fennel and lemon, and ahi tuna with soba noodles. The name Pairs reflects the owners' helpful recommendations, which pair each dish with a complementary wine.

Pearl. 1339 Pearl Street, Napa; (707) 224-9161 $$$
This casual, upscale restaurant serves some of the best food in the lower Napa Valley. Among the menu highlights are fresh Tomales Bay oysters, a marvelous smoked chicken and roasted pasilla quesadilla, mouth-watering soft tacos filled with chopped ginger flank steak, chiles, cilantro, and onion, and accompanied by a beautifully smooth and spicy guacamole; and fresh fish cooked to perfection. Best of all, you can call ahead, and order the food to be taken out—for the perfect Wine Country picnic.

River City. 505 Lincoln Ave., Napa; (707) 253-1111 $$
Every place ought to have a restaurant overlooking water, and this is Napa's version of a steak and seafood house on the river. It's especially interesting because many visitors are unaware that the Napa River runs through town and that, due to the influence of tidewater, it is much broader here than it is up-valley (steamboats once docked here, at the head of navigation).

Showley's at Miramonte. 1327 Railroad Ave., St. Helena; (707) 963-1200 $$$

This homey dining room in a 19th-century hotel building serves very good food in a somewhat eclectic vein. For appetizers, the signature dishes are stuffed pasilla peppers or house-smoked sturgeon. Try wild mushrooms in a pinot noir butter sauce. For the main course, choose from pork tenderloin, steak, lamb, duck, or fresh seafood. Breads are baked fresh twice daily. On warm nights you can dine under the fig tree in the courtyard and, yes, there are fig dishes in season.

Spring Street Restaurant. 1245 Spring St., St. Helena; (707) 963-5578 **$$**

This homey bungalow serves great, home-style meals in a very comfortable atmosphere. Since Roy Breiman, former chef at Meadowood, has taken over, dishes have become more subtle and elegant than those served at the "old" Spring Street.

☆ **Terra Restaurant.** 1345 Railroad Ave., St. Helena; (707) 963-8931 **$$$**

This comfortable, friendly restaurant serves truly great food in the converted work room of a stone-walled turn-of-the-century foundry. Chef Hiro Sone (formerly of Los Angeles's Spago) goes in for a vaguely southern French/Northern Italian style of cookery with all sorts of unexpected Asian twists that make his dishes truly delightful. He has a light hand with sweetbreads and just the right touch with quail, which may come deep-fried with a golden glaze that makes the skin alone worthy of Lucullus. He achieves hard-to-master East-West harmonies other chefs vainly strive for. Seasoning is very accomplished, assuring that the dishes go well with local wines. The wine list has some older, very hard-to-find Napa Valley bottlings.

Tomatina. 1016 Main St., St. Helena; (707) 967-9999 **$**

This family restaurant (brought to you by the same folks who created Mustard's and Tra Vigne) is popular with locals because the food is both good and inexpensive. It's also fast—you order at the counter and pick a table. Favorites include minestrone, tomato salad, the thin-crust pizzas, and pasta dishes. Don't worry if there's a line out the door: things move very quickly here. Besides small, private tables, there are also long European-style communal tables. In sunny weather you can sit outside in the courtyard. You can't miss the place: its sign sports a big red tomato.

☆ **Tra Vigne Restaurant.** 1050 Charter Oak Ave., St. Helena; (707) 963-4444 **$$$**

It's hard to say whether this restaurant is most appealing in spring, when the wild-

TRA VIGNE RESTAURANT

flowers in the small vineyard out front are in full bloom, or on a rainy winter day, when the bright decor and friendly staff are sure to take the chill from your bones. The food has California-Mediterranean's good flavors and textures. The wine list is divided between California and Italy, with some hard-to-find bottlings from small wineries.

Trilogy. 1234 Main St., St. Helena; (707) 963-5507 $$$$
A lovely restaurant. Chef Diane Pariseau has an especially deft but delicate touch with chicken and seafood. Dinners are three-course *prix fixe* only. The wine list for the restaurant and at the wine bar is among the valley's best, including 650 wines. Reservations recommended.

✯ **Wappo Bar & Bistro.** 1226 Washington St., Calistoga; (707) 942-4712 $$
The menu at this comfortable restaurant is eclectic, ranging from fish tacos to a steak sandwich with aioli, but the flavors are rustic Mediterranean. Portions are more than ample—order one dish at a

time. In warm weather, try to snag a table under the vine-covered trellis of the patio.

Wine Spectator Greystone Restaurant. 2555 Main St. (Hwy. 29), St. Helena; (707) 967-1010 $$
When this restaurant opened at the Culinary Institute of America's St. Helena campus a couple of years ago, there was talk that it might become the new culinary trendsetter for Napa Valley food. It didn't. Reviews have, in fact, been somewhat mixed. But the restaurant seems to have found its stride with broad-based Mediterranean cookery matched to local wines.

Wine Train of Napa Valley. 1275 McKinstry St., Napa; (707) 253-2111 $$$$
A restaurant that won't hold still while you eat. During lunch or dinner it chugs from Napa to St. Helena and back, through industrial neighborhoods and past wineries, but doesn't stop to let you taste local bottlings.

❖   ❖   ❖   ❖   ❖

■ SONOMA COUNTY

Applewood (restaurant). 13555 Highway 116, Guerneville (707) 869-9093 $$$$-
A very comfortable place just south of the Russian River (and part of an equally comfortable inn; see page 266). The food here is great: Chef David Frakes, who learned his craft from Gary Danko (of San Francisco Ritz Carlton fame), has been gaining high praise ever since he took over the inn's kitchen. Menu

highlights include pan-seared salmon with creamed white potatoes, braised bok choy, and seasoned eggplant chips, oven-roasted summer squash with herbed blue cheese gratinee, shitake and garlic ragout; and pork loin with fried multi-seasoned torpedo onions. For desert, Frakes makes a great creme brulee (enhanced with fresh seasonal fruits), cheesecake, and beautiful sorbets.

Babette's Restaurant. 464 First St. East, Sonoma; (707) 939-8921 **$$$$** This French-inspired restaurant *cum* wine bar is the absolute favorite of Sonoma food critic Michele Jordan. Daniel Patterson is the chef. Don't miss what he does with Sonoma foie gras. The menu changes weekly. Elizabeth Ramsey takes care of the dining room. Prices are much lower at the wine bar out front. Perhaps that explains why it has become a hangout for local characters.

Bear Republic. 345 Healdsburg Ave., Healdsburg; (707) 433-2337 **$** This wide-open hall of a brewpub on the Healdsburg Plaza is one of the most fun places around. The beers are uncommonly tasty, the food is delicious, and the service is friendly and fast. In warm weather, there's outdoor seating with a view towards the creek. This pub is where the fun locals hang out, the ones who like to socialize, and don't mind laughing in public. In this respect, the pub is a welcome relief from the serious demeanor of some local vintners and wineries.

✯ **Bistro Ralph.** 109 Plaza St., Healdsburg; (707) 433-1380 **$$** A very friendly, fun place, where the winemaker entertaining at the table next to you may offer you a glass of the latest, not-yet-released wine. The food is classy bistro fare, simple but tasty and very seasonal, since it's primarily made from fresh local ingredients. The kitchen does as spectacular a job with shoestring potatoes as it does with ahi tuna. In spring, the grilled marinated asparagus is incredible. The menu changes regularly, but there's something for every palate: filet mignon with onion rings, lamb meatloaf, grilled Columbia River sturgeon, Dungeness crab ravioli, and, you hope, Szechuan pepper calamari. The wine list is excellent, including such rarities as Preston viognier, Frick cinsault, and Seghesio sangiovese, but be sure to ask for the "Local Stash" as well. Try to get a table out front or in the front of the restaurant for the best people-watching. Chef/owner Ralph Tingle has a sense of humor. The menu ends by stating, "We accept local checks, travelers checks, MC, VISA, greenbacks or KP duty." Judging by the laughter emanating from the kitchen, the latter might not be a bad way to pay.

The Cafe at Sonoma Mission Inn. 18140 Sonoma Hwy., Boyes Hot Springs; (707) 938-9000 **$$$** This place is less snooty than—and serves food at least as good as—**The Grille,** the resort's more formal restaurant and whose spelling we find silly. Appetizers are the best dishes in the house and big enough to be a meal. The wine list is good, as is the service.

Cafe Citti. 9049 Sonoma Hwy., Kenwood; (707) 833-2690 **$** A Tuscan trattoria popular with locals. Go for plain fare, like spaghetti with olive oil and garlic, the focaccia sandwiches, or the rotisserie chicken.

✱ **Cafe Lolo.** 620 Fifth St., Santa Rosa; (707) 576-7822 **$$**
A fun downtown restaurant with a simple bistro atmosphere, serving delicious soups and salads, as well as other California-style fare.

Catelli's The Rex. 21047 Geyserville Ave., Geyserville; (707) 433-6066 **$$**
If you wonder where winemakers ate before new-age bistros opened in Healdsburg, you've found the place. The Rex has been around, pretty much unchanged, since 1936—though it seems to be expanding behind the facades of adjoining buildings. The food is basic: steaks and the works, traditional Italian-American fare, sumptuous desserts. The wine list is locally famous.

Chateau Souverain. "The Cafe at the Winery." 400 Souverain Rd., Geyserville; (707) 433-3141 **$$**
A simple bistro in a great Wine Country setting, with views across the vineyards. Locals consider this to be the quintessential Wine Country restaurant, perhaps because of the cafe's atmosphere, but also because the food is so good, and so well matched to the splendid wines

CHATEAU SOUVERAIN

created by winemaker Ed Killian. Open on weekends only. Reservations recommended.

Costeaux French Bakery & Cafe. 421 Healdsburg Ave.; Healdsburg; (707) 433-1913 **$$**
An upscale European-style pastry shop/cafe with outdoor seating. Simple lunches and rich pastries.

Della Santina's. 133 E. Napa St., Sonoma; (707) 935-0576 **$$**
A true Tuscan trattoria, run by owner/chef Quiroco Della Santina (who is from Lucca) and his extended family. All pastas are made in-house, and the meats are roasted on a rotisserie. Don't miss the lasagna Bolognese, or the roasted rabbit, duck, or chicken.

Equus Restaurant. At Fountain Grove Inn, 101 Fountain Grove Pkwy., Santa Rosa; (707) 578-0149 **$$$$**
An elegant dining room serving a robust version of California cuisine. Chef Mark Dierkhising bases his dishes on local produce. The wine list has at least one bottling from each Sonoma County winery.

Freestyle. 522 Broadway, Sonoma; (707) 996-9916 **$$$**
This bright, upscale restaurant brought to you by the folks who created San Francisco's Rubicon has carved out a niche for itself in the burgeoning Sonoma restaurant scene with such San Francisco-style dishes as salmon tartare with baby greens, herb and pepper seared tuna with horseradish-smashed potatoes,

and oven-roasted chicken with rustic bread stuffing. A cheese plate of local "artisanal" cheeses is a dessert highlight.

Girl and the Fig. 13690 Arnold Dr., Glen Ellen; (707) 938-3634 **$$**

While the food is beautifully presented, the quality can be less than consistent. It ranges from simple hamburgers, pastas, and yummy pizzas to splendid soups and crunchy salads. Figs add interest to many of the dishes. A wine-tasting sampler allows you to taste several different wines of one variety, such as viognier or syrah. Make reservations.

✫ **Glen Ellen Inn.** 13670 Arnold Dr., Glen Ellen; (707) 996-6409 **$$**

This cafe in a creekside house is small enough that you can converse from the dining room with the chef in the open kitchen, making it almost seem like you're dining in someone's home rather than in a restaurant. The exceptionally tasty food is prepared simply from fresh local ingredients; the wine list is short but well selected. Prices are reasonable.

Healdsburg Restaurant Charcuterie. 335 Healdsburg Ave., Healdsburg; (707) 431-7213 **$**

Under new owners Patrick and Robin Martin, this very pleasant, airy restaurant just off the plaza serves not only great burgers and steak sandwiches but a variety of superb pastas: fusilli with smoked chicken, rigatoni with roasted eggplant, cheese ravioli with sun-dried tomato, a delectable smoked chicken breast salad, as well as assorted salads

and sandwiches. Best of all, you can take out some of this food for a picnic.

John Ash & Co. 4330 Barnes Rd., Santa Rosa; (707) 527-7687 **$$$$**

John Ash does not cook anymore at this elegant, eponymous restaurant (he's gone north to work as Fetzer Vineyards' culinary director) but the food here is better than ever. The wine list is large and reasonably priced.

✫ **Kenwood Restaurant & Bar.** 9900 Sonoma Hwy., Kenwood; (707) 833-6326 **$$**

Kenwood serves a great variety of dishes (the menu changes constantly) from perfectly sauced meat dishes to hearty ham-

KENWOOD RESTAURANT

burgers. The bird feeder at the end of dining patio is a nice touch: you can watch the birds' antics and compare them to the behavior of fellow diners. The wine list is very good, especially when it comes to local bottlings.

Kitchen. 8989 Graton Rd., Graton; (707) 824-0563 **$$$**

With its wide veranda, this corner clapboard building on Graton's main drag looks like an old-fashioned American family restaurant. But the food is something else. Owner-chef Jan Salisbury has expanded the loyal following she had when she ran Samba Java in Healdsburg a few years back, and it's easy to see why. She has a truly magic touch in the kitchen, magically transforming such dishes as bouillabaisse, turkey meatloaf, vegetables, and steak. Service is just what you'd expect in a place of this caliber. Be sure to make reservations well ahead of time.

Lo Spuntino. 400 First St. East, Sonoma; (707) 935-5656 **$**
This down-to-earth Italian deli affiliated with Viansa Winery stands where the Creamery used to. Relax all day at the wine bar or the espresso bar, grab a delicious sandwich, or opt for a hearty Italian meal of beef stew, polenta lasagna, or grilled chicken infused with rosemary and wine. Very friendly and laid-back.

✯ **Mes Trois Filles.** 13648 Arnold Drive, Glen Ellen; (707) 938-4844 **$$-$$$**
The simple look and reasonable prices of this place are deceiving: the food is sophisticated and presented with flair; service is excellent. The crab cakes are superb, as are the roasted breast of duck in bing cherry sauce, the tournedos of beef with crushed peppercorns in a cabernet sauvignon sauce, the pork with red cabbage and pickled ginger, and the ragout of organic vegetables baked in parchment. The moderately priced wine list has some uncommon local bottlings.

✯ **Ravenous.** 117 North St., Healdsburg; (707) 431-1770 **$$**
This tiny restaurant (seven tables) attached to a movie theater serves incredibly delicious and well-prepared food from an open kitchen that seems larger than the dining room. Chef Joe Pezzolo's menu changes daily—so you're never quite sure what to expect, but you don't have to worry. It will be delicious. There are always great sandwiches and pastas and wine by the glass, including hard-to-find Bannister zinfandel. Reservations are not taken—so get there early or expect a long wait, since no one is ever rushed. Some locals consider this one of the best restaurants in Sonoma County—and they may just be right.

Swiss Hotel. 18 W. Spain Street, Sonoma; (707) 938-2884 **$**
This restaurant in the 1840 Salvador Vallejo adobe, serves hearty fare popular with locals and good-old-boys who like to hang out in the bar. Upstairs are several recently renovated guest rooms.

Vineyards Inn. 8445 Sonoma Hwy., Kenwood; (707) 833-4500 **$**
Casual Mexican food and pasta in an informal setting at the turnoff to Sugarloaf Ridge State Park. A great place for refreshing yourself if you've been hiking through too many wineries or woods.

✯ **Willowside Cafe.** 3535 Guerneville Rd., Santa Rosa; (707) 523-4814 **$$**
A roadhouse on the way from the Santa Rosa suburbs to the Green Valley wine country, serving some very delicious

food under chef Richard Allen's sure hand. He prepares delectable calamari, as well as perfectly grilled tuna and rabbit. A long wine bar takes up much of the front of the house, and the wine list is reasonably priced. This should not come as a surprise since the Willowside is a favorite of local vintners.

WILLOWSIDE CAFE

❖   ❖   ❖   ❖   ❖

■ MENDOCINO COUNTY

Boonville Hotel and Restaurant. 14040 CA 128, Boonville; (707) 895-2210 **$$$**

Under the guidance of chef John Schmitt (whose parents, Don and Sally Schmitt, put Yountville's French Laundry on the culinary map), this small dining room has blossomed into a very comfortable restaurant where local winemakers love to hang out. Both the decor and the food are simple but tasteful. Several upstairs rooms make up the hotel part of the enterprise. They are

BOONVILLE HOTEL & RESTAURANT

simply, almost austerely furnished. After retiring in 1993, Don and Sally Schmitt also settled in Boonville in 1995.

Broiler Steak House. 8400 Uva Dr., Redwood Valley; (707) 485-7301 **$$**

This ultimate steak house specializes in huge hunks of tender meat seared to perfection over fires of local oak. A place of pilgrimage for lovers of red meat.

Floodgate Store and Grill. 1810 Hwy., 128, Philo; (707) 895-2870 **$**

A small cafe serving uncommonly gourmet fare for a backcountry eatery. But that's to be expected, since the Floodgate is the closest restaurant to some of the Anderson Valley wineries.

Horn Of Zeese. 14025 Hwy. 128, Boonville; (707) 895-3525 **$**

This local coffee shop is the last place where visitors may still be able to hear Boontling, the unique local lingo invented by the locals to keep outsiders from butting into their conversations.

L O D G I N G

Good company, good wine, good welcome,
can make good people.
—*Shakespeare, King Henry VIII*

WINE COUNTRY LODGING CAN BE VERY SPECIAL, turning a weekend in the country into a truly romantic experience. We've listed below favorite lodgings, blessing with a star [☆] those we find particularly wonderful. But, we must admit, Wine Country lodging can be expensive and at times hard to come by. For this reason, we've followed this list with the names of chain accommodations, many of which are very comfortable and more modestly priced. Remember that outlying towns may have inexpensive accommodations, yet be near to the wineries and restaurants you wish to visit and enjoy.

One further note. It's tempting to compare California's wine country to European wine districts and to see how the wine, food, and lodging stack up. All of the places listed here would fit right in—and do very well—anywhere in Europe.

> *P*rices designations for lodging, per couple:
> $ = less than $79; $$ = $80–$124; $$$ = $125–$199; $$$$ = $200 plus

■ NAPA COUNTY

The Ambrose Bierce House. 1515 Main St., Saint Helena; (707) 963-3003 **$$** Yes, Ambrose Bierce, America's favorite literary curmudgeon, did indeed live here—until 1913, when he became bored with the peaceful wine valley and vanished into Pancho Villa's Mexico, never to be seen or heard from again. The two suites have private baths.

Auberge du Soleil. 180 Rutherford Hill Rd., Rutherford; (707) 963-1211 **$$$$** This deluxe French country inn is the valley's most famous lodging. Set in an old olive grove and overlooking the valley, the Auberge has stunning views. Guest rooms and suites have French doors, terracotta tiles, and a private terrace. The more deluxe rooms have fireplaces and whirlpool baths.

Brannan Cottage Inn. 109 Wapoo Ave., Calistoga; (707) 942-4200 **$$-$$$** One of the last three of the cottages remaining from Sam Brannan's 1860 Calistoga Hot Springs Resort, and the only one still on its original site. The six rooms have private entrances and baths.

El Bonita Motel. 195 Main St. (Hwy. 29), St. Helena; (707) 963-3216 **$**
Clean and inexpensive, this small motel is a bargain-hunter's dream. Charming vintage details.

Embassy Suites Napa Valley. 1075 California Blvd., Napa; (707) 253-9540 **$$$**

EMBASSY SUITES AT NAPA VALLEY

All of the rooms in this large, sprawling mission-style complex are small suites, with large, separate, and very well appointed and comfortable living and bedrooms—allowing for maximum privacy. Even though you're just off busy CA 29 (which here is a freeway), all you hear at night is the strange, almost eerie cry of the black swan living on the courtyard pond. A big, tasty breakfast of eggs, bacon, rolls and/or sausages is served in the restaurant, and comes with all the

coffee you can drink. Embassy Suites is located on the western outskirts of Napa and thus only about an hour's drive from the Bay Area. It is close to wineries of the lower Napa Valley and Stags Leap District to the north and to the Carneros to the west. It is also about equidistant between Calistoga and the Sonoma Valley wineries.

Fanny's. 1206 Spring St., Calistoga; (707) 942-9491 **$**
This simple, quiet, craftsman cottage—painted wine red—is a quiet retreat just a couple of blocks off Calistoga's busy main street. It was built in 1915, with a full-length front porch (to accommodate rocking chairs and cats, of course), and it's about as quiet as any place in this bustling spa town can get. All bedrooms have private baths and window seats. The living room and dining room are spacious, allowing for extra privacy. The sumptuous breakfast alone is worth the stay. Besides, owner/innkeeper Deanna Higgins knows the valley, its wineries, and vintners very well and is

FANNY'S

ever willing to help plan forays into the hidden nooks and crannies of the Valley. To top it off, she's a good hiking trail guide as well. No smoking.

Inn at Southbridge. 1020 Main St., St. Helena; (707) 967-9400 or (800) 520-6800 **$$$$**
This comfortable new hotel at the south end of St. Helena has become very popular, because it's right in the heart of things, with a winery (Merryvale) next door, and an adjacent restaurant (Tomatina). Tra Vigne, one of the wine country's most beloved restaurants, is on the same block, and the shops and restaurants of St. Helena are within easy walking distance. If you don't feel like going out, you can order room service from Tomatina next door.

☆ **La Residence.** 4066 St. Helena Hwy., Napa; (707) 253-0337 **$$$–$$$$**
Comes in two parts, a mansion built in

LA RESIDENCE

1870 by a riverboat captain from Louisiana, and Cabernet Hall, which is supposed to resemble a French barn. The mansion is ornate and looks indeed like it was built by a well-to-do riverboat captain. If French peasants, however, had luxurious barns like Cabernet Hall, they all would have gone to the guillotine during the revolution. Cabernet Hall is about as comfortable as lodgings come on either side of the big pond. (The first thing I could think of when I saw the deep, tiled bathtub was, "I want it!") A heated swimming pool and rose gardens separate the two buildings. All of the rooms in the "barn" have private entrances, private baths, private balconies or patios. But there are some truly special touches.

Other inns have wine and cheese hours, but none are as special as the ones at La Residence (it's the quality of the wine and food, plus the ambiance). Breakfast is served in a sunny dining room that speaks of a relaxed, effortless elegance of a kind you only find in the very best country houses (those whose owners don't have to "prove" their social status). Not only do huge bouquets of flowers brighten up the room, but the food is tasty, the coffee is rich, and service is attentive. There's also a piano to put you in the right mood for the day (the inn supplies the player). A very special touch is the orange tree that grows on the south side of the barn, protected from harsh Carneros winds by a redwood. Here you can realize the ultimate California dream, the one that has brought millions of migrants to the Golden State: You can step outside your door, pick an orange, and squeeze fresh juice from it. It doesn't get better than this. If you also happen to have some sparkling wine handy, you can take the dream one step further and make a swell mimosa.

✸ **Meadowood Resort.** 900 Meadowood Lane, St. Helena; (707) 963-3646 **$$$$** I have a bias in favor of Meadowood. I think it's a truly great resort and a cozy

MEADOWOOD RESORT

place to hide out in. Not only are the guest rooms spacious, well-insulated, and perfectly quiet, but they are spaced all over the property in small clusters, touching the nine-hole golf course on one side and the oak woods on the other. There's a great hiking trail running around the perimeters of the property. Here you can meet deer in the glades, and see wildflowers in spring. Down by the ponds at the south end of

the golf course, a flock of colorful wood ducks hangs out. If you feel active, you can work out on the professional croquet ground, on the tennis courts, in the pool, or in the spa, which is equipped with every imaginable gadget men and women use to inflict pain on their bodies. If you care for a more intellectual lifestyle, John Thoreen, the wine tutor, will instruct you in the arcane secrets of local wines, or you can hang out at one of the two restaurants (see "The Grill at Meadowood" page 253). At night, the place gets so quiet, you can hear owls hoot or coyotes howl in the distance— and all that within brisk walking distance of downtown St. Helena. Lodging is not inexpensive but, considering the attention to detail, well worth the price. The concierge, by the way, can get you into restaurants and wineries that may be difficult to get into on your own.

Napa Valley Lodge. 2230 Madison St., Yountville; (707) 944-2468 **$$$–$$$$** Elegant and comfortable, this lodge is very popular and quite difficult to get into.

NAPA VALLEY LODGE

✰ **Villa St. Helena.** 2727 Sulphur Springs Avenue, St. Helena; (707) 963-2514 $$$$

A hideaway in the oak woods of the Mayacamas Mountains. After you arrive, it's hard to believe you're only a couple of miles west of St. Helena—it's that peaceful. Architecturally, the place is a grand Mediterranean-style villa. It was built in 1941 for the elaborate entertaining of movie stars (Rita Hayworth once stayed here). Since only three of the rooms are used as guest accommodations, this makes for plenty of room and privacy. Enjoy the serene peace of the tiled cloisters, hike in the nearby woods, or just sit quietly and enjoy the panoramic views across the Napa Valley. A simple continental breakfast is served.

White Sulphur Springs Resort & Spa. 3100 White Sulphur Springs Rd., St. Helena; (707) 963-8588 $–$$$

What makes this place unique, is that it

WHITE SULPHUR SPRINGS RESORT

feels like a mountain resort, even though it is just a few minutes drive from the center of St. Helena. The lodge, squeezed between the narrow road and a steep mountainside, the rushing creek, and the rust, very comfortable cabins make you feel like you're far, far away in a quiet valley.

❖　　❖　　❖　　　❖　　❖

■ SONOMA COUNTY

✰ **Applewood—an Estate Inn.** 13555 Hwy. 116, Guerneville; (707) 869-9093 $$$-$$$$

If you think a pink Mediterranean-style villa does not fit into a landscape of redwoods and apple trees, look again. Applewood is about as snug a fit as you can hope for. This is a truly great place, with splendidly comfortable rooms, inviolate privacy, and some of the best breakfasts in the wine country—all within walking

distance of Guerneville. Best of all, owner Jim Caron is also an expert on local wines and can direct you to and

APPLEWOOD

put you in contact with small, virtually unknown wineries of the Russian River Valley. I was a bit worried when I heard that Applewood was about to expand, but the addition fits right in and is, if anything, even more luxurious than the original villa. Applewood also serves *prix fixe* dinners Tuesdays through Saturdays. When they're prepared by co-owner Darryl Notter, they're truly sumptuous. Here's a little known secret: The best place for breakfast is in the kitchen, with Jim Caron cooking and dishing up the stuff fresh and hot in front of you. Applewood is truly one of the great inns of the wine country.

★ **Camellia Inn.** 211 North St., Healdsburg; (707) 433-8182 **$$–$$$**
One of those quiet, tucked away, seemingly innocuous places that turn out to be more fun than you ever expected. It's in a truly old building, dating back to 1869 and predating the wine country's current fascination with things Mediterranean by being built in an Italianate style. Later, the house served as a doctor's office and Healdsburg's first hospital. The current owners recall that, after they bought the place, several old-timers stopped by to tell them they had been born in the house. The more than fifty varieties of camellias go all the way back to Santa Rosa horticulturist Luther Burbank, who was a family friend. Innkeeper Ray Lewand is an accomplished amateur winemaker (he's been winning gold medals at the fair) who knows his way around wineries and the Wine

CAMELLIA INN

Country. You couldn't ask for a better cicerone. You'll learn more about local wineries at happy hour on the swimming pool terrace than you will on many winery tours. There's a sumptuous breakfast that could double for lunch. The rooms have private baths, several have private entrances, and one has a private porch as well. Several rooms have whirlpool tubs; several have gas fireplaces. Best of all, the Camellia Inn is only a couple of blocks from the Healdsburg Plaza and its shops and restaurants. This is truly a splendid place, that feels about as much like home as any inn can.

★ **El Dorado Hotel.** 405 First St. W., Sonoma; (707) 996-3030 **$$**
Goes back to the days before Anglos arrived in the wine country, when it was the home of Gen. Mariano Vallejo's never-quite-respectable brother Salvador. The place has been extensively restored (with a second, wooden story

attached during the Yanqui occupation), but guest rooms tend to be small except for the new, ground-level suites beyond the patio and pool. These are about as luxurious as they get hereabouts. Breakfast, best enjoyed under the courtyard fig tree, is a pleasant experience. Since the El Dorado fronts on the Plaza, it's in easy walking distance of everything.

Fountaingrove Inn. 101 Fountaingrove Pkwy., Santa Rosa; (707) 578-6101 **$$** This is a truly splendid hotel, conveniently close to the Russian River and other Sonoma wine districts. It's a great place, with quiet, luxurious rooms, a sumptuous breakfast buffet, and a first-class restaurant where Mark Dierkhising, formerly of All Seasons in Calistoga, runs the kitchen. The food at the inn's Equus restaurant has gotten splendid reviews since Dierkhising took over.

✯ **Gaige House Inn.** 13540 Arnold Dr., Glen Ellen; (707) 935-0237 **$$$ –$$$$** Occupies a Queen Anne home built in 1890 for the wealthy town butcher. Today it is a very quiet, though not at all staid, bed and breakfast with modern

paintings, art objects, and some of the most gorgeous orchids you've seen outside a greenhouse. The rooms are bright and airy, and if you miss a piece of furniture you can't do without, like say a desk, the staff will set it up in your room. A large garden with a swimming pool runs down to a bank above Swan Creek. This is a very quiet spot at night, its silence disturbed only by the purling of the creek, the croak of a lonely frog, and the wind soughing in the boughs of the trees. There's a hammock hanging from the trees that just invites you to snooze under the stars. Breakfasts are outrageously good, prepared by a professional chef, and are served either at individual tables in the dining room or out on the terrace, weather permitting. The meal—of brunch proportions—might include freshly squeezed orange juice, coffee, and the inn's famous scrambled eggs with smoked salmon served in a very light, flaky pastry shell. It's a lot lighter than your run-of-the-mill croissant and, if it were served anywhere in France, would make the place so popular that none of us could get in. As it is, however, it's one of the Wine Country's best kept secrets. Gaige House is under new owners, but better than before; a truly delightful place. Greg Nemrow and his staff have upgraded the rooms and added several more, as well as more small garden spaces, turning this into one of the most pleasant inns in the Sonoma Valley.

GAIGE HOUSE

Hope-Merrill House. 21253 Geyserville Ave., Geyserville; (707) 857-3356. $$$
A carefully restored 1870 Eastlake-style house with its own vineyard of chenin blanc and zinfandel grapes. This is the B&B for you if you like old-fashioned architecture crammed full of Victoriana. The inn is not only located within easy driving distance of most Alexander Valley and Dry Creek Valley wineries, it is also within easy walking distance of downtown Geyserville and the Russian River—where you can dangle your feet in the water on a hot summer evening, or plunge into a shaded swimming hole.

KENWOOD INN & SPA

☆ **Kenwood Inn & Spa.** 10400 Sonoma Hwy., Kenwood; (707) 833-1293 $$$$
Looks more like a small Mediterranean village, with its compound of sun-colored buildings surrounding a flowery courtyard and with oak woods rising to one side of the road and vineyards to the other. The Kenwood Inn offers perhaps the most "Wine Country" experience of any lodgings in the Napa or Sonoma valleys and it's so unabashedly, romantically Mediterranean you'd expect an operatic soprano bursting onto the balcony of one of the upstairs rooms, and a warbling swain to pop from a rose bush to serenade her with love songs. Actually, the courtyard is very quiet, except for the tinkling of falling water. You can hear the buzzing of bees and smell the flowers while sipping wine and reading a book. The rooms are spacious and have private baths. Breakfast—which may amount to a substantial quantity of muffins and scones, white beans, sausage, and poached eggs, plus a fruit platter, orange juice, and coffee—is served in the restaurant-sized dining room with a very Mediterranean open kitchen (there's even a wine barrel on the tiled floor) and small tables—allowing you to eat by yourself or with friends, if you wish. You'll never feel crowded here, since the place has only 12 suites.

☆ **Raford House.** 10630 Wohler Rd., Healdsburg; (707) 887-9573. $$-$$$
Considered a "Healdsburg bed and breakfast," though the place is quite a ways out of town, in the heart of the Russian River Wine Country (and a short distance south of one of the favorite local swimming holes). Built in the 1880s as the logistical center of the flourishing Wohler hop ranch, the Raford House today is surrounded by vines (all right, there is a squash field

RAFORD HOUSE

in the place may well be the Strawberry Room, which overlooks the flower garden and has more than its share of admirers. The words of one guest, written into the guest book, say it best: "Strawberry Room Forever."

Sonoma Mission Inn & Spa. 18140 Sonoma Hwy., Sonoma; (707) 938-9000 $$$$

Pink, expensive, and popular. The resort consists of 170 guest rooms, an Olympic-sized pool, tennis courts, and two restaurants.

SONOMA MISSION INN & SPA

down in the valley) on a knoll that rises above even the highest floods (as the spring of 1995 amply proved). But what you'll notice most, on first sight, are the tall palms that were planted as status symbols in the 19th century and now tower above the house. That smacks of snobbism, but there's no snobbish air about this place. Under the cheery management of Carole and Jack Vore, it's very comfortable and down-to-earth. There's not only a delicious breakfast, but an afternoon wine and "appetizers" session that's so sumptuous it might kill your appetite for dinner. If it does and all you're up for afterwards are more snacks, the Vores gladly direct you to the nearest deli, at Speers Market, just up the hill. But be advised, if you're planning to enjoy your picnic dinner on the porch or patio by yourself, chances are one of the resident cats will butt in and demand a share. The most private room

✱ **Timberhill Ranch.** 35755 Hauser Bridge Rd., Cazadero; (707) 847-3258 $$$$

A truly incredible place, at the edge of the Sonoma Wine Country. It's like a summer camp for adults with luxurious cabins and a grand dining room with private chef offering multi-course dinners every night, whether the place is full or empty. The rooms (that is, cabins) are the ultimate in luxury and comfort, the grounds are extensive and at the raw edge of the wild, the food is delicious, the wine list laudable. Besides, you just have to love a place where the maids tuck fresh flowers between the bathroom towels. At night it's so quiet you can hear leaves fall and owls hoot, yet Timberhill is only a short drive from the Russian River Wine Country. Expensive but worth it.

TIMBERHILL RANCH

❖   ❖   ❖   ❖   ❖

■ CHAIN AND MOTEL LODGING IN NAPA COUNTY

CALISTOGA

Calistoga Spa Hot Springs
1006 Washington St.; (707) 942-6269

Calistoga Village Inn & Spa
1880 Lincoln Ave.; (707) 942-0991

Comfort Inn–Napa Valley North
1865 Lincoln Ave.; (707) 942-9400

Golden Haven Spa Hot Spring Resort
1713 Lake St.; (707) 942-6793

Hideaway Cottages
1412 Fair Way; (707) 942-4108

Dr. Wilkinson's Hot Springs
1507 Lincoln Ave.; (707) 942-4102

NAPA (TOWN OF)

Best Western Inn
100 Soscol Ave.; (707) 257-1930

Chablis Lodge
3360 Solano Ave.; (707) 257-1944

Napa Valley Budget Inn
3380 Solano Ave.; (707) 257-6111

Napa Valley Travelodge
853 Coombs; (707) 226-1871

Napa Valley Marriott
3425 Solano Ave.; (707) 253-7433

Discovery Inn
500 Silverado Trail; (707) 253-0892

Wine Valley Lodge
200 S. Coombs; (707) 224-7911

RUTHERFORD

Rancho Caymus Inn
1140 Rutherford Rd.; (707) 963-1777

ST. HELENA

Vineyard Country Inn
201 Main St.; (707) 963-1000

Wine Country Inn
1152 Lodi Lane; (707) 963-7077

■ CHAIN AND MOTEL LODGING IN SONOMA COUNTY

HEALDSBURG

Best Western Dry Creek Inn
198 Dry Creek Rd.; (707) 433-0300

Vineyard Valley Inn
178 Dry Creek Rd.; (707) 433-0101

SANTA ROSA

Best Western Garden Inn
1500 Santa Rosa Ave.; (707) 546-4031

Hillside Inn
2901 4th St.; (707) 546-9353

Days Inn–Santa Rosa
175 Railroad St.; (707) 573-9000

Santa Rosa Motor Inn
1800 Santa Rosa Ave.; (707) 523-3480

Hotel La Rose
308 Wilson St.; (707) 579-3200

Motel 6
2760 Cleveland Ave.; (707) 546-1500

Motel 6
3145 Cleveland Ave.; (707) 525-9010

Super 8 Lodge
2632 Cleveland Ave.; (707) 542-5544

Travelodge Downtown
College Ave. & Mendocino Ave.;
(707) 544-4141

SONOMA

Best Western Sonoma Valley Inn
550 Second St. W.; (707) 938-9200

Private functions may be arranged at many of Napa Valley's wineries.

R E F E R E N C E

Listings

■ TRAVEL TIPS

■ AREA CODES

(707) is the area code for all the Napa and Sonoma valleys. Nearby San Francisco is (415) and the East Bay—Berkeley and Oakland—(510).

■ METRIC CONVERSIONS

1 foot = .305 meters
1 mile = 1.6 kilometers
Centigrade = Fahrenheit temp. minus 32, divided by 1.8

■ CLIMATE/ WHEN TO GO

People often talk of California's Napa and Sonoma valleys as having a Mediterranean climate. The temperatures year-round and the precipitation patterns are almost identical to those of Greece, Sicily, southern Italy, and Cyprus. This is a climate characterized by winter rainfall and summer drought accompanied by often stifling heat. The farther up (northwards) in the valleys you go, the hotter it gets during summer, a result of increasing distance from the cold waters of San Pablo Bay (San Francisco Bay's northern extension). Yet the heat is often mitigated by cool fogs generated by the cold California current. These roll in through gaps in the mountains and blanket the valleys. Between October and April, but particularly during winter months, Pacific storms roll ashore and drench the area with rain. Thus, in summer the Wine Country hills are scorched brown and gold, and in winter they're green. As a result of sea fogs and the region's varied terrain, there are an astonishing number of micro-climates in the Wine Country which in turn

CLIMATE ❖ INFORMATION

provide prime conditions for a variety of wines *(see* "Vintages," *page 277).* The chart below outlines the kind of weather one may expect throughout the year if visiting St. Helena or the town of Napa in Napa County, or Santa Rosa or Healdsburg in Sonoma County.

City	January High Low	April High Low	July High Low	October High Low	Record Temps Annual Rain High Low
Napa precipitation	53 42 4.81"	68 47 1.31"	78 53 0	75 48 1.22"	110 17 22.71"
St. Helena precipitation	56 35 7.24"	72 42 2.06"	91 50 0	77 44 1.42"	115 11 32.15"
Santa Rosa precipitation	57 36 6.07"	70 41 1.96"	82 49 0	77 44 1.54"	112 15 20.57"
Healdsburg precipitation	56 38 8.69"	72 41 2.15"	92 56 0	76 46 1.76"	116 17 38.89"

■ GETTING THERE

By car. From the city of San Francisco, cross the Golden Gate Bridge and head north on US 101, then east on CA 37. From the East Bay head north on US 80 and turn east on the Columbus Parkway, then north on CA 29. If you're driving south from Oregon, you have two choices, both very close in distance and driving time. Take US 101 south from Crescent City through the redwoods to the Sonoma Wine Country. Or take Interstate 505 south to Vacaville, then head west on Interstate 80, and take CA 12 west to CA 29 and Napa or Healdsburg.

For a shorter, but windier, road, take CA 128 west from Winters to Napa (via CA 121).

By air. If you are flying into the Bay Area, you may arrive at San Francisco or Oakland airports. Oakland, the smaller airport, is easier to get around in (and out of) than San Francisco and is half an hour closer to the Wine Country. Airline and rental car rates also tend to be lower in Oakland.

■ INFORMATION NUMBERS

California Welcome Center, Rohnert Park, (707) 586-3795
Healdsburg Chamber of Commerce & Visitors Bureau, (707) 433-6935
Napa Chamber of Commerce & Visitors Bureau, (707) 226-7455

■ FESTIVALS & EVENTS

JANUARY

Winter Wineland. Mini-seminars, tastings, entertainment at Russian River Wine Road wineries. Third weekend. (707) 433- 6782/ (800) 723-6336.

Knights of Columbus Cioppino Feed. Villa Chanticleer, Healdsburg. Fourth weekend. (707) 433-4020.

FEBRUARY

Cloverdale Citrus Fair. Middle of month. Gourmet food show and wine tasting. (707) 894-3992.

MARCH

Russian River Wine Road Barrel Tasting. First weekend. (800) 723-6336.

Annual Alexander Valley Spaghetti Dinner and Auction. Alexander Valley Hall. First Saturday. (707) 433-5247.

Barrel Tasting Preview. At historic Alexander Valley wineries. Special food and wine pairings and special discounts. First Saturday. (707) 433-1944.

APRIL

Passport to Dry Creek. A weekend of adventure, feasting, and education. Approximately $60 per person. Sign up early, for this is a very popular event and sells out early. (707) 433-3031.

MAY

Opening of Healdsburg's Saturday Farmers Market. North Plaza parking lot, North and Vine streets. Fresh produce, cookbooks, flowers. 9:00 a.m. to noon. First weekend. (707) 431-1956.

Discover Alexander Valley. An annual food and wine adventure. Tickets $20.00. (707) 433-2319.

Luther Burbank Rose Festival. Third weekend. Santa Rosa. (707) 546-7673.

Russian River Wine Festival. Healdsburg Plaza. Wine tasting, food, music. Admission fee includes souvenir glass and five tasting tickets. (707) 433-6935.

Healdsburg Country Fair. Fourth weekend. Livestock show and chile cook-off. (707) 431-7644.

JUNE

Annual Ox Roast. Sonoma Plaza. A truly fun event with great food and wine to boot. Plan to get there early (before 11:00 a.m.) or parking will be difficult. Remember the free parking lot between the Sonoma Barracks and Depot, north of the Plaza. This is as good a barbecue as you'll find anywhere and well worth a special trip. Yes, there's vegetarian food. (707) 996-5947.

Bear Flag Days. Sunday closest to Flag Day (June 14th). Celebration of Bear Flag Revolt which turned California into an independent nation for a couple of weeks. (707) 996-2337.

Napa Valley Wine Auction. The nation's top food and wine event, sponsored by the Napa Valley Vintners

Association and held at Meadowood Resort on the last weekend in June. Tickets sell out early. (707) 963-5246.

JULY

Napa County Fair. Fairgrounds, Calistoga. A chance to see the real Napa Valley: rustic and laid back. First weekend. (707) 942-5111.

Fourth of July Celebration. At many wineries. With fireworks.

Bastille Day Celebration. French Independence Day, July 14th. Domaine Chandon. (707) 944-2280.

Annual Wine Showcase and Auction. Various Sonoma County wineries. Last weekend. (707) 586-3795.

AUGUST

Shakespeare at Buena Vista. Sonoma. Every Sunday in August and September. Informal, fun, and educational. Bring a picnic meal, and buy a bottle of wine before the action begins. (707) 938-1266.

Sonoma County Chefs' Tasting. Held at Saralee's Vineyard and Richard's Grove, Windsor. Last weekend of the month. (707) 546-3276.

SEPTEMBER

Valley of the Moon Wine Festival. Sonoma Plaza. One of the most fun, unsnooty wine festivals anywhere—with some of the best wine in the world. There's good food, too. (707) 996-1090.

OCTOBER

Sonoma County Harvest Fair. Sonoma County Fairgrounds. Professional and amateur wine judging. Notorious grape stomp. "Tallest weed" contest. First weekend. Great showcase for Sonoma County produce. (707) 545-4203.

Soroptimists Annual Beer & Sausage Tasting. Villa Chanticleer, Healdsburg. Local sausages, local mustards, and two dozen breweries. (707) 431-8088.

NOVEMBER

Napa Valley Wine Festival. Town & Country Fairgrounds, Napa. First weekend. (707) 253-3563.

Annual Holiday Crafts Fair. Healdsburg Senior Center. Handmade gift items made of wood, ceramics, and wool, plus embroidery. (707) 431-3324.

Healdsburg Certified Farmers Market. North Plaza. Holiday crafts and produce market, Saturdays, 9:00 a.m. to noon, through mid-December.

DECEMBER

Santa Comes To Town—on his firetruck. Healdsburg. First Sunday of the month. (707) 433-6935.

■ VINTAGES: 1984–1997

It's a naive domestic burgundy without any breeding,
but I think you'll be amused by its presumption.

—*James Thurber*

We're a bit reluctant to give you vintage listings, since these work best for small, self-contained districts, like France's Chablis or Germany's Rheingau. Large, sprawling wine regions, like those of Northern California's Wine Country, have too many micro-climates with unique conditions to ever allow their wines to be squeezed into a definitive vintage chart. Knowing the grower/winemaker and knowing about local conditions is much more important. For example, in 1989, the harvest was interrupted by heavy rains in mid-September. Some wine writers immediately wrote off the entire vintage. Yet good wines were made from grapes harvested before and after the rains. Not only that: not all regions were equally affected. While the floor of the Napa Valley experienced some real gully washers (I know—I sat out on the broad porch at the Hudson House at Beringer, cheering on the lightning and thunder), Howell Mountain, a couple of miles uphill to the east, had a mostly normal harvest.

Keep in mind that vintage descriptions are a rough guide and should never be a substitute for tasting the wine. Even in France, where wineries often lower their prices in off-years (something that has yet to happen in California), you can find some great wines among a sea of average ones. In other words, once the vintage description has pointed you into a specific direction, you must still visit a winery and sniff, taste, and make up your own mind.

1984 A hot year, making for early maturing wines. Most of the chardonnays and sauvignon blanc should have been drunk by now—but you can never tell with wine, there are always surprises. Cabernet sauvignon and zinfandel, made in a heavier style, are not only ready to drink, but may be at the peak of enjoyment. Determine on a bottle by bottle (and winery by winery) basis.

1985 A year of big, hard, well-structured reds with some real blockbusters, especially cabernet sauvignon, which need a decade or more to mature and show their best—which means they're ready to drink now. A few may have faded. But well-made cabernet sauvignon and petite sirah may be held for several more years in a properly insulated cellar (if they were made in a late-maturing style and handled properly). A very good to great year for (red) zinfandel which may be aged for several more years. Sonoma County merlot also showed well, but it has been made in so many different styles that only experimentation —over time—will tell which ones age well and which do not (heaviness alone is no reliable indicator, nor are high tannins). Many cabernet sauvignons are at their peak and highly enjoyable, but some Sonoma County ones (from the better producers) could still age for a few more years. Zinfandels are also ready to be enjoyed to the fullest, though here again, those made in a more robust style can age for a few more years (but it depends on which winery made them).

1986 Wines were more delicate than 1985, with more elegant fruit, especially in Napa and Sonoma County chardonnays. Napa County chardonnays should have been drunk by now; while Sonoma County chardonnays may be aged for a few more years (they always seem to last a bit longer). A good year for Sonoma County merlot, cabernet sauvignon, and sauvignon blanc. Cabernet sauvignons can be cellared for several more years—six if they were made right and have been properly stored. Napa County zinfandel should be drunk now; Sonoma County zinfandel can be held for another two or three years.

1987 A very good vintage, combining the backbone of 1985 with the elegant fruit of 1986. A very good year for merlot and sauvignon blanc. Most of these wines should have reached their peak or gone beyond. Zinfandel can be held for several more years. Napa chardonnays are fading earlier than Sonoma ones. Not a great year for Carneros and Russian River pinot noir (except for those made into sparkling wines). Napa Valley cabernet sauvignons from this vintage are holding up very well and can be cellared for several more years. Top-ranked Sonoma cabernets from this vintage may age for another decade, or longer.

1988 A warm and dry growing season (drought year) with a short crop producing some big, luscious, very complex wines marked by intense fruit. Cabernets with intense varietal character, although a few may have been a bit overripe, with little backbone, and have begun fading early. A good year for pinot noir and a great one for Sonoma County sauvignon blanc. Sonoma County merlot is probably at its prime now, but may be cellared for several more years if properly made and stored.

1989 Rain at the height of the harvest in mid-September induced some wine writers to declare this vintage a disaster. It was anything but, though a few lots of Carneros and Napa Valley chardonnay came in with diluted fruit. Grapes from well-drained slopes and mountain vineyards—such as Spring and Howell mountains—showed few if any of these symptoms. Some Napa Valley chardonnays developed better than the critics predicted, but even the best are ready to drink now. Despite the climatic vicissitudes, this proved to be a great year for Sonoma County merlot and sauvignon blanc.

1990 A "Vintage of the Century" year: a warm, even growing season created wines of extraordinary balance, with good aging potential. Napa chardonnay and Sonoma sauvignon blanc were tops. Also an exceptionally good year for Napa Valley sauvignon blanc—but what there was is beyond its peak now. A very good year for zinfandel, pinot noir, and merlot, which are drinkable now, but will improve with several more years of cellaring. A bit cool for cabernet sauvignon, though the wines are aging well and can be held for several more years. A truly great vintage for zinfandel—some of which might last well into the next century.

1991 A long, cool growing season. A spell of warmer weather, lasting late into the harvest, gave the grapes a ripening boost with deeply colored fruit and intense flavors. Since rain fell in late September, this vintage was not universally successful, but a top year for Napa County chardonnay and Sonoma County sauvignon blanc; good for Napa merlot and Sonoma chardonnay and zinfandel. Some very elegant cabernet sauvignon and merlot from the Carneros district. Most wines can age for a few more years. Also a very good year for Dry Creek reds. For those wineries who brought in their grapes before the rains, this was another vintage of the century. Some fine sweet wine was made from botrytis-affected grapes after the rains. Cabernet sauvignon and chardonnay should age well. A good vintage for zinfandel as well, though not as outstanding as 1990.

1992 The third year of very good vintages in Napa, with rich, fat, full-bodied white wines; one of the most normal years in Sonoma, despite the continuing drought. Moderate summer temperatures led to a slow, even ripening of grapes. Early harvest. Excellent Sonoma County reds, especially from the Dry Creek Valley. Sonoma County cabernets among the finest of recent vintages; should age well for several years, till the late 1990s. Chardonnays may be drunk now, but can age for several more years.

1993 A long, relatively cool growing season with a hot spell at the end that ripened the grapes all at once. Some early-harvested grapes suffered from a lack of definition. Cool weather returned in September and vineyards not yet harvested regained good acid balance with complex flavors and tannins. Good, ripe fruit for reds in the Dry Creek Valley; good ripe fruit with proper acidity for whites. A great year for Napa and Sonoma County chardonnays. Some very fine Russian River and Carneros pinot noirs. Wines can age for several more years.

1994 A cool growing season without heat surges, yet with high crop yields at harvest for some wineries, although overall the crop was down. Excellent fruit quality with almost perfect acid levels. An excellent year for all types of grapes in many diverse growing regions. A long, cool harvest—some growers were picking cabernet sauvignon and merlot in October, and chardonnay and sauvignon blanc as late as November. Viognier and some of the other new varieties planted in Sonoma County did very well. A great year for Sonoma County zinfandel. The zinfandel crop was down 30 to 40 percent, making for intensely flavored wines that should develop beautifully with age. A vintage to enjoy in the 21st century.

1995 The end of the drought. Heavy spring rains washed out some vineyards but hardly affected others, because they fell when the vines were still dormant. But cold weather and rains during bloom caused low fruit set, making for an exceptionally small—but excellent—crop, causing wineries to scramble for extra grapes. Expect prices to go higher because of the short supply of high quality grapes. Because the crop was light, the flavors of the wines will be more intense. Early barrel samples show powerful fruit. Expect some great wines from this vintage.

1996 A strange year with low yields but good fruit. Rain during blossoming of the vines and fruit set cut quantity in many areas, but a warm fall and summer made up for much of that. Even so, this seems to have been a vintage that ripened very late. Some red wine grapes were picked as late as November. Most winemakers seem very happy with the results. Chardonnays are drinkable now, as is viognier, marsanne, and perhaps sangiovese. Cabernet sauvignons and zinfandels should be cellared for several years.

1997 Everybody's dream vintage. Yields were up (Napa had its biggest harvest ever) but so was quality. Some wineries had to hire tank cars to store all that bounty. Grapes for sparkling wines saw their earliest harvest ever. Rains in late summer worried some growers, but everybody seems to have come out just fine. Chardonnay, viognier, and marsanne are drinkable now, or should be held for only a year or two. Sangiovese also shows signs of early maturity. Cabernet and zinfandel are surprisingly enjoyable.

■ RECOMMENDED READING

Darlington, David. *Angel's Visits.* New York: Henry Holt & Co., 1991. An inquiry into the mystery of zinfandel. A delightful book written by someone who got his hands stained in a winery to learn what makes great zinfandel.

Heintz, William F. *Wine Country: A History of Napa Valley. The Early Years: 1838-1920.* Santa Barbara, CA: Capra Press, 1990. A very thorough—and very readable—historical treatise of the founding years of the valley's most important industry.

Jones, Idwal. *Vines in the Sun: A Journey through California Vineyards.* New York: William Morrow, 1949. A small book loaded with anecdotes, character sketches, and description of Wine Country scenes and places as they looked in the 1940s. The book has been criticized by some historians because it is not always accurate—Jones the novelist triumphs over Jones the historian. Even so, it is good reading and gives an interesting picture of the Wine Country as it was.

Lee, W. Storrs. *California: A Literary Chronicle.* New York: Funk & Wagnalls, 1968. A comprehensive selection of excerpts from writings about California. Especially good for the early years. A good source book.

Melville, John Robert. *Guide to California Wines.* Garden City, NY: Doubleday, 1955 (rev. ed. by Melville in 1960; by others, 1968, 1972, 1978). A good look at the California Wine Country just before the revolution.

Menefee, Campbell Augustus. *Historical and Descriptive Sketchbook of Napa, Sonoma, Lake and Mendocino.* Napa City, CA: Reporter Publishing House, 1873 (Repr. Fairfield, CA: John D. Stephenson, PhD, 1993). Contains biographical sketches of pioneer vintners as well as descriptions of the countryside while it still lay primarily untilled.

Muscatine, Doris, Maynard A. Amerine, and Bob Thompson, editors. *The University of California/Sotheby Book of California Wine*. Berkeley & Los Angeles, CA/London: University of California Press/Sotheby Publications, 1984. An essential book for anyone interested in California wine. What makes this book so valuable are the essays by historians, enologists, and vintners on the topics they know best, from the early days of California wine to the 1980s, including essays by Eleanor McCrea on chardonnay, Forrest Tancer on pinot noir, Paul Draper on zinfandel, and Brother Timothy Diener on corkscrews.

Starr, Kevin. *Americans and the California Dream, 1850–1915*. New York: Oxford University Press, 1973. A delightfully written analysis of why the Wine Country is the way it is and how the region is seen against the backdrop of greater California.

Sterling, Joy. *A Cultivated Life: A Year in a California Vineyard*. New York: Villard Books, 1993. A pleasantly readable, informative account of all the things it takes to make a winery successful, by one of the proprietors of Iron Horse.

Sullivan, Charles L. *Napa Wine: A History from Mission Days to the Present*. San Francisco, CA: The Wine Appreciation Guild, 1994. A comprehensive history of the Napa wine industry, with many historical photos.

Thompson, Bob. *The Wine Atlas of California and the Pacific Northwest: A Traveler's Guide to the Vineyards*. New York: Simon & Schuster, 1993. A thorough and user-friendly guide to the wine growing districts of California (and beyond), with excellent maps.

The WPA Guide to California. Written and compiled by the Federal Writers' Project of the Works Progress Administration for the State of California. New York: Hastings House, 1939 (Reprint: New York: Pantheon Books, 1984).

GLOSSARY

G L O S S A R Y

Acidity. The tartness of a wine, derived from the fruit acids of the grape. Not to be confused with sourness. Acids stabilize a wine, serve as a counterpoint to its sugars (if any) and bring out its flavors. Wine without acid is flat. Acid is to wine what salt is to cooking: a proper amount is necessary but too much spoils the taste. Tartaric is the major acid of a wine but malic, lactic, and citric acids also occur in greatly variable concentrations.

Aftertaste. The way a wine lingers on the palate after you have swirled it around in your mouth. Good wines have a long-lasting aftertaste of many complex flavors and aromas.

Aging of Wine. Some wines, if properly stored, will improve with some aging in barrel or bottle. Aging makes them more smooth and complex and, with time, develops a pleasing bouquet. But most wines do not age well. Wine ages by reacting to oxygen at a very slow rate through the pores in the wood, and even this small amount of oxidation is too much for most wines. It can make some wines appear heavy and awkward while it may maderize lighter wines.

Alicante Bouschet. A grape that is widely cultivated in France since it was created as a cross between petit bouschet and grenache. The juice of this grape is blended with other varieties since it makes dull wine on its own. It was widely planted in California during Prohibition because of its intensely red juice which could be stretched with much sugar and water and still stay red.

Appellation. American Viticultural Appellation (AVA). The legally binding geographical definition of a wine-growing region. When the label lists the appellation, as in, for example, Dry Creek Valley or Sonoma Mountain, 85% of the grapes from which the wine was made must come from that region.

Aroma. The scent of young wine derived directly from the fresh fruit. This fresh grape aroma diminishes with fermentation and is replaced by a more complex bouquet as the wine ages. The term may also be used to describe special fruity odors like black cherry, green olive, ripe raspberries, or apples.

Astringent. What a layman might call "sour." By common agreement of the experts there is no such thing as a "sour" wine, just astringent or tart wine.

Balance. A winemaker's term describing a wine whose various elements are in harmony. A well-balanced wine has a special "mouth-feel," which is difficult to describe verbally but has to be evaluated by the olfactory, gustatory, and tactile senses.

Barbera. An Italian wine grape from the Piedmont. It grows well in several North Coast micro-climates, where it produces deeply colored, full-bodied wines with tarry, spicy, earthy character and a backbone of balancing acid. It goes very well with Italian food.

Blanc de Blancs. A fancy term denoting a white wine made from white grapes. Most commonly used in the marketing of sparkling wines, to distinguish them from off-white sparklers made from pinot noir grapes and called blanc de noirs.

Blending. An art. The careful mixing or "marriage" of several wines to create a wine of greater complexity (or a more enjoyable one, as when a heavy wine is blended with a lighter one to create a more readily approachable medium-bodied wine).

Body. The substance of a wine as experienced by the palate. A full body can be an advantage in the case of some reds but a disadvantage in many lighter whites. Wine has soul as well as body, and the latter are more enjoyable when they have more soul than body.

Bouquet. This term describes the different odors a mature wine gives off when opened. They should be diverse but pleasing, complex but not confused, and give an indication of the wine's grape variety, origin, age, and quality. A good bouquet appeals to anyone, not just to wine experts.

Brut. A dry sparkling wine. (*See also* Demi-sec)

Burgundy. The English name for Bourgogne, a prime French wine growing region making both red and white wines. It is sometimes used on labels of inferior California red wines to indicate a cheap, generic red wine. Needless to say, this is a silly custom, since all California wine can stand on its own and does not need to borrow foreign names.

Cabernet Franc. A noble grape of France's Bordeaux region, cabernet franc produces very aromatic red wines which are softer and more subtle than those of the closely related cabernet sauvignon, and age more quickly. Cabernet franc is often blended into cabernet sauvignon to soften the wine of that somewhat harsher grape.

Cabernet Sauvignon. This superb red wine grape is the noble grape that has made the clarets of Bordeaux renowned. It grows also very well in parts of California. Its wine is deeply red, tannic, and requires a long period of aging to become enjoyable. For this reason it is often blended with cabernet franc, merlot, and other related red varieties, to soften it and to make it enjoyable earlier.

Carignane. This French variety of Spanish origin can make good or indifferent wine depending on whether it is grown in austere hillside vineyards or in fertile bottomlands.

Champagne. *See* Sparkling Wines

Chablis. A prime French wine growing region making austere white wines. It is sometimes used on labels of inferior California wines to indicate a cheap, generic white wine, though it has also been used for pink and red wines.

Chardonnay. Chardonnay is the noble grape variety making the great white burgundies of Montrachet, Meursault, and Chablis in France, as well as the lesser whites of Pouilly-Fuissé and Mécon. It is also one of the principal varieties of the Champagne region.

Chenin Blanc. A noble old French white grape variety that has recently fallen from grace in California because it does not make "big" wine, the way chardonnay does. It is very fruity and, in good years, may be aged—when it develops a beautiful, complex bouquet that makes the wine eminently enjoyable.

Chianti. A pleasantly quaffable Italian red wine made primarily from the sangiovese grape, which goes beautifully with Italian food.

Cinsaut. A productive French red wine grape also grown in California where it is also known under the name black malvoisie. It adds softness and fragrance to Rhone-style blends of carignane and grenache.

Claret. "Claret" is a name that was once applied to red wines from Bordeaux that were shipped to Britain's discriminating wine connoisseurs. The term came into disrepute when it was applied to California bulk wines. It is, however, regaining respect as a name several California premium wineries are bestowing on their red Bordeaux blends.

Clarity. A requirement for a good wine. Wine should always be clear (though it can be dark or dense); it should never be cloudy.

Cloudy. While an occasional cloudy day can be good for the human psyche, a cloudy wine never is. It will taste dusty or even muddy—quite definitely off. Set the bottle, at a slant, into a place where it will not be disturbed, then let the sediments settle. Decant the clear liquid collecting above and discard the sediments. If the wine remains cloudy pour it out. It has been badly made or is spoiled.

Complexity. Layers of different flavors and aromas in harmony with the overall balance of a wine, and perhaps—in an aged wine—a pleasing bouquet and a lingering aftertaste: in short, all the elements that make a good wine such a rewarding experience.

Cooperage. A collective term used to describe all the containers of a winery in which wine is stored and aged before bottling. It includes barrels, casks, vats, and tanks of different materials and sizes.

Corky or Corked. Off-flavors and aromas created by leaky corks which allow too much contact between the wine and the air and will, with time, spoil the wine.

Crush. The California term for the vintage in which grapes are made into wine. Not all of the grapes grown in the state go into wine—some go to fresh market, others are made into raisins. These are not part of the "crush" but are counted as part of the grape harvest.

Cuvée. A blend of sparkling wines.

Demi-sec. In the convoluted language of sparkling wine this means "sweet."

Dessert Wines. Sweet wines that are big in flavor and aroma but may be quite low in alcohol, or wines that have been "fortified" with brandy or neutral spirits and may be quite high in alcohol (from 17–21%).

Dry. In California, this means more than just "not sweet" but is a philosophical category because of the long fight the wine industry has had weaning consumers away from sweet wines.

Dry Creek. A major Sonoma County growing region northwest of Healdsburg.

Estate Bottled. For a winery to be allowed to label a wine as "estate bottled," both the winery and the vineyards from which the grapes were harvested must be located in the same viticultural area.

Fermentation. The process in which enzymes generated by yeast cells convert the grape sugars of must into alcohol and carbon dioxide and by which the grape juice becomes wine.

Fermenter. Any vessel small or large in which wine is fermented.

Filtration. A purification rite in which the wine is pumped through filters to rid it of suspended particles. If not handled right, the filtration can remove a wine's flavor.

Fining. Traditional method of clarifying a wine by adding crushed egg shells, isinglass, or other natural substances to a barrel. As these solids settle to the bottom, they take suspended particles with them, thus clarifying the wine. A more tedious and slower process than filtering, but one that makes better wine.

Fortification, Fortified. Wines to which brandy or natural spirits have been added to stop fermentation and increase their level of alcohol. This makes them more stable after a bottle has been opened than regular table wines.

Foxiness. The odd flavor of native grapes such as *Vitis californica* which grow wild in Napa and Sonoma valley woods and thickets. An acquired taste for some East Coast enophiles.

Free Run. Juice that runs from the crushed grapes before pressing and is more intense in flavor than pressed juice (and also has no or fewer off-flavors).

Fruity. Aromatic quality of a wine that has nuances of fresh fruit like fig, raspberry, apple, etc. A sign of quality in young wines; replaced by bouquet in aged wines.

Fumé Blanc. Term coined by Robert Mondavi to describe a dry, crisp sauvignon blanc, but now used so indiscriminately by some wineries that it has lost any special meaning. Often a wine quite similar to what was once known as California "sauterne."

Gamay (also called Gamay Beaujolais). A vigorous, productive French red grape variety which is widely planted in California. It produces pleasant reds and rosés that should be drunk young. There is some confusion as to which California plantings are the true gamay and which are actually clones of pinot noir.

Gewürztraminer. A German/Alsatian pinkish grape variety that makes excellent aromatic, almost spicy white wine in Mendocino County's Anderson Valley. It is also planted elsewhere in California.

Green. Wine made from unripe grapes with a pronounced leafy flavor and a raw edge.

Grenache. A southern French red wine variety of Spanish origin *(garnacha)* with limited plantings in the California wine country, where it makes good rosés. Its popularity has increased with the rise of the new Rhone-style blends. (*See also* Carignane and Cinsaut)

Grey Riesling. Not a riesling, but a grape of dubious origin which makes indifferent wine yet is quite popular with some consumers.

Horizontal Tasting. A tasting of wines of the same vintage from several wineries.

Late Harvest, Select Late Harvest, Special Late Select Harvest. Wine made from grapes harvested later in the fall than the main lot and thus higher in sugar levels. These terms are vague, however, and have no legal meaning in California. They may simply indicate that the grapes got too ripe and that the resulting wine is sweet and cloying. In fact, one recent wine was labeled "VT," for "very tardy."

Lees. The deposits thrown by a wine as it ages in a barrel. Wine left on the lees for a time improves in complexity. It has become a very popular way of aging chardonnay and sauvignon blanc.

Malbec. A French cabernet-type red wine grape which makes deeply colored, somewhat tannic wine. Less aromatic than cabernet sauvignon, it is softer and ages earlier and is therefore commonly blended with cabernet in Bordeaux reds as well as in California meritage wines.

Malolactic Fermentation. A secondary fermentation in the tank or barrel which changes harsh malic acids into softer lactic acid and carbon dioxide, making the wine smoother.

Marsanne. A white wine grape of France's northern Rhone Valley that can produce a rather full-bodied, overly heavy wine unless handled with care. Blended with rousanne, it makes the famous White Hermitage. It gives very good wine in California.

Meritage. High quality wine blended from red or white wines in which none of the component wines reach the legal level of 75% the law requires of the designated grape variety. These wines are designed to allow the winemaker more flexibility with the blends, and most are in no way inferior to varietal wines. Most Meritage wines carry vintage dates. A few wineries use proprietary names like Insignia or Trilogy instead of the Meritage designation.

Merlot. Known in its native France as merlot noir, for the dark, blue-black color of its berries, this grape is more productive than cabernet and gives a softer, more supple wine that may be drunk at a younger age. Until recent years, merlot was not widely planted in California, but it has experienced a boom.

Meunier (also called Pinot Meunier). A relative of the pinot noir whose dusty-black grapes are made mostly into white or off-white Champagne. It is more productive than pinot noir but its quality is not as good. There are limited plantings of meunier in the California Wine Country.

Mourvèdre. This red wine grape was once moderately popular in California under its Spanish name mataro. It has gained a

new following under its French name mourvèdre, under which it has been made into Rhone-style wines. Wine made from mourvèdre is alcoholic, deeply colored, very dense, and at first harsh, but it mellows with several years of aging.

Muscat Blanc (also called Muscat de Frontignan or Muscat Canelli). An ancient and very aromatic grape variety that may have been brought to France by Greek colonists who settled Provence before the Roman empire. It has been planted in California since the middle of the 19th century, but never on a large scale.

Must. Crushed grapes and/or their juice ready to be fermented into wine or in the process of being fermented.

Nebbiolo. The great red wine grape of Italy's Piedmont region, where it makes such renowned wines as Barolo, Barbaresco, and Gattinara. Considered one of the greatest red wine grapes in the world, it has only recently been planted in California's Wine Country. Its full-bodied, sturdy wines are fairly high in alcohol and age splendidly.

Noble Rot. *Botrytis cinerea,* a fungus mold attacking certain ripe grapes and perforating their skin. This shrivels the grapes through dehydration and concentrates the sugars and flavor elements in the remaining juice while preserving the grape's acids. This helps keep the resulting sweet wine from becoming cloying.

Nose. Both the overall fragrance (aroma or bouquet) given off by a wine as well as the facial appendage with which a winetaster sensually evaluates (and enjoys) wine—since the flavor of wine is mostly aroma.

Oaky. Wine that has been aged in new oak for too long and tastes more of the vanilla-like flavors of the wood than of the grape. Once praised as a virtue in California chardonnays, it is now considered a fault.

Petite Sirah. A noble red wine grape of California whose origin is shrouded in mystery. It was once thought to be the true syrah grape of France, but it is not. Neither is it the durif, or any of several other French vinifera hybrids. Since it is a true vinifera it may be a sport or natural hybrid that occurred in a mid-19th-century California vineyard —much like the equally mysterious zinfandel.

pH. An indicator of a wine's acidity. It is a reverse measure, that is, the lower the pH level, the higher the acidity.

Phylloxera (*Phylloxera vastatrix*). A root louse, native to the central and eastern United States. It attacks grapevine roots, first weakening, and ultimately destroying them.

Pinot Blanc. A white sport of the pinot noir grape which, when treated properly, makes a wine much like chardonnay.

Pinot Noir. An ancient French grape variety, this noble grape may, under perfect conditions, make the best red wine in the world. It does so only rarely, even in the best vineyards of its native Burgundy. Until quite recently, it rarely made more than ordinary wine in California. But recent wines made from new plantings in the cooler growing regions of the Carneros District and the Russian River Valley, combined with improved vinification methods, hint that pinot noir will have a great future in California.

Pinot Noir Blanc. White wine made from the black pinot noir grape, most commonly as sparkling wine, when it is called blanc de noirs. "White" is relative here, since the wine more often than not has a rosy tinge and can even be rather pink.

Pomace. The spent skins and grape solids from which the juice has been pressed; these are commonly returned to the fields as fertilizer.

Racking. Moving wine from one set of cooperage into another, to drain it off the lees; the wine may or may not be fined or filtered in the process.

Residual Sugar. Sugar left over from fermentation that is above the threshold of perception of 0.5 percent.

Riesling. (Also called Johannisberg Riesling or White Riesling). The noble white wine grape of Germany was introduced to the California Wine Country in the middle of the 19th century by immigrant vintners. This cool-climate grape has rarely made great wine here, although at times it has made very sweet ones.

Rosé. French term for pink wine. This is usually made from black (red wine) grapes with the juice left on the skins only long enough to give it a tinge of color. Rosés can be pleasant and versatile food wines, especially when they are made from premium grapes like cabernet sauvignon, grenache, or pinot noir.

Rounded. A well-balanced, complete wine. While this quality indicates good wine, it does not necessarily imply that the wine is distinctive or great.

Roussanne. A noble white wine grape of France's Rhone Valley that gives a full-bodied, distinguished wine. Blended with marsanne it makes the famous White Hermitage. It makes very good wine in California..

Sangiovese. The main red grape of Italy's Chianti district and of much of central Italy. It is a surprisingly versatile grape. Depending on how it is grown and vinified, it can be made into vibrant, light-bodied to medium-bodied wines, as well as into long-lived, very complex reds (like Italy's renowned Brunello di Montalcino). Sangiovese was once widely planted in California—it went into the famous Tipo Chianti made by the Italian Swiss Colony before Prohibition—but has made a comeback only recently.

Sauvignon Blanc. The sauvignon blanc, the "wildling," may well be the native wild grape of France's Bordeaux region. Sauvignon blanc does very well in the California Wine Country and makes more interesting wine than the more popular chardonnay. A dry, austere wine made from this grape is sometimes marketed as fumé blanc.

Sauvignon Vert. A simple white wine grape that is not a true sauvignon, but makes a pleasant, easily drinkable wine. It is made as a varietal by only one winery, the Napa Valley's Nichelini Vineyards.

Semillon. A white Bordeaux grape variety that has made—blended with sauvignon blanc—some of the best sweet wines in the world. Like the riesling, it can be affected by the noble rot, which concentrates the juices and intensifies the flavors and aromas.

SO_2 (sulphur dioxide). Sulphur dioxide is added to must, especially to that of white wines, to prevent browning through oxidation and to inhibit natural yeasts which can wreak havoc with the winemaker's plans. An excessive amount of sulphur dioxide in a wine, however, is an unacceptable fault.

Sparkling Wines. Sparkling wines are, despite the mystique surrounding them, nothing more or less than wines in which carbon dioxide is suspended, making them bubbly. Because sparkling wines were invented in Champagne, France's northernmost wine district where wines tend to be a bit acid

...cause grapes do not always fully ripen, sparkling wines have traditionally been naturally tart, even austere.

Sylvaner. A white wine grape from Central Europe that makes good, rather than great, wine. The wine is greenish yellow in color and has a light body and aroma. In the past, much of California's sylvaner wines were labeled "riesling," a practice which benefitted neither wine.

Syrah. A red wine grape from France's hot-climate Rhone region. It gives the best wine when grown in austere soils, and loses its noble qualities when the vines are planted in fertile, irrigated bottomlands. At its best, the wine made from this grape is big-bodied and complex and needs to be aged to bring out its qualities. It was long thought that California's petite sirah (note the slightly different spelling) was of this variety. It is not, despite the name, but may be a natural sport or hybrid that originated in California in the 19th century. Plantings of true syrah were once very limited in California but have increased in recent years, partly due to the new popularity of Rhone-style wines, partly because of the success syrah has had in Australia (where it is called shiraz).

Table or Dinner Wine. Federal regulations require a table wine to have at least seven percent alcohol but not more than 14 percent by volume. Such wines may be labeled Table Wine only, without a listing of their exact alcohol content on their label. The term is sometimes used, incorrectly, by consumers to denote an inexpensive wine.

Tannins. Tannins are phenols (like a grape's color pigments) that taste astringent and make the mouth pucker. Because tannins settle out in the natural sediments red wine throws as it ages, older reds have fewer tannins than young ones.

Tartrates. Tartaric acid is the principal acid of wine, some of which is deposited in the form of crystals as the wine settles in a cask. Sometimes, in unstable wines, it is also deposited in the bottle—which causes consumers to return the bottles because of "broken glass" in the wine (tartar crystals look like tiny shards of glass but are not harmful).

Ullage. The air space left in a barrel as a liquid slowly evaporates through the barrel's pores (in brandy-making this is called "the angel's share"). The barrel needs to be topped off regularly to avoid exposing too much of the wine to the air and thus cause rapid oxidation.

Varietal. A wine which takes its name not from a town, district, or vineyard—as is the case in much of Europe—but from the grape variety from which it is made, such as chardonnay, merlot, sangiovese, etc. According to law, a wine labelled as a varietal must contain wine that is made from at least 75% of the grape variety printed on the label as its varietal name.

Vertical tasting. A tasting of wines of one or more varietals from the same winery, but of different vintages, generally starting with the youngest and going back in time to the oldest.

Vinifera Grapes. The great wine grapes of the old world which—despite their widely and wildly varying character—all belong to just a single species, *Vitis vinifera,* the true Old World wine grape of Eurasia. Many varieties of vinifera grapes have been successfully transplanted to the New World and give our best wines—unlike the native grapes of the New World which tend to have odd flavors (*see* Foxy).

Vintage. The grape harvest and the year in which the grapes are harvested. In California the term "crush" may be used for the harvest as though it were synonymous with vintage. A vintage date on a bottle of wine always indicates the year in which the grapes were harvested, never the year in which the wine was bottled.

Viognier. A white wine grape of France's Rhone Valley that gives a distinguished wine of special character—golden, with a unique, fruity bouquet.

Viticultural Area. (*See also* Appellation) A new class of appellation in the United States, delineating a significant grape-growing region whose geography and boundaries are recognized and strictly defined by the federal government. When a "Viticultural Area" is used on a label, a minimum of 85% of the grapes used in making the wine must come from that area.

Wine. A natural libation. One of only a few beverages not invented by man, and the only alcoholic one that can make itself: fully ripe grapes, stacked in a watertight container, will crush under their own weight. The skins will burst, and the natural yeasts will mingle with the liberated grape juice and ferment its sugars into alcohol. The end product may be rough, but it is wine and needs only to be strained off the skins to be drinkable.

Woody. A wine that has been stored in a wooden barrel or cask for too long and has picked up excessive wooden aromas and flavors. It has the "mouth-feel" you get when you've chewed on a wooden toothpick too long.

Zinfandel. Much has been written about the origin of this red wine grape, but try as they may, scientists have been unable to pin it down. We shall assume that it is a sport or natural hybrid that happened in a mid-19th century California vineyard—perhaps in that of Agoston Haraszthy, the father of Sonoma wine. It is likely that an already existing name was attached to this new hybrid (nomenclature among California grapes has long been hairraisingly chaotic; *see also* Syrah and Petite Sirah). But let's not quibble. Whatever its origin, this grape can give great wine. At its best, it gives complex, well-balanced wine that ages as well as the best French clarets.

...ERY MASTER LIST

	Region	Phone (707)	Tasting Room	Page #
...na Spring Cellars	Napa Valley	965-2675	by appt.	205
Alderbrook	Dry Creek	433-9154	open	180
Alexander Valley	Alexander Valley	433-7209	open	194
Arrowood	Sonoma Valley	938-5170	open	172
B. R. Cohn	Sonoma Valley	938-4064	by appt.	162
Bannister Wines	Russian River	433-6402	no visitors	185
Beaulieu Vineyards	Napa Valley	963-2411	open	101
Beringer Vineyards	Napa Valley	963-7115	open	111
Benziger Family Winery	Napa Valley	935-3000	open	168
Bouchaine Vineyards	Carneros	252-9065	by appt.	150
Buena Vista Carneros	Sonoma/Carneros	252-7117	open	159
Burgess Cellars	Napa Valley	963-4766	by appt.	213
Cakebread Cellars	Napa Valley	963-5221	by appt.	82
Canyon Road Cellars	Alexander Valley	857-3417	open	197
Carneros-Alambic	Carneros/Napa	253-9095	open	148
Carneros Creek	Carneros	253-9463	open	149
Caymus Vineyards	Napa Valley	963-4204	open	84
Chappellet Vineyard	Napa Valley	963-7136	by appt.	216
Charles Krug	Napa Valley	963-2761	open	116
Chateau Montelena	Napa Valley	942-5105	open	201
Chateau Potelle	Napa Valley	255-9440	open	96
Chateau Souverain	Alexander Valley	433-8281	open	196
Chateau St. Jean	Sonoma Valley	833-4134	open	170

Winery	Region	Phone (707)	Tasting Room	Page #
Chateau Woltner	Napa Valley	963-1744	by appt.	214
Chimney Rock	Napa Valley	257-2641	open	90
Cline Cellars	Carneros	935-4310	open	145
Clos du Bois	Alexander Valley	857-1651	open	197
Clos du Val	Napa Valley	259-2200	open	91
Clos Pegase	Napa Valley	942-4981	open	128
Cuvaison	Napa Valley	942-6266	open	130
Davis Bynum	Russian River	433-5852	open	178
Domaine Carneros	Carneros	257-0101	open	148
Domaine Chandon	Napa Valley	944-8844	open	75
Dominus Estate	Napa Valley	944-8954	no visitors	76
Dry Creek	Dry Creek Valley	433-1000	open	188
Duckhorn	Napa Valley	963-7108	open for sales	130
Dunn	Napa Valley	965-3642	no visitors	215
Far Niente	Napa Valley	944-2861	no visitors	81
Ferrari-Carano	Dry Creek Valley	433-6700	open	189
Field Stone	Alexander Valley	433-7266	open	195
Fisher	Sonoma County	539-7511	by appt.	172
Flora Springs	Napa Valley	963-5711	by appt.	104
Foppiano	Russian River	433-7272	open	180
Freemark Abbey	Napa Valley	963-9694	open	120
Frog's Leap	Napa Valley	963-4704	by appt.	136
Geyser Peak	Alexander Valley	857-WINE	open	196
Gloria Ferrer	Carneros/Sonoma	996-7256	open	146
Green & Red	Napa Valley	965-2346	by appt.	205

	Region	Phone (707)	Tasting Room	Page #
...Cellar	Napa Valley	963-2784	open	103
	Lake County	987-2385	open	204
...ch-Bundschu	Sonoma Valley	938-5277	open	160
...ley Cellars	Anderson Valley	895-3876	open	220
...itz Wine Cellars	Napa Valley	963-3542	open	131
The Hess Collection	Napa Valley	255-1144	open	94
Hop Kiln	Russian River	433-6491	open	179
Husch	Anderson Valley	895-3216	open	219
Inglenook	*see* Niebaum-Coppola Vineyards			
Iron Horse	Russian River	887-1507	by appt.	174
J Wine Company	Russian River	431-5400	open	181
Johnson's	Alexander Valley	433-2319	open	194
Joseph Phelps	Napa Valley	963-2745	by appt.	130
Kenwood	Sonoma Valley	833-5891	open	170
Kistler	Sonoma Valley	823-5603	no visitors	175
Korbel Champagne	Russian River	887-2294	open	177
Kunde Estate	Sonoma Valley	833-5501	open	168
Landmark	Sonoma Valley	833-0053	open	171
Laurel Glen	Sonoma Valley	526-3914	no visitors	172
Livingston Wines	Napa Valley	963-2120	no visitors	104
Long Vineyards	Napa Valley	963-2496	by appt.	217
Louis M. Martini	Napa Valley	963-2736	open	105
Lytton Springs	Dry Creek Valley	433-7721	open	192
Mark West Estate	Russian River	544-4813	open	180
Matanzas Creek	Sonoma Valley	528-6464	open	168

Winery	Region	Phone (707)	Tasting Room	Page #
Mayacamas	Napa Valley	224-4030	by appt.	95
Merryvale	Napa Valley	963-2225	open	108
Mont St. John Cellars	Carneros	255-8864	open	149
Mumm Napa Valley	Napa Valley	942-3300	open	85
Nalle	Dry Creek Valley	433-1040	no visitors	192
Navarro	Anderson Valley	895-3686	open	219
Nichelini	Napa Valley	963-0717	open wknds	215
Niebaum-Coppola	Napa Valley	963-9099	open	100
Opus One	Napa Valley	944-9442	by appt.	81
Pedroncelli	Dry Creek Valley	857-3531	open	191
Porter Creek	Russian River	433-6321	open wknds	178
Preston	Dry Creek Valley	433-3372	open	188
Quivira	Dry Creek Valley	431-8333	open	188
Ravenswood	Sonoma Valley	938-1960	open	161
Raymond	Napa Valley	963-3141	open	103
Robert Mondavi	Napa Valley	963-9611	open	80
Robert Sinskey	Napa Valley	944-9090	open	87
Rochioli	Russian River	433-2305	open	179
Roederer Estate	Anderson Valley	895-2288	open	219
Round Hill	Napa Valley	963-5251	sales only	132
Rutherford Hill	Napa Valley	963-1871	open	132
Rustridge	Napa Valley	965-9353	open	206
Rutz	Sonoma Valley	823-0373	no visitors	175
Saint Clement	Napa Valley	963-7221	open	116
Saintsbury	Napa Valley	252-0592	by appt.	149

	Region	Phone (707)	Tasting Room	Page #
	Napa Valley	963-4507	open	82
	Alexander Valley	433-2285	open	194
...enberger Cellars	Anderson Valley	895-2065	open	219
...amsberg	Napa Valley	942-4558	by appt./sales	121
...hug Carneros Estate	Carneros/Sonoma	939-9363	open	148
Sebastiani Vineyards	Sonoma Valley	938-5532	open	158
Seghesio Winery	Alexander/Dry Creek	433-3579	no visitors	185
Silver Oak	Napa Valley	944-8808	open	78
Simi	Alexander Valley	433-6981	open	185
Sonoma-Cutrer	Russian River	528-1181	by appt.	180
Spring Mountain	Napa Valley	967-4188	no visitors	117
Stag's Leap Wine Cellars	Napa Valley	944-2020	open	89
Stags' Leap Winery	Napa Valley	944-1303	no visitors	88
Sterling	Napa Valley	942-3344	open	128
Stonegate	Napa Valley	942-6500	open	127
Stony Hill	Napa Valley	963-2636	by appt.	120
Storybook Mountain	Napa Valley	942-5310	by appt.	200
Trefethen	Napa Valley	255-7700	open	74
Truchard	Napa Valley	253-7153	by appt.	150
Viansa	Carneros/Sonoma	935-4700	open	143

BOTTLE SIZES

New metric sizes have replaced the traditional bottle sizes of gallon, quart, fifth, etc., but the old names linger:

Tenth: 375 ml (12.7 oz)

Fifth: 750 ml (25.4 oz), the most commonly used wine bottle.

Magnum: 1.50 L (50.8 oz)/the equivalent of two regular bottles.

Half Gallon: 1.75 L (59.2 oz)

Double Magnum or Jeroboam: 3.0 L/the equivalent of four 750-ml bottles.

Rehoboam: 4.5 L (approx.)/the equivalent of six 750-ml bottles.

Methuselah or Imperial: 6.0 L (approx.)/the equivalent of eight 750-ml bottles

Salmanzar: 9 L (approx.)/the equivalent of twelve 750-ml bottles.

Balthazar: 12 L (approx.)/the equivalent of sixteen 750-ml bottles.

Nebuchadnezzar: 13—15 L/the equivalent of fifteen to twenty 750-ml bottles of wine, depending on who made the bottle, and when and where the wine was made.

Case: A box or carton of 12 bottles of wine, usually of the same variety and vintage. A magnum case contains six 1.5 L magnum bottles.

Barrel: A cylindrical storage container with bulging sides; usually made from American, French, Slavonic, or Baltic oak. A full barrel holds the equivalent of 240 regular 750-ml bottles, or 20 regular cases.

I N D E X

COMPASS AMERICAN GUIDES

Critics, Booksellers, and Travelers All Agree: You're Lost Without a Compass.

Compass American Guides are compelling, full-color portraits of America for travelers who want to understand the soul of their destinations. In each guide, an accomplished local expert recounts history, culture, and useful information in a text rife with personal anecdotes and interesting details. Splendid four-color images by an area photographer bring the region or city to life.

"This splendid series provides exactly the sort of historical and cultural detail about North American destinations that curious-minded travelers need."
— *Washington Post*

Boston (1st Edition)
1-878-86776-8
$18.95 ($26.50 Can)

"This is a series that constantly stuns us; our whole past book reviewer experience says no guide with photos this good should have writing this good. But it does."
— *New York Daily News*

Minnesota (1st Edition)
1-878-86748-2
$18.95 ($26.50 Can)

"Of the many guidebooks on the market few are as visually stimulating, as thoroughly researched or as lively written as the Compass American Guides series."
— *Chicago Tribune*

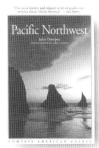

Pacific Northwest (1st Edition)
1-878-86785-7
$19.95 ($27.95 Can)

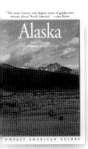

"Good to read ahead of time, then take along so you don't miss anything."
— *San Diego Magazine*

"Compass has developed a series with beautiful color photos and a descriptive text enlivened by literary excerpts from travel writers past and present."
— *Publishers Weekly*

Alaska (1st Edition)
1-878-86777-6
$18.95 ($26.50 Can)

Compass American Guides are available in general and travel bookstores, or may be ordered directly by calling (800) 733-3000. Compass American Guides are available at special discounts for bulk purchases for sales promotions or premiums. Special editions, including personalized covers and corporate imprints, can be created in large quantities for special needs. For more information, write to Special Marketing, Fodor's Travel Publications, 201 E. 50th St., New York, NY 10022; or call (800) 800-3246.

COMPASS AMERICAN GUIDES

Critics, Booksellers, and Travelers All Agree You're Lost Without a Compass

Arizona (4th Edition)
0-679-03388-2
$18.95 ($26.50 Can)

Chicago (2nd Edition)
1-878-86780-6
$18.95 ($26.50 Can)

Colorado (4th Edition)
0-679-00027-5
$18.95 ($26.50 Can)

Hawaii (3rd Edition)
1-878-86791-1
$18.95 ($26.50 Can)

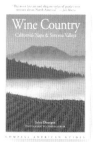

Wine Country (2nd Edition)
0-679-00032-1
$18.95 ($26.50 Can)

Montana (3rd Edition)
1-878-86797-0
$18.95 ($26.50 Can)

Oregon (3rd Edition)
0-679-00033-X
$18.95 ($26.50 Can)

New Orleans (3rd Editic
0-679-03597-4
$18.95 ($26.50 Can)

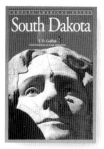

South Dakota (2nd Edition)
1-878-86747-4
$18.95 ($26,50 Can)

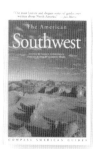

Southwest (2nd Edition)
0-679-00035-6
$18.95 ($26.50 Can)

Texas (2nd Edition)
1-878-86798-9
$18.95 ($26.50 Can)

Utah (4th Edition)
0-679-00030-5
$18.95 ($26.50 Can)

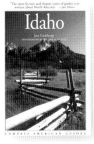

Idaho (1st Edition)
1-878-86778-4
$18.95 ($26.50 Can)

New Mexico (3rd Edition)
0-679-00031-3
$18.95 ($26.50 Can)

Maine (2nd Edition)
1-878-86796-2
$18.95 ($26.50 Can)

Manhattan (2nd Edition)
1-878-86794-6
$18.95 ($26.50 Can)

Las Vegas (5th Edition)
0-679-00015-1
$18.95 ($26.50 Can)

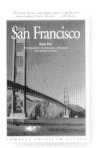

San Francisco (4th Edition)
1-878-86792-X
$18.95 ($26.50 Can)

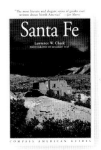

Santa Fe (2nd Edition)
0-679-03389-0
$18.95 ($26.50 Can)

South Carolina (2nd Edition)
0-679-03599-0
$18.95 ($26.50 Can)

Virginia (2nd Edition)
1-878-86795-4
$18.95 ($26.50 Can)

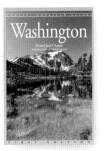

Washington (1st Edition)
1-878-86758-X
$17.95 ($25.00 Can)

Wisconsin (2nd Edition)
1-878-86749-0
$18.95 ($26.50 Can)

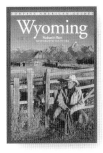

Wyoming (3rd Edition)
0-679-00034-8
$18.95 ($26.50 Can)

■ ABOUT THE AUTHOR

John Doerper is the publisher and editor of *Pacific Epicure, A Quarterly Journal of Gastronomic Literature,* and has worked as a food and wine columnist and editor for numerous publications. His articles about food, wine, and travel have appeared in *Travel & Leisure* and *Pacific Northwest Magazine,* among others. He is also the author of several books including Compass American Guides' *Coastal California* (with Galen Rowell) and *Pacific Northwest,* as well as *Washington Shellfish Cookery: Absolutely Delicious Recipes from the West Coast.*

■ ABOUT THE PHOTOGRAPHER

Charles O'Rear has photographed 24 major articles for *National Geographic* including a feature story on Napa Valley. For CD-ROMs and books, he continues to document the subject of wine and wine harvests around the world. His photographs have received awards from the American Society of Magazine Photographers, *Communication Arts* magazine, and the National Press Photographers Association. He lives in St. Helena.

Comments, suggestions, or updated information?
Please write:
Compass American Guides
5332 College Ave., Suite #201
Oakland, CA 94618
or visit us at www.Fodors.com